Understanding and Training your Dog or Puppy

Understanding and Training your Dog or Puppy

H. Ellen Whiteley, D.V.M.

SUNSTONE PRESS

SANTA FE

© 2006 by H. Ellen Whiteley, D.V.M.
All rights reserved.

No part of this book may be reproduced in any form or by any electronic or mechanical means including information storage and retrieval systems without permission in writing from the publisher, except by a reviewer who may quote brief passages in a review.

Sunstone books may be purchased for educational, business, or sales promotional use. For information please write: Special Markets Department, Sunstone Press, P.O. Box 2321, Santa Fe, New Mexico 87504-2321.

Library of Congress Cataloging-in-Publication Data:

Whiteley, H. Ellen
   Understanding and training your dog or puppy / H. Ellen Whiteley.
     p.cm.
   Includes index.
   Originally published: New York : Crown Trade Paperbacks, c1996.
   ISBN: 0-86534-510-4 (alk. paper)
   1. Dogs--Behavior. 2. Dogs--Training. I. Title.

SF427. W42 2006
636.7--dc22
                                2006044250

WWW.SUNSTONEPRESS.COM
SUNSTONE PRESS / POST OFFICE BOX 2321 / SANTA FE, NM 87504-2321 /USA
(505) 988-4418 / ORDERS ONLY (800) 243-5644 / FAX (505) 988-1025

To George and Bear, who share their love for each other and for this mountain with me.

Special thanks, also, to Brandt Aymar, my editor, for his kindly guidance; to Jane Jordan Browne, my agent, for her hard work on my behalf; to the staff of the Northeast New Mexico Rural Bookmobile for their research assistance; and to my friends, neighbors, clients, and family who have shared their favorite dogs with me.

And here I was this May day sitting on a mountainside, Pat [the dog] beside me saying in his own way that life was good and life was ours, his and mine, whenever we chose to go out together and savor it. And I thought how stupid were those who said that man had made the dog his degraded slave, how completely they had missed the essential relationship of man and dog.

Hal Borland, *The Dog Who Came to Stay*

Contents

Preface	x
1. Yesterday and Today	*1*
In the Beginning	2
Domestication	2
Diversity	6
Dog's Work	7
People and Dogs	8
Question: Burying Treats	14
2. Relationships—Dogs and People	17
The Human-Animal Bond	18
Client, Patient, Veterinarian	22
Question: Allergy-Proofing Pets	28
3. The Way Dogs Are	*31*
The Ancestral Type	32
Dogs Big and Small	33
Genetics	37
Personality Plus	39
Question: Pit Bull Controversy	44
4. Choosing Dogs	47
Matching Owner and Pet	48
Roommates	51
The Heart Factor	53
Where to Find a Dog	55
Lemon Laws	57
Choosing	58
Question: Frostbite in Dogs	60
5. Puppies—The First Weeks	63
Before and Following Birth	64
Two to Four Weeks	68
Four to Twelve Weeks	72
Recommendations	77
Question: Introducing a New Baby	79

6. The Dog Senses — 81
    Hearing — 82
    Balance — 86
    Vision — 86
    Smell — 90
    Taste — 94
    Touch — 95
    Other Senses — 97
    Question: Deformed Puppy — 102

7. Intelligence and Communication — 105
    Intelligence — 106
    Communication — 109
    Question: Aggressive Puppy — 124

8. The Essentials — 127
    Air — 128
    Water — 129
    Food — 129
    Shelter — 140
    Question: Reverse Sneeze Syndrome — 144

9. Teaching — 147
    How Dogs Learn — 149
    Training Methods — 152
    Naming — 156
    Housetraining — 157
    Crate Training — 159
    Obedience Training — 160
    Exercise Training — 162
    Swimming — 162
    Tricks — 163
    Question: Training a Watchdog — 165

10. Aggression and Other Misbehavior — 167
    Contributing Factors — 168
    Types of Aggression — 169
    Bites — 178

Other Misbehavior *181*
Question: Limping for Attention *186*

11. The Sick, Injured, and Neurotic *189*
General Signs of Illness *190*
Pain *190*
Stress *191*
Diseases Affecting Behavior *192*
Emotional Disorders Causing Behavioral Changes *201*
Question: Allergic Dog *208*

12. Sex, Pregnancy, and Parenthood *211*
The Female *212*
The Male *214*
The Mating Act *216*
Pregnancy and Lactation *220*
Parenthood *223*
Birth Control *226*
Question: Spaying Dog with Nymphomania *229*

13. Aging *231*
Life Expectancy *232*
Old Dogs and New Tricks *236*
The Aging Body *238*
Geriatric Care *238*
Behavioral Problems Associated with Aging *244*
Neurological Conditions in Aged Dogs *244*
Question: Sibling Rivalry *246*

14. Preparing for the Inevitable *249*
Grief *250*
Euthanasia *253*
Making Arrangements *256*
Surviving Pets *260*
Question: Hospice Care *265*

Index *267*

Preface

My husband and I live in dog country. At the local post office, we are greeted by four to six dogs, large breeds for the most part—chows, shepherds, and mongrels—and in town, Rottweilers and pit-bull crosses ride by in the backs of pickups or lounge by the corner bar and on the doorstep of the gas company.

This is rural America; the entire county had less than 4,500 human inhabitants last census; who knows how many dogs there are, as no county dog licenses are available to keep up with the canine population. Although we—people and dogs—share our environment with coyotes, porcupines, raccoons, skunks, and other wild critters, we know that cats, now America's most popular domestic pet, come in second around here.

My husband, dogs, and I know intimately the people and dogs inhabiting our small community. Smokey is the 150-pound, cat-hating malamute who howls at the mailman; Chow is a friendly, black-tongued extrovert prone to wandering; Tiffany is the hyperactive canine companion to a five-feline household; and you'll meet Tiger in nearly every chapter.

A four-pound Chihuahua, Tiger rules his home with sharp teeth and a snarl that is more reminiscent of a rattlesnake than the feline species for which he is named. Tiger "trees" bears, who seem not to know that one swat from a large paw would send the bearer of that ferocious bark to Kansas or Oz, whichever is farther. Tiger can bluff, but he himself is hard to fool.

If Tiger's human companions, an accommodating couple in their seventies, want to travel via foot, four-wheeler, or car and leave Tiger at home, they can't say "go" or "vamoose" (Tiger knows Spanish, too), nor can they spell *G O*. Tiger knows what's being communicated and becomes excited at any hint of an impending trip, raising h—— if left behind.

Tiger's owners try nonchalantly to sidle away before Tiger realizes that he's being left behind. In this scenario Tiger has trained his owners by his loud protests not to leave him, and more often than not, they take him along, even when they don't want to.

The move to a close neighborhood has rekindled my interest in the canine species. My own dog, an elderly keeshond inherited by marriage over nine years ago, has proved to me that dogs, like people, are a product of their community and environment. In the city where my husband and I previously resided, our dog named Bear was, frankly, a nuisance. He barked excessively, jumped on people, dug up the yard, had a phobia for thunder and rainstorms and escaped—or attempted to escape—from the fenced yard on a regular basis. Here on the mountain where we now live, however, Bear is transformed.

He rides down the mountain in the pickup camper or back of our four-wheel-drive vehicle to "woof" a greeting to the canine gang at the post office. All the people on the mountain know Bear and call him by name; he seems to feel no need to seek their attention by jumping on them. Here our dog runs free, and he has never abused the privilege by running away. He is happy—you can tell by the alert way he holds his head and ears, the waving of his curled tail, the lilt of his bark when he spies us picking up our walking sticks for a stroll, and his jump off the porch after an intruder. Bear is our security guard, a job that he likes, barking at and chasing away wandering bears, marauding raccoons, and pesky Steller's jays.

Although Bear is still frightened by thunderstorms (I have not bothered to treat the phobia by methods covered in chapter 11), his other behavioral problems have disappeared. Apparently, his misbehavior was the result of a setting that he perceived as stressful. When the stress was eliminated, the motivation for the undesirable behavior was removed, as well.

An owner must understand what motivates his dog's behavior in order to take steps that will bring about desired change in that pet's actions. This is what this book is about: understanding dog behavior, and steps that you as canine caretaker can take to ensure that your dog or puppy's actions will be the most appropriate for life in your household and environmental setting. It is an important task—understanding and training your dog or puppy—because the alternatives—misunderstanding and lack of appropriate training—are major reasons why dogs are relinquished to animal shelters. At one large-city humane society, 25 percent of its dogs were surrendered because of owner-reported behavioral problems, while 65 percent of adopted dogs were returned to the shelter owing to misbehavior.

Factors influencing behavior are varied and broad, encompassing communication, breeding, conditioning, training, environment, and the physical and mental health of the individual dog and others, human and animal, in the household. I use observations of my dog and my canine neighbors, interactions with canine patients and their owners, correspondence with readers of numerous pet-related magazine and newspaper columns I have written, and research in the field of animal behavior to help you understand and better control the factors influencing your pet's behavior.

The goal is to have an enjoyable relationship with your canine companion, whether that companion is a toy poodle in a New York City high-rise or a Great Dane protecting your island paradise in the Puget Sound.

Understanding and Training Your Dog or Puppy

1
Yesterday and Today

In the Beginning

There were no dogs in the Garden of Eden, prompting many canine lovers to surmise that a garden with serpents but devoid of dogs was not a true paradise.

Early, after mammals evolved into four-legged creatures with hair, there were, and there remain today, wild animals belonging to the Canidae family. These animals share a similar arrangement of teeth, size, and habits; some can mate with other members of the Canidae family, producing fertile offspring. They are found all over the globe. These are the dholes of Asia; the hunting dogs and jackals of Africa; the dingoes of Australia; the wolves and foxes of Europe, Asia, and North America; and the coyotes of our country.

One or more of these wild canids is the probable ancestor of our modern dog. Most authorities favor the wolf as the dog's "father and mother." I, while not an ethologist, find the theory that *Canis familiaris* evolved from more than one ancestral source almost simultaneously in different parts of the world more in keeping with how things could have happened.

As is usually the case, there is still another school of thought: that the dog is descended from a now-extinct primordial canid. The fact that no bony remains of such a creature have been found is a major limit on the credence of this theory.

Domestication

To understand the evolution of man's best friend, one must study the evolution of man. Before the end of the last Ice Age, people lived a nomadic life, following the seasonal migration of herds of large mammals, such as reindeer, bison, mammoth, sheep, goats, and horses, across miles of tundralike vegetation.

After the planet warmed and the large glaciers retreated about 14,000 years ago, the migrating herds of large mammals dwindled, prompting their human hunters to devise additional means of survival, namely fishing, farming, and herding. For the first time, people began to stay put, to live in small villages on a more permanent basis, allowing conditions more conducive to animal adoption.

Carl Sagan, in an adaptation of *Pale Blue Dot: A Vision of the Human*

Yesterday and Today

Evolution of the Dog

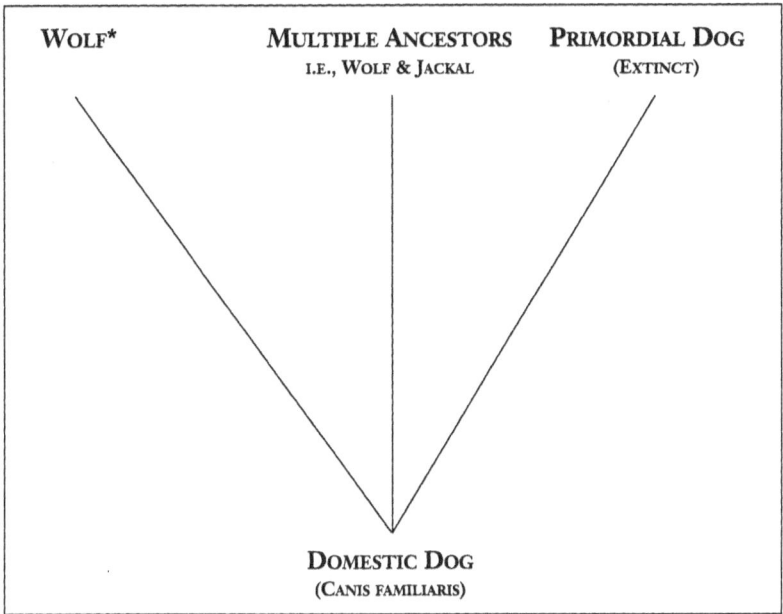

*Most popular theory

Future in Space, for *Parade* magazine, writes: "In the last 10,000 years—an instant in our long history—we've abandoned the nomadic life. We've domesticated the plants and animals. Why chase food when you can make it come to you?"

Unlike those entering Noah's ark, animals came to us at different times. The dog came first and is, in fact, the first animal species to become domesticated—approximately 12,000 years ago, prior to the domestication of the pig, duck, reindeer, sheep, or goat. The cat, domesticated about 5,000 years ago, is a newcomer compared to dogs.

Which canine characteristics made him most appealing for adoption and hence domestication? Were they utilitarian—cooperative hunting skills and guarding—or companionable traits? Whatever the reasons why humans began a closer association with wild canids, there must have been at least some willingness on the part of the wolves or jackals to associate with humans. There must have been some mutual agreement to come to and to be with us.

Gradually, as litters were raised in close association with human caretakers, the canids forgot to be wild. They lost their ferociousness and distrust of humans and eventually, as in the case of modern dogs, lost the ability to survive on their own.

Stephen Budiansky, senior writer at *U.S. News and World Report* and author of *The Covenant of the Wild: Why Animals Chose Domestication*, in the article "A Special Relationship: The Coevolution of Human Beings and Domesticated Animals," *Journal of the American Veterinary Medical Association*, writes:

> This loss of survival skills is closely linked to the retention into adulthood of juvenile traits, an evolutionary process known as neoteny. All domesticated animals have a whole suite of juvenile traits. Adult dogs, for example, have much more puppy-like heads (domed heads, shorter muzzles, floppy ears) than have adult wolves; they also display many juvenile behaviors (playfulness, curiosity, care-soliciting, food-begging) that disappear in the wild type with maturity and with the activation of adult hunting and courtship behaviors.

Call of the Wild

Physical appearance and behavior are different for domesticated and wild canids. As closely as some dogs are in appearance to wolves, you can tell which is which.

I was working not long ago in a small animal hospital for a veterinarian away on vacation. While I was in the exam room with a small poodle and his owner, a young woman and her pet appeared at the reception desk right outside the open exam-room door. I could feel the poodle shrink back against the far wall of the exam table. I glanced at the animal outside the door, and knew immediately that he was a wolf. There was a "look" about the animal's eyes and a stance that gave him away.

The wolf's owner tried to pass the animal off as a German shepherd mix. Before the medical record had been completed by the receptionist, the young woman said that her pet was a wolf hybrid (a cross between a dog and a wolf), and before the visit was finished, she admitted that the animal before us was a wolf.

Yesterday and Today

It was there—an almost undefinable wildness that one can admire in an individual but that has no place in the average pet-owning household for numerous reasons, including hazards to humans, other animals, and to the captive animal himself.

It seems that more and more people are trying to make wolves into domesticated animals. In our small local newspaper was the following ad under the category of "Pets for Sale":

> Big beautiful intelligent wolf pups
> Male $150, female $100.

I have no doubt that the pups are indeed big, beautiful, and intelligent; my objection is that they are being sold as pets.

The American Veterinary Medical Association (AVMA), of which I am a member, has the following to say about wild animals as pets:

> People acquire wild animals as pets because they like to possess unusual pets or regard them as status symbols. Problems associated with wild animals include disease, diet, exercise, housing and traumatic injury. Wild animals kept as pets are frequently subjected to various surgical procedures for the sole purpose of making the animal more sociably acceptable to its owner. Disposing of a wild animal can be a traumatic experience for both the animal and its owner. Frequently, legitimate zoos will not accept them and they are "too domesticated" to return to the wild; therefore, euthanasia may be the only alternative. Veterinarians should exert their influence to discourage the keeping of wild animals as pets.

Although I may be belaboring the point, I can't resist one last argument. I know a veterinarian who works as a wildlife rehabilitator. This is what Dr. Jessica Porter has to say about her experiences:

> While at the wildlife center, I set up a refuge for wolves. For the most part, we took pet wolves and retrained them to be wild. We kept a core pack of wolves just to train the others to behave like their species. It was common for people to buy the cute little furry fellows when they were pups and then give them up when they grew into large unruly adoles-

cents. We had cases of three- and four-year-old wolves that had been kept in a three-by-five-foot cage for their entire lives. When they were put into a larger enclosure, they still paced three-by-five. We had about a 50 percent success rate, meaning we released half to the wild and had to destroy the other half because they couldn't learn to be wolves.

DIVERSITY

Like all individuals, certain dogs are imbued with traits of behavior, proficiency, or physical appearance that are suppressed or lacking in other dogs. Some of these attributes come about by congenital defects and mutation of genes, and they can be enhanced and propagated by breeding the individuals carrying the desired trait.

As man and woman depended upon their new canine companions to pull a sled, to protect the tepee, to keep tabs on the reindeer herd, to help in the hunt, or to provide novelty or companionship, they began to favor individuals who provided such skills. The offspring of these individuals were kept, and ancient breeding programs begun.

Selective breeding produced three canine types in terms of function, which also dictated behavior and physical form: herding, hunting, and companion dogs. It helped, for example, for hunters to be long-legged and fast, with hair that provided camouflage and weather resistance; herders must have exquisite senses and timing, and companion dogs need congeniality or unusualness.

One of the first breeds to be represented in ancient art, more than 6,000 years ago, is the African basenji, a hunting dog. Egyptian frescos portray dogs looking much like mastiffs, greyhounds, and salukis—again dogs who functioned primarily as hunters. Archaeological digs in this country produced the remains (over 10,000 years old) of a small, light-limbed dog similar to a fox terrier, a dog who might function as a herding and/or hunting dog.

Historians theorize that dog breeding in China began around 12,000 B.C., producing not only working breeds such as the chow chow but also exotics such as the Pekingese, who served primarily as companions. Selective breeding of dogs has been going on a very long time.

There have been, it is believed, approximately 2,000 distinct breeds of dogs existing in the world at different times; today there are more than 400 breeds. They have originated primarily from Europe, Africa, and China. The diversity in physical appearance that these breeds represent is astounding. A 1-pound Chihuahua is a dog, just as is a 200-pound Saint Bernard. No other mammalian species shows such contrast.

This type of diversity is not seen in domestic cats. All cats look much alike and all cats remain in a relatively constant size range. Dr. Donna Brown, an animal behaviorist, writes, in the article "Cultural Attitudes Toward Pets," *Veterinary Clinics of North America*, "Lack of selective breeding meant that breeding for specialized functions did not occur in the cat as it did in the dog, and domestication was not accompanied by enhancement of desired traits. Only recently has such selective breeding occurred in the cat. This is reflected in the fact that there are far fewer cat breeds than dog breeds, and cat breeds exhibit less variation in many physical and behavioral traits."

Dog's Work

Throughout history, dogs have worked side by side with man. Jack London chronicles this sharing of labors in *The Call of the Wild*: "Here were many men, and countless dogs, and Buck found them all at work. It seemed the ordained order of things that dogs should work. All day they swung up and down the main street in long teams, and in the night their jingling bells still went by. They hauled cabin logs and firewood, freighted up to the mines, and did all manner of work that horses did."

Although many of us see our pet dogs as leading a life of comfort requiring little in return except loyal friendship, modern dogs do have jobs. Most dogs, like most people, relish performing worthwhile tasks, and some behavioral problems stemming from boredom and lack of useful activity are remedied by teaching dogs to perform tricks or tasks.

I know one man who trained his Labrador, named Ben, to open the refrigerator and pick up a beer in his teeth and deliver it to his master, who would be lounging in the hot tub or recliner. Now, that's my kind of dog, especially if he can be taught to put the empties in the trash.

Some canine job descriptions never change. Others, however, are created daily by ingenious owners and their dogs. Table 1.1 demonstrates some of the jobs available in the past and present.

PEOPLE AND DOGS

The relationships that people have had in the past and have today with dogs are varied. Attitudes are based on factors as diverse as religion, economic status, and emotions such as love and fear.

Religion

Societal views about dogs vary from those who believe in canine deification to those who appreciate the dog as a food protein source, from those who treat the dog as an equal to those who believe in domination of the canine species.

The Egyptian god Anubis is depicted as having a human body with the head of a jackal or dog. This god acted as an intermediary between the living and the dead, and therefore presided over the process of embalming or mummification.

Other cultures came to the same conclusion: dogs, loyal to the end, were helpful as guides into the spirit world. In the first century A.D., the Roman writer Pliny recorded the story of a faithful dog belonging to a slave condemned to capital punishment: "When he [the dead slave] had been flung out on the steps of lamentation [the dog] would not leave his body, uttering sorrowful howls to the vast concourse of the Roman public around, and when one of them threw it food it carried it to the mouth of its dead master, also when his corpse had been thrown into the Tiber it swam to it and tried to keep it afloat, a great crowd streaming out to view the animal's loyalty."

The idea of the dog as guide to the afterlife may have been the impetus for burying dogs with their masters. Archaeologists have found burial sites containing humans and dogs in the Americas, Asia, Europe, and Africa.

One of the oldest graves, found in northern Israel, contained the remains of an elderly human and a puppy buried together 12,000 years ago. Interestingly, the bond appeared to be a strong one because the person's hand was placed for eternity on the shoulder of his canine companion.

Table 1.1
Canine Job Description

YESTERDAY

hunting/fishing, guarding, herding, beast of burden, fighting, bull and bear baiting, pulling sleds/tepees, turning spits, source of meat/hair, scavenger, rodent/badger control, weapon of war, object of religious worship, detecting truffles, entertainment, companionship, water/alpine rescue, coach/barge/firetruck mascot

TODAY

Service Dogs—seeing eye, hearing ear, service (carries packs, opens doors, etc.), therapeutic (visits nursing homes, hospitals, psychiatric treatment), educational (schools, prison programs), medical research

Racing Dogs—greyhound, whippet, sled dog, hound, lurcher ("sight hounds" such as Afghans, Irish wolfhounds, borzois, salukis, whippets chase an artificial lure along a random course through an open field)

Police/Military/Home-Business—scout, sentry/guard, search (bombs, drugs and contraband), trackers (escaped prisoners, lost persons)

Herding—sheep, cow, hog, general

Hunting—retrievers, pointers, other

Pack—expedition (used by explorers such as Will Steger), business (carries supplies/finished product in remote regions)

Performers—advertising, entertainment (movies, TV, circus, rodeo)

Competition—show, agility, obedience, field trial, Frisbee contests, fighting (illegal)

Pest Control—termite detection

Companionship

I've known people who want to be buried side by side with a beloved dog. Some believe, I think, that heaven would not be heaven without their canine companions, and others believe that they and their dog belong together in death as in life (similar to husband and wife being buried in the same plot). I don't know the problems that these devoted dog lovers encounter with burial regulations, but cemetery by-laws excluding animals seemed for many to be of greater concern than having their dogs prepare the way to the spirit world.

There was, and perhaps in some places still exists, a religious attitude about selling dogs, and the dog involved is called a Catahoula. I was raised in Catahoula Parish, a land of swamp and water in central Louisiana, the origin of the Catahoula. I find this dog fascinating and hope you will forgive an extensive explanation of a dog his owners would not sell.

The Catahoula is a hog dog, weighing from forty to fifty pounds, with trim, muscular body, blue leopard spots, and light-blue "glass" eyes; it is fairly close to being an ancestral dog type. (The ancestral dog is covered extensively in chapter 3.)

The breed, it is believed, resulted from the mating of domestic Indian dogs and possibly red wolves with Spanish war dogs or mastiffs. In 1686, French explorer Henri de Tonty told of seeing dogs with white eyes and mottled spots. Jim Bowie, the famous frontiersman, owned a pair of Catahoulas in the mid-1800s, and in the early twentieth century, President Teddy Roosevelt became acquainted with Catahoula swamp dogs on his historic hunting trip to Louisiana.

The Catahoula hog dog was the only known breed that could maneuver swamp hogs to a designated point with their cunning, and they could catch and hold the most ornery boar.

Swamp hogs were a mixture of domestic breeds and wild hogs. They had long snouts and legs; a tuft of bristles stood up, manelike, along the backbone from the neck to the middle of the back. I remember them from the time I was a child and traveled through the swamp to the closest city, Alexandra, and the hogs looked as if they'd be as tough to eat as they were in temperament.

Wild hogs could not be driven; they invariably turned on an enemy for a fight to the finish. If one pig squealed or gave the distress signal, every hog within hearing distance charged to his rescue with raised bristles and clamping teeth.

Yesterday and Today

The Catahoula's technique for "driving" hogs was this: the dog looked for a couple of stragglers and provoked them into giving the rally signal. The dog took position on the side of the drove, leading toward an enclosure, and tantalized the lead boar into chasing him. When the entire hog herd was led through the corral, the hog dog jumped over the back fence. It was a risky job for a dog, and many were slashed by tusks before they escaped over the fence.

A dog learned his trade in a season. When a man wanted a puppy, a neighbor would give him one, but they were never sold because Deuteronomy 23:18 (King James version) admonishes: "Thou shall not bring ... the price of a dog into the house of the Lord thy God...."

The land of the Catahoula has changed. With new levees, locks, and dams, the floods don't come as often. The woods have been cut and the swamps drained to make way for soybeans, the major crop in the area now. The swamp hog has disappeared.

The Catahoula hog dog, however, remains. His cunning and speed make him a good stock dog. In July 1979, Governor Edwin Edwards signed a bill making the Catahoula hog dog the official state dog of Louisiana. Called by some the ugliest dog in the country, the hog dog is, nonetheless, a survivor and a wonderful representative of my roots.

Selling dogs is an abomination even today to some persons, especially animal rights activists, who believe that all living beings have equal rights and that buying and selling dogs is akin to the human slave auctions of times past. Even use of the words *pet* and *owner* are distasteful for those who believe that pet ownership exploits animals.

Others counter this proposition with Genesis 1:26: "And God said, let us make man in our image, after our likeness; and let them have dominion over the fish of the sea, and over the fowl of the air, and over the cattle, and over all the earth, and over every creeping thing that creepeth upon the earth."

The eating of dogs has, in some instances, been a religious act. Where dogs were valued as spiritual allies, totems, or tribal symbols, eating was a ritual believed to transfer respected canine characteristics such as keen senses and swiftness to those eating its flesh. In certain North American Indian tribes the killing of a beloved canine companion and the sacrificial offering of its cooked flesh to a friend or visitor was evidence of the esteem the host held for the guest.

If you are curious about the subject of eating dogs, I can offer the following quote by the American explorer John C. Fremont; if you've had your fill already, better skip this paragraph:

> The dog was in a large pot over the fire, in the middle of the lodge, and immediately on our arrival was dished up in large wooden bowls, one of which was handed to each. The flesh appears very glutinous, with something of the flavor and appearance of mutton. Feeling something move behind me, I looked round, and found that I had taken my seat among a litter of fat young puppies. Had I been nice in such matters, the prejudices of civilization might have interfered with my tranquility, but, fortunately, I am not of delicate nerves, and continued quietly to empty my platter.

Economics

Never is a motive clear-cut, and this applies to those who have used dogs as food. In some instances, what started as a religious act turned into an economic one as people discovered that eating dogs could sustain them when protein sources were low.

In Mexico, it was the Aztec custom to sacrifice a small dog when someone died and to bury it with the body. The Aztecs believed that the dog had mystical powers that could guide the dead person's soul across the nine deadly rivers of the underworld. If a surplus of dogs, the ancestors of today's Chihuahua, occurred, the Aztecs fattened and ate them. In southern China, Polynesia, and Central America dogs have been raised as food animals.

Of course, we are horrified at the thought of eating Rover, as are most people in the world. It is not only those who eat dogs, however, who refrain from keeping them as pets or companion animals. Some sociologists believe that a strong human bond with dogs is peculiar to affluent industrialized countries, and that in poor underdeveloped countries, economics dictates that the emotional bond between people and dogs not be as strong. It doesn't take a mathematician to figure out that the more mouths one has to feed on a limited amount of food, the less there is for each family member. There's just nothing left for the care and sustenance of pets.

It was Sophie Tucker who is credited with saying: "I've been rich and I've been poor; rich is better." Apparently, rich was better if you wanted to own dogs in the old days. It was the wealthy classes and royalty who kept the companion animals depicted in early art and literature and who selectively bred dogs for sport and recreation. However, the writings of Pliny quoted earlier about the slave and his loyal dog prove that this was not entirely true.

And working dogs have more than earned their keep in both the past and present. It is economically feasible to care for dogs who pull your sled, catch your warthog or swamp hog, herd your sheep, protect the castle from intruders and rodents, fight in your armies, catch your criminals, find the booty, rescue lost travelers, help with the hunt, provide services for handicapped persons . . .

Love and Fear

Love and fear are discordant emotions; it is extremely difficult to love that which you also fear. There are places in the world where dogs pose a physical threat to humans, as carriers of parasites and of diseases such as rabies.

Rabies has been recognized in humans and animals for over 4,000 years. It was recorded in Mesopotamian laws before 2300 B.C., when responsibility and retribution for dog bites were placed on the owner. Aristotle described the clinical signs of the disease in the third century B.C.

The bite of the mad dog or rabid dog was often the "kiss of death," until Louis Pasteur developed his rabies vaccine in the late 1800s. Before that, ancient Greeks believed that throwing the victim into a river or lake and forcing him to swallow water was curative. I suppose you can't get rabies if you drown first.

Rabies in dogs is still a threat. In India and the Philippines, rabies causes thousands of human fatalities yearly. Canine rabies is a significant threat to human health in Central and South America, Africa, the Middle East, and parts of Asia. The disease potential is one reason why people in certain areas of the world do not form as close an attachment to dogs as we do.

It has not been terribly long in this country since rabies was a reason to fear dogs; there were 6,949 cases of canine rabies in 1947 versus 182 laboratory-confirmed rabies cases in dogs in 1992. However, control of rabies plays only a minor part in the development of the strong human-dog bond that has developed during the last half-century.

Dr. Donna Brown, in "Cultural Attitudes Towards Pets," *Veterinary Clinics of North America*, writes:

> The change in the role of the pet, particularly the dog, in modern society has been attributed to changes in family composition and size. Industrialization has decreased the average size of the family unit and reduced contact with extended family members. The dog presumably gained status as it filled the void left by the reduction in the number of family members in the home. There were significant changes in patterns of pet-keeping, particularly after World War II; for example, the family dog was no longer banished to the barn or kept under the back porch but was more often allowed to live in the house.

And so it is that Rover, King, Blacky, and Monique have moved from guarding our house to being a family member with all the rights and privileges thereof. It is those canine traits that we define in our own terms—acceptance, forgiveness, and love—that make dogs such worthwhile companions, especially when all others seem to have forsaken us. In the book *Mondo Canine*, Tammy Faye Bakker is quoted, "As I lay on the floor in the dark, empty room, Tuppins, my puppy, licked at the tears running down my face. 'Oh, Tuppins,' I sobbed, 'Why has God forsaken me?'"

Dogs are friends, confidants, surrogate children, and yes, if we have no reason for fear to enter into the relationship, we love them.

QUESTION

Dear Dr. Whiteley,

We have a four-month-old female cairn terrier. On occasion we give her treats. When she gets the Milk-Bone dog treat (with real bone marrow) she very often buries or hides it. Is it the bone marrow in the treat? Why does she bury these treats?

Curious in Texas

Yesterday and Today

Dear Curious,

Will Cuppy, author of *How to Become Extinct*, is credited with saying, "If an animal does something, we call it instinct; if we do the same thing for the same reason, we call it intelligence." It is natural instinct for a dog to bury a bone. She does it for the same reason that we put money in savings accounts and a squirrel hides nuts in a hollow tree—to save for a "rainy day." Give most dogs a leftover soup bone, and they will store it under the cool, dark earth, while we intelligent beings store our leftovers in the old Frigidaire.

Apparently, the Milk-Bone maker has created a product that has the same appeal as the real thing. Dogs are influenced more by smell than by sight. I think your puppy buries the Milk-Bone treats because they smell like bone.

Best Wishes!
H. E. W.

2
Relationships—Dogs and People

The Human-Animal Bond

The word *bond*, in this case, refers to a binding element or tie between people and animals. The Indian chief Seathe, in 1855, said, "What is man without the beasts? If all the beasts were gone, man would die from great loneliness of spirit, for whatever happens to the beasts also happens to man. All things are connected."

This wise man knew that we need the connection with animals, that without contact with growing living things—plant and animal—our spirit suffers a lack that is almost as acute as lack of food for some of us. I didn't realize how much this communion with nature meant to me until I moved to the mountains, surrounded by trees, birds, and other animals. A walk through the woods is a meditation to me. In city apartments we also need that communion with living entities other than our own species; pets, houseplants, and parks serve this vital need.

More than half the families in the United States own some kind of pet; pet owning is the cultural norm. According to a 1988 AVMA study, families who own dogs tend to be larger and have children; households in smaller communities are more likely to own a dog than those in larger communities. This same study cited that dog-owning households are more likely to own their own home than those without dogs. Depending on how one interprets the statistics, you might surmise that if you want a house, you should buy a dog. It might be wiser, however, to purchase a savings bond.

For most of us, obtaining a dog or puppy is less a financial and more an emotional decision. Aaron Katcher, M.D., writes in *New Perspectives on Our Lives with Companion Animals:* "Urban Americans tend to class family pets as family members, attributing human characteristics to them. In interactions with pets people use a style of talking that resembles the kind of talk used between adults and young children and between intimates."

The facial expressions and blood-pressure readings of people who talk to animals indicate that talking to animals is easier than talking to unfamiliar adults, according to Dr. Katcher. This may be one reason why pets serve as social lubricants, easing interactions with others of our own species. If I meet you and your dog Rover at the park, smiling and saying something cute to Rover is easier than acknowledging you, whom I do not know and who might think me forward for speaking directly to you.

Relationships—Dogs and People

In some cases, it is easier to talk to Rover than to the kids or spouse. Rover almost never reciprocates our communication with a sassy retort or hurtful remark. We may even consider Rover nicer than our spouse.

This reminds me of a patient, Dominick, and a client, Mrs. Woods. Dominick was an ancient standard poodle suffering from chronic kidney failure. He was my boss's patient, but everyone at the animal hospital where I worked knew Dominick because he came in often to be treated. As fate would have it, the old poodle went into terminal kidney failure while my employer, Dr. Cheever, was on an extended leave from the practice. In spite of what the rest of us at the hospital did or didn't do, Dominick died.

It was my duty to offer condolences and deliver Dominick's effects—his favorite blanket and toys—to the bereaved owner and her daughter, who had come for them prior to making the dog's funeral arrangements. I stood in the exam room clutching the patient's soiled yellow blanket tightly to my chest, while Mrs. Woods reminisced about the times when everyone had thought Dominick was a goner, but Dr. Cheever, bless his heart and expertise, had managed to pull him back from the brink of death. Alas, if only Dr. Cheever . . .

Then, Mrs. Woods and her daughter discussed the burial. "This is just killing Mom," Miss Woods said, patting her mother on the shoulder.

"Yes," Mrs. Woods said, "losing Dominick is so much worse than when Mr. Woods died, but Mr. Woods was not a nice man and Dominick was a wonderful dog."

The bond between people and dogs varies from nonexistent, or negative in the case of those who abuse and neglect them, to those who suffer phobias and allergies, to those who consider a dog just a pet, to those who consider their dog a surrogate child, to those who esteem them more than members of their own species. The degree of bonding depends upon cultural norms, our early background, our relationships with others, and our lifestyle.

Phobias Between People and Dogs

My dictionary defines *phobia* as "an irrational persistent fear of some particular thing or situation." Most people who have phobias about dogs or other animals have suffered a past trauma involving the species. The inciting experience or experiences may be either conscious or hidden deep within the unconscious. Treatment by a psychologist or psychiatrist is recommended for people with phobias.

Since a phobia is a fear, perhaps there is another, more generic approach to ponder. I call upon the experiences and advice of Peace Pilgrim, a woman I have admired for many years. Now deceased, Peace Pilgrim was an advocate for inner peace and world peace, and she often addressed the subject of fear, which is an emotion incompatible with peace. The book *Peace Pilgrim: Her Life and Work in Her Own Words* quotes the gentle woman: "Almost all fear is fear of the unknown. Therefore, what's the remedy? *To become acquainted with the thing you fear.*"

A woman who was afraid of house cats asked Peace Pilgrim's advice about curing her irrational fear of felines. After following Peace's advice by adopting a small, vulnerable kitten and by feeding, caring, and playing with him, the woman found that her fear had disappeared. When it came time to give the kitten back to his original owner, the woman couldn't bear to part with her feline companion.

We can take Peace Pilgrim's story and apply it to someone who is afraid of dogs. Adopt a small, cute, dependent puppy and nurture him until fear turns to love. Of course, it makes sense to investigate the type of puppy and his care and training first (topics addressed in later chapters). But for just a preview, pick a breed known for congeniality, such as a lab or collie, rather than a chow chow or pit bull.

Do dogs have phobias about specific people? In my experience they do, and the phobias usually are expressed as fears of a specific gender or race or profession (veterinarians, groomers; I don't know about lawyers).

The Gender Gap

I have known dogs who liked only women. One was a huge Great Dane who hated men with the exception of his owner, a single middle-aged man. Strangely enough, the owner was shy and uncomfortable around women, but set aside his own comfort for that of Buck, who liked me and had growled and threatened to bite the male veterinarians he had visited. In those days, female veterinarians were few and far between. Buck and his owner were always gentlemen in

Relationships—Dogs and People

my presence, and I'll never forget this lovable dog who died at a relatively young age of cancer.

At the opposite end of the spectrum are dogs who hate women. I used to have a habit, one I have abandoned, of walking into the exam room, patting the patient on the head, and saying something like "Nice Poochie." One day a shepherd sideswiped my hand with his fangs while his astute owner said, "Ole Shep don't like women."

Now, I give the patient time to adjust to me via his senses by offering my upturned palm for him to sniff; I venture to touch only if he indicates it is okay.

Race Relations

Dr. Donna Brown, in the journal *Veterinary Clinics of North America*, talks about racial attitudes toward dogs:

> One occasionally hears the statement, "Blacks (substitute any minority group) are afraid of dogs." It is probably more accurate to say that some black (or other minority group) people are afraid of *White* people's dogs, and probably for valid reasons. Certainly, it is true that some suburban dogs that were raised without exposure to integrated schools or working environments may be exposed only infrequently to black people. Dogs are somewhat neophobic and often react to unfamiliar stimuli with fear and aggression. For dogs living in white suburbs, the presence of blacks may be a rare occurrence and disruptive of normal routines, thereby generating aggressive behavior on the part of white-owned dogs. Perhaps black people who have been exposed to white-owned dogs in white neighborhoods have learned to be cautious around them, as white people may have learned to be cautious of dogs raised in predominantly black neighborhoods.

I have had some experience with this topic. My first job as a practicing veterinarian was working in a small clinic located in a suburb of New Orleans. Although the clinic owner's wife occasionally served as receptionist for the practice, Richard, who had worked in the clinic for twenty years as assistant, kennelman, and groomer, and I were the staff most of the time.

Occasionally, a white owner looked at Richard, a muscle-bound black man, and said something like, "My dog doesn't like train porters." Richard would gracefully back away and busy himself elsewhere. I never had a black client say to me, "My dog doesn't like secretaries," but had there been, I'm doubtful that I would have had Richard's grace, good humor, and good sense to take what was said as a warning and respond in kind.

Of course, stereotypes are sometimes an advantage. Once when a belligerent and drunk client was giving me a rough time, Richard appeared in the door, looking mean as a junk-yard dog; my tormentor stopped yelling in mid-sentence and exited the office in a flash.

The above stories are a roundabout way of stressing that dogs are prejudiced, as are people; often it is a fear of someone different or instinctively taking on their owner's fears. Things are improving, I believe, for both dogs and people. Very few professions are now identified as male or female, or white or black. With more interaction between races, our dogs will have no reason to perceive members of another race as different and, thus, frightening.

As far as dog training goes, we can condition dogs to accept people of different races and genders; it's as Peace Pilgrim said, "Become acquainted with that you fear." After all, we're all just people or just dogs, as the case may be.

CLIENT, PATIENT, VETERINARIAN

Veterinary Services

The veterinary community offers more varied services than ever before—specialty practices, house calls, mobile clinics, small one-veterinarian clinics, large multi-veterinarian hospitals, veterinary teaching hospitals, Humane Society veterinary services, emergency hospitals, and recently, veterinary services in large pet-supply stores, such as PetsMart.

In the old days, veterinarians were generalists, treating any animal for which the owner solicited their services. This was the James Herriot type of practice, and it still exists today. The veterinarians in my rural area are mixed-animal practitioners for the most part, and perform a worthwhile service for their clients and patients.

More frequently, however, veterinarians are specializing, either by

Relationships—Dogs and People

discipline, such as surgery, dermatology, or behavior, or by species, such as equine, feline, exotic animals, or birds. A veterinary radiologist told me why she decided to specialize: "I began to feel isolated in private practice and felt that I was losing capabilities that I didn't want to lose.... I finally realized that I could stay where I was and do little bits of lots of things, or I could narrow my focus and concentrate on knowing more about less. I decided to learn more about less."

As veterinary medical knowledge expands, it becomes increasingly difficult to keep up with everything. The general practitioner can offer his clients the latest knowledge by referring to a specialist those cases he or she is not equipped to handle. It is also the right of every client to ask for a referral to a specialist or for a second opinion.

Because of the narrow focus of their practice, however, most specialists are located in large cities. If the need is great enough, the majority of us are willing to travel to a city with a veterinary-school teaching hospital, which is loaded with specialists, or to a private specialty practice. Also, experts are available to consult with you as pet owner and with your veterinarian via telephone consultation.

House-call practices are considered new offerings, yet in the old days, most veterinarians made house calls. As I owned a house-call practice with the creative name of Cat Clinic (I've done almost everything), I'll list what my practice brochure described as its selling points and how it operated:

> Dr. Whiteley comes to you. This eliminates the need to transport your pets or wait in the waiting room of a veterinary clinic. Your pet is not exposed to other animals. This serves to reduce the potential for exposure to infectious diseases or a confrontation with an unruly animal. Your animal remains in his home surroundings. Uneasiness during the trip to a clinic is eliminated. Appointments can be made at your convenience. Any waiting is done at your home....
>
> Cases requiring anesthesia, radiographs, surgery and intensive care will be transported by Dr. Whiteley in her mobile van to the home hospital. Emphasis of Cat Clinic is feline medicine and surgery. Although Dr. Whiteley will gladly provide veterinary service for dogs at your home, hospital service will be provided only for cats, rabbits and

small dogs. Orthopedic surgery will be referred to a veterinarian who specializes in orthopedics.

Of all my practice endeavors, Cat Clinic was the most fun. I developed a close relationship with most clients and patients and had firsthand knowledge of the pet's home environment. If there was a downside (most things have a downside), it was the excessive time required to travel to a client's home, transport pets requiring hospitalization back and forth, and keep a fresh inventory of drugs and supplies for what was a limited number of patients.

A close cousin to the house-call practice is the mobile practice, a self-contained clinic on wheels that comes to you. Examinations and surgery are usually performed in the mobile hospital. Combinations—full-service hospitals with mobile units or house-call services—are becoming common.

Veterinary hospitals such as the ones located in PetsMart operate on a volume principle—they see many patients and buy supplies and drugs in large quantities—so they can usually offer low prices. Some veterinary facilities provide seven-day, twenty-four-hour operations with grooming and boarding and a pet store all in one. Obviously, a one-veterinarian practice cannot offer all these amenities.

One of the best things to come along since I've been a veterinarian is the veterinary emergency hospital. These hospitals are open after hours and on weekends and holidays, when most veterinary clinics and hospitals are closed. After the patient is stabilized, he is referred to and/or transported back to the regular veterinarian for follow-up care. Emergency hospitals are equipped with both personnel and surgical and diagnostic equipment to handle trauma cases and other emergencies.

Rabies Clinics

I used to wonder why people showed up in such numbers for rabies vaccination clinics held at the local fire station, when, in some cases, the cost of the vaccination was the same or cheaper at their local veterinary hospital.

For some people it is what I'll call the circus factor. Vaccination clinics are a great place to watch people and dogs; you can often see the veterinarian bitten by a chow; a mongrel escape from his owner,

Relationships—Dogs and People

trailing ten feet of logging chain; and catch a fight between a Chihuahua and a Rottweiler. For others, it's the hassle factor. They don't want to be hassled with the veterinarian or staff at the local veterinary hospital mentioning parvo vaccinations and heartworm preventative. And for still others it's a civic response to a plea in the newspaper to protect the public from rabies. I am tempted, while on the subject, to tell another story.

Over twenty-five years ago in Louisiana, I volunteered to help at the yearly rabies drive in Orleans and Jefferson parishes. I was assigned to the Barataria area, located at the southern tip of Jefferson Parish, down the Mississippi River from New Orleans.

Lafitte was the solitary community, consisting of a school, tavern, cafe, and post office. I set up "shop" in the schoolyard. While other veterinarians might boast of vaccinating a thousand dogs at a New Orleans fire station, I saw less than a hundred animals. But oh, what a good time had I.

Barataria is an area wealthy in history and charm. It was the home of the French pirate Jean Lafitte, who aided Andrew Jackson at the Battle of New Orleans during the War of 1812. I could envision a pirate's hideout in the little coves off the river, surrounded by moss-covered oaks and cypress. Shrimp boats loitered at small wooden piers, while nets lay drying on wooden planks. Sounds of frogs and crickets made backup music for the occasional horn of a tug on the river, and the rich smells of fish and of rotting humus hung over the area like a mosquito net.

The rabies clinics were always in the spring, before biting insects became unbearable. The clinic in Barataria seemed to serve as social event for its residents—native Cajuns with a thick dialect and dark features reminiscent of their French Canadian forefathers. When I arrived at the schoolyard, they would be waiting with their animals.

The dogs were hunting breeds, hounds of every variety, a Catahoula, a coon hound, and the big mixes. One baying hound would be the cue for the rest to join in chorus.

I crawled into a pickup filled with six hounds; the owner held, I triggered the syringe, and my assistant frantically tried to catch the particulars for the rabies certificates.

"Well, this un's Mama. That's River Rat and Ole One Eye. Let's see, I reckon Ole One Eye must be close to two now, cause he's from Ole Five Tits's second litter. After he got in a fight with a nutria, me and my brother sewed him up with some fishing line, and he done just fine," the owner said. And other than his battle scars, Ole One Eye did look just fine.

There would be cats in gunny sacks, issuing hisses and yowls that made me shake in my tennis shoes. A teenage girl held a raccoon on a leash, away from the dogs that were straining toward it. A small kitten, frightened by the activity, was clutched to the bosom of an elderly matron.

I proceeded slowly, dispensing free veterinary advice for animals that had never seen a veterinarian. I heard the classic cough of congestive failure from heartworm disease, saw the pale gums characteristic of hookworm infection. The home remedies were revealed. "Old Shep had the worst darn case of red mange you'd ever see, and we cured it with coal oil and axle grease," someone would say.

I occasionally recognized an owner or animal from the previous year, and people stopped to talk to me at the cafe, where I treated myself to a supper of boiled crawfish after my chores at the school were done.

When the overwhelming, swift pace of life catches me in its whirlwind, I remember Barataria, and I hope it hasn't changed.

I don't know why some people go to rabies vaccination clinics, but I go for the people and for the dogs and for the communion and for the circus, and of course, to protect all of us from rabies.

Pet Clubs

Pet clubs are new. Pet owners join the club by paying an annual fee, and in return they receive a quarterly newsletter and complimentary and discounted services from participating veterinarians, kennels, grooming parlors, and coupons for a variety of products sold in grocery stores, in pet shops, and at veterinary practices. A representative of National Pet Club can answer your questions by calling 1-800-PET-CLUB.

Pet Health Insurance

Two companies offer health insurance policies for dogs: Medipet, a member of Fireman's Fund Insurance; and Veterinary Pet Insurance (VPI). Both companies offer plans similar to human health in-

Relationships—Dogs and People

surance policies. Premiums depend on coverage, deductible, and age of pet, but they average $75 to $100 per dog per year. Most policies cover medical treatment, surgery, diagnostic tests, and hospitalization for illness or injury of the insured pet; elective surgery such as neutering is not covered.

Individual veterinarians or groups of veterinarians may offer health maintenance organization–type pet insurance plans. With HMO plans, the pet owner pays a flat fee at certain intervals and then receives future veterinary services at a reduced rate or for free. Each HMO sets its premiums and coverage. If you elect this type of pet insurance, you must use the veterinarian or group of veterinarians offering the coverage. With Medipet and VPI, you are free to use the services of any licensed veterinarian in a state offering the plans.

For more information about insurance plans for dogs, contact your veterinarian or the office of your state insurance commissioner. Details about Medipet are available by calling 1-800-345-6778 (1-800-742-5678 in Connecticut) and about VIP by calling 1-800-USA-PETS (1-800-VPI-PETS in California).

The Best Relationship

Finding the best veterinarian and veterinary services for you and your pets depends upon what you want. I have worked many years as a relief veterinarian, and have observed that, generally, each veterinarian attracts a certain type of client. I could take a large group of veterinary clients and match them at better-than-random chance with the correct veterinarian (one in whose practice I have worked).

Most pet owners are attracted to a veterinarian whose personal or practice style is compatible with their needs and wants, whether those needs and wants are cheap prices, the latest in medical techniques, equipment, and facilities, convenience, or table-side manner. Other reasons may be because their children are on the same soccer team or they attend the same church, have a similar professional appearance, or they prefer a more laid-back doctor dressed in jeans and boots. There are numerous other factors that can go into the doctor-client relationship.

In the same way, people may choose a veterinarian based on the facility he or she works from—the hospital on the next corner, the one offering separate waiting rooms for cats and dogs, one with a cozy home atmosphere or sophisticated surroundings, with a waiting room corner or baby sitter for the children, or one that has one-stop shopping.

Most practices are happy to offer a tour of the hospital at the convenience of the staff, of course. Others provide a glimpse of the "back" through photo albums, practice brochures, also touting policy and hours, and periodic newsletters. Some provide an opportunity for owners to watch patient surgery while others object to this type of disruption. Volunteer programs are available in some hospitals for people who want to experience veterinary medicine firsthand.

Regardless of the surroundings, one of you, you *or* your pet, should like and trust the veterinarian you choose. If *both* you and your pet like and trust the veterinarian, consider it a match made in heaven and place this lucky veterinarian on your Christmas list. For more guidelines on choosing a veterinarian, see Table 2.1.

Table 2.1

Client-Veterinarian Relations

1. You should expect confidentiality.

2. You may ask for a referral.

3. Copies or summaries of your pet's medical records and radiographs should be made available upon your request within a reasonable time (usually 10 working days).

4. Unless you request otherwise, repackaged drugs should be supplied in safety closure containers.

5. After-hour emergency service should be available, provided by your veterinarian or by an alternative source.

6. Your pet's medical records should be maintained for a period of at least three years from the last visit.

Relationships—Dogs and People

7. You may ask about fees or estimates of fees for specific procedures.

8. You should not ask for a guaranteed cure; it is against the law for your veterinarian to make a guarantee.

9. You should pay for services as rendered.

10. You should not expect your veterinarian to fill a prescription or otherwise prescribe for the treatment of an animal for which a patient-doctor relationship has not been established.

QUESTION

Dear Dr. Whiteley,

My husband and I will be keeping our grandson, age seven, while his parents are learning Spanish in Costa Rica; my grandson will be staying for the entire summer. We have a good relationship with the child and are looking forward to having him to ourselves. The one problem which I can foresee is our grandson's allergies, particularly to dogs and cats.

We own an elderly pug and a middle-aged spayed female cat, both inside pets. Is there anything we can do to assure our son and daughter-in-law that the pets won't cause medical problems for our grandson?

Concerned in St. Petersburg

Dear Concerned,

I can't prescribe treatment for your grandson, and I urge you to consult with your grandson's physician. However, I can and will offer suggestions for allergy-proofing your pets and home.

Brush the dog and cat daily with a soft brush to remove allergy-causing dander (hair and dandruff) and saliva. An antishedding spray such as Shed-Guard might be helpful. Wipe pets daily with a towel or sponge moistened with distilled water.

Consider, also, a product called Allerpet (marketed by Veterinary Products Laboratories through veterinarians and pet stores), designed to reduce the allergens in dander and saliva. To use, wipe the dog or cat's hair with a damp sponge saturated with Allerpet once weekly; when using the product, do not apply the wet towel treatment.

Shampoo pets every two weeks with a mild pet shampoo and cream rinse. Feed both animals a balanced diet containing natural fat. If either suffers dryness of hair, ask your veterinarian about adding fatty acid supplements to his diet.

Change the cat's litter box when your grandson is outside. Use a dust- and perfume-free litter product, and take care of the box daily.

Allergic persons are especially sensitive to odors; therefore remove pet food dishes and wash them after feeding time. Clean pet beds often, and avoid the use of insecticides and perfumed products on the pets.

Most people who are allergic to animals are also allergic to dust, pollen, and mold. Forbid smoking, and vacuum often when your grandson is away. Eliminate dust catchers, such as dried flower arrangements, and sources of mold in damp areas, such as in bathrooms and basements. Use non-allergic, polyester-filled pillows and comforters in your grandson's room.

Best wishes for a great visit with your grandson!
H. E. W.

3
The Way Dogs Are

The Ancestral Type

There is a theory that says that the dog, if not selected and bred with specific objectives of form and function in mind, will revert to the original, or ancestral, type—that is, the dog who appeared shortly after the wolf, and possibly other canids, became domesticated. Present-day dogs, breeding at random for generations, may revert to this type of generic dog, called a pariah, meaning "outcast."

Pariah dogs, found worldwide, look similar: mid-size in weight (forty to seventy pounds) and stature, ears dropped in the puppy but erect in the adult, with colorations such as yellow, light-brown, white, or combinations of these, and a coat varying from short to shaggy. Old Yeller, the canine protagonist from the novel by Fred Gipson, was probably a pariah: "We called him Old Yeller. The name had a sort of double meaning. One part meant that his short hair was a dingy yellow, a color that we called 'yeller' in those days. The other meant that when he opened his head, the sound he let out came closer to being a yell than a bark."

Because of more effective animal control and leash laws in this country, the pariah dog is seen less often than in times past. The best representative of the pariah that I know is the junkyard dog.

There was a song popular many years ago that said something about the "baddest man" in town being "meaner than a junkyard dog." Lyrics like those didn't make the life of English teachers any easier, nor have they enhanced the image of the junkyard dog. The junkyard dog had a bad reputation; he was an outcast.

Years ago, in New Orleans, I worked at a veterinary hospital located in close proximity to a scrap metal company I'll call Delta Scrap, and I became doctor to a succession of junkyard dogs. I doubt any of my patients from Delta Scrap had ever seen a veterinarian before, but like Little Orphan Annie, they found Daddy Warbucks when they became residents of Delta Scrap.

I never met the owner of that junkyard; the dogs were brought in by employees, often in a big, expensive car. The instructions were always the same: "Give him the works, and send the bill to Delta Scrap."

The "works" included a complete overhaul from ears to anal sacs. After the dog was made more aesthetically pleasing with a bath and

The Way Dogs Are

dip, I administered vaccinations and other needed medical treatment. The dog brought in with a dirty piece of rope or rusty chain left with a new, shiny collar and leash.

The junkyard dogs I knew fit the description of the ancestral type; their only papers were the ones on the bottom of the cage while they were visiting the veterinary hospital. However, their hybrid vigor must have made them survivors.

For some reason, there never seemed to be more than one dog residing at Delta at the same time. Did other dogs respect his territory until the present resident decided it was time to move on? Did the junkyard dog, used to fighting for the bones in life, present a side of his personality that earned him a reputation to his own kind? I don't know.

I do know that the junkyard dogs I worked with were the best of patients. They loved the attention and presented the most mild-mannered personality to those ministering to them. I found another irony in life's assumptions: we should all be as mean as a junkyard dog and as generous as his anonymous benefactor.

This long dissertation about pariahs, ancestral, and junkyard dogs does have a point: the ancestral dog represented the principle of survival of the fittest, and the further from this generic dog that we get via selective breeding, the more problems we create, both physically and behaviorally, for breeds that would never have survived except for the intervention of man.

Dogs Big and Small

Small Dogs

The smallest dog I have known is a half-pound Chihuahua. The little fellow was about six months old when I examined him, and he was anemic owing to an infestation of hookworms. I administered a blood transfusion and a prayer before worming him. Thankfully, he survived the treatment.

Tiny dogs are less likely to survive than their slightly larger peers. The smaller the dog, the greater the body surface area compared to body mass, allowing more heat loss than can be produced or maintained. This is the reason toy-breed dogs shiver and shake, seeking refuge from the cold under blankets and warm sweaters. Rarely do miniature dogs suffer heat prostration.

While there is great disparity in the general size of dogs (largest at 200-plus pounds and smallest at 1/2 pound), there is not much variation in size and weight of the brain; the brain of the biggest dog is only about 2 1/2 times larger than that of the smallest dog.

Interestingly, the smallest wolf has a brain larger in size than the largest dog. According to some experts, that extra brain capacity is needed to survive in the wild. Need is also the reason why wolves have larger teeth and longer jaws than dogs. Little Red Riding Hood said to the wolf, "What big teeth you have!" I'm sure you remember what the wolf said back.

In dogs smaller than the ancestral dog, the skull and bones forming the bony canal surrounding the spinal cord are compressed, in some cases squeezing the brain, spinal cord, and nerves. In extreme cases, the sutures where the bones of the skull should meet (fontanelles) and become bone remain open (the same as when the soft spot on a baby's head remains soft) because there is just not enough room.

In many of these dogs, fluid accumulates in the chambers of the brain, leading to hydrocephalus (water on the brain) with destruction of brain tissue resulting from the pressure. This problem may be noticeable as a bulging of the skull at the top of the head. Other signs are hyperactivity, high-pitched voice, and resistance to house training. The condition is seen most frequently in tiny dogs, such as Chihuahuas, Pomeranians, miniature pinschers, and teacup poodles. The Chihuahua, by the way, is the most apple-headed of all dogs; his skull is rounded in every direction to various degrees.

In other cases, a failure of the small bones of the neck vertebrae to form solid bone near the junction with the head leads to "wobblers" and unsteady gait.

In the tiny dog, also, a condition affecting the hip occurs more often than in large dogs or short dogs, such as dachshunds, with large bones and blood vessels. In the small-structured hip, the openings of the blood vessels are so small they offer inadequate blood supply to the head (ball) of the femur (large bone of the rear leg). If an injury occurs to the hip, the femoral head begins to die owing to inadequate blood circulation. As humans selected breeding animals for reduced leg size, the limbs of the offspring became crooked and the ligaments grew weak, resulting in movement and twisting of the stifle (knee of the rear leg) and dislocation of the patella (knee cap).

I often see my Chihuahua neighbor, Tiger, carrying one of his rear legs as he runs around his yard challenging intruders. I would never invoke Tiger's wrath by wiggling his knee (bears are not the only ones afraid of this diminutive terror), but I'd be willing to bet money on a diagnosis of luxating knee cap.

Large Dogs

At the opposite end of the scale are the large breeds; these, too, have a size limit. In extremely large dogs, the body surface is not sufficient to eliminate the large amount of heat produced by excessive body mass. Giant dogs are prone to heat stroke and circulatory and heart failure. Generally, the larger the breed, the shorter the life span. Bigger is not always better or healthier.

There are laws of mechanical structural design that probably apply to dogs. For example, an architect designing a building triples the bracing when the building height is doubled. As large dogs spurt up in height, the bracing (muscles and ligaments) is often inadequate for the job, contributing to problems such as hip dysplasia (a painful condition caused by poor "fit" between the bones of the ball and socket of the hip joint) and osteochondritis dissecans, a condition causing soreness in the shoulder of big dogs.

Hip dysplasia is a major problem in some breeds, such as the German shepherd. The breed has changed during the last century from a lighter dog, closer in body type to the ancestral dog, to a canine carrying more weight, with a body conformation emphasizing depth and breadth, especially in the chest.

Dr. Wayne H. Riser, in the pamphlet titled "The Dog: His Varied Biological Makeup and Its Relationship to Orthopaedic Diseases," says:

> One wonders if this change in weight and body conformation could have influenced or intensified the incidence of orthopaedic disease.... In hip dysplasia, there is evidence that increased weight, height, and early increased growth have increased the incidence of this condition.

Acute gastric dilation and torsion of the stomach were unknown in this breed [German shepherd] 50 years ago, now it is recognized and it is associated with large dogs that have deep and wide bodies.

A working dog, the German shepherd is known as a police and military dog. But the U.S. military is using fewer German shepherds for scout and sentry duty now in favor of Malinois; the Malinois is lighter and closer to the ancestral type in build and has a lower incidence of hip dysplasia than the German shepherd.

Let's not pick on only the German shepherd. The Saint Bernard is a good representative of a giant breed, with large head and excess, loose skin on the head and neck regions. His teeth are flared and slant outward, creating a pocket inside the mouth at the corners in which saliva collects and spills over, creating a drooler. The loose skin around the eyes contributes to a condition called ectropion, a turning out or drooping of the eyelids.

The breed risk for bone tumors is also high in the Saint Bernard. Bone cancer occurs more frequently in heavier, taller dogs because there are a lot of bone cells undergoing division and change while experiencing the stress of weight and compression.

Short Dogs and Others

I use the term "short dogs" to describe breeds such as the dachshund and basset hound, which were developed from a congenital anomaly that produced stocky dwarfs of the ancestral dog. The head and trunk are essentially normal, but the legs are unusually short. Abnormal changes occur in the cartilage of the vertebrae in these dogs soon after birth, leading to an increased susceptibility to intervertebral disc protrusion and back problems.

The English bulldog, also short in stature, has had to pay for that unusual and pugnacious appearance. The squashed face and nose may be great for holding on to a bull, but the anatomical features are a setup for breathing problems. The huge head and shoulders add strength, but make whelping a difficult, rather than a natural, phenomenon for the female.

Dogs such as the shar-pei, who have wrinkled skin (writer Roger Caras describes the shar-pei as a miniature hippopotamus with badly fitting panty hose), are cute, but obviously all those folds set up this type of dog for skin problems. It's a similar situation as that experienced by long-eared dogs like bassets and cockers, prone to ear problems: no air can get to the ear canals (in dogs with floppy ears) and into skin creases (in dogs with folds and wrinkles), and these areas remain moist, an ideal situation for bacterial and fungal growth. See Table 3.1 for a breakdown of breeds by size.

GENETICS

The dog, as does the wolf, has 78 chromosomes (39 pairs). Genes that determine behavior, personality, and physical traits are located

Table 3.1

Breeds by Size

TOY BREEDS *(LESS THAN 10 POUNDS)*	**SMALL BREEDS** *(10–20 POUNDS)*
Yorkshire terrier	West Highland terrier
Toy poodle	Beagle
Chihuahua	King Charles spaniel
Miniature pinscher	Miniature poodle
Pomeranian	Pug
Maltese	Cairn terrier
MEDIUM BREEDS *(20–50 POUNDS)*	**LARGE BREEDS** *(50–75 POUNDS)*
Airedale terrier	German shepherd
Basset hound	Labrador
Springer spaniel	English/Irish setter
Keeshond	Collie
Siberian husky	Labrador retriever
French bulldog	Greyhound

GIANT BREEDS
(GREATER THAN 75 POUNDS)

St. Bernard, Irish wolfhound,
Newfoundland, Pyrenean mountain dog,
Great Dane, Hungarian komondor

on the chromosomes; one member of each chromosome pair comes from the mother and one from the father, thus both parents contribute equally to the genetic makeup of their offspring.

In cases of inherited disease, a defective gene must be contributed by both parents in some cases, by only one parent in other cases, and in still other cases, the effects of defective genes are influenced by the presence or absence of genes located elsewhere on the chromosome or by sex chromosomes.

The configuration of sex chromosomes are XX for female and XY for male. All offspring receive an X chromosome from the mother and either an X or a Y from the father. If the father donates the Y, he will sire a son, an X, a daughter.

The gene for hemophilia A is found on the X chromosome but not on the Y. If mother passes an X chromosome that carries the defective gene for hemophilia to her son, he develops the disease. If she passes the same defective gene to her daughter, the daughter still has one normal X gene, which prevents the disease but makes her a carrier. Very few males carrying the defective gene live to become fathers; if they did, daughters would have the potential for inheriting two "bad" genes and thus the disease. This is a complicated way of saying that some inherited diseases appear in one sex only.

There's a similar situation when certain genetic problems occur in conjunction with color. For example, if two merle (dappled coat with normal and bluish pigmentation) collies are mated, the offspring have a 25 percent chance of being white and suffering inherited deafness and eye problems.

The color of a dog's coat can be used in some instances to predict behavior. The golden cocker spaniel is more likely than cockers of another color to develop rage syndrome, in which aggression appears without warning and then disappears just as suddenly. No one knows exactly why this occurs, but a genetic abnormality associated with the color gene seems a likely explanation.

There are many inherited diseases, some mild, others fatal, that affect dogs. Some show up at or before birth, others later in life. And close inbreeding (mating parent and offspring or sibling to sibling) is likely to enhance certain features. Unfortunately, hidden defects are also more likely to be exposed. Purebred animals are, of course, much more inbred than mongrels.

The Way Dogs Are

In an article that appeared in *Time*, author Michael D. Lemonick writes: "Today, 15 to 25 percent of the 20 million purebred dogs in America have or carry a genetic disease, while many others suffer from lesser genetically related problems." These genetic disorders are estimated to cost breeders and owners close to one billion dollars in lost revenues and veterinary bills.

What we have been doing to man's best friend has been going on for years. Konrad Lorenz, the famous Austrian who studied animal behavior, wrote in *Man Meets Dog*: "One is probably less likely to obtain in a mongrel a nervous, mentally deficient animal than in a dog with eight champions in its pedigree."

That's one solution—stick with a mutt. Science is helping, too. Dr. Donald Patterson, chief of the medical genetics department at the University of Pennsylvania School of Veterinary Medicine, is creating a computerized genetic-disease database that will list over 300 genetic problems affecting dogs. He and other researchers are isolating the genes responsible for many genetic diseases, enabling breeding clubs to adopt stricter standards and to educate their members to cease breeding dogs carrying defective genes. (For more information on inherited diseases, see Table 3.2.)

PERSONALITY PLUS

Old Yeller, a representative of the ancestral type, was a great dog, loving and loyal, and those of us of my generation who remember the movie, and Fess Parker's shooting the dear fellow when he contracted rabies, get tears in our eyes just thinking about it. Most dogs have great personalities, and that's the reason we've chosen them for our best friends.

Through selective breeding, personality traits have been enhanced or changed, just as physical traits have been. But there is a genetic "catch," which applies to both physical and personality traits: to achieve or excel on one side, or in one direction, something must be taken away on the other.

Let me give an example. Chips, a collie-husky cross, was aggressive and sometimes mean. After he bit the garbage man, his owners did what many of us have wanted to do: they signed over their rebellious canine offspring to the army, and this was in wartime, too—

Table 3.2

Inherited Diseases Named for Affected Breeds

DISEASE AND SYMPTOMS

Afghan myelomalacia:
Reported in Afghan hounds 3–13 months of age; symptoms of hopping gait, paralysis, and death

German shepherd posterior paresis:
In dogs 7–10 years of age; wobbly gait, leading to paralysis

Collie eye syndrome:
Abnormality of retina that can progress to blindness

Dalmatian bronzing syndrome:
Partial hair loss accompanied by reddish-brown skin color

Scottie cramp:
Muscular contractions and cramps, causing stiff-legged gait

Lhasa apso disease:
Kidney disease varying from slight to severe

Norwegian elkhound anomaly:
Progressive deterioration of kidney

Grey collie syndrome:
Blood disease of collies linked to coat color

Beagle pain syndrome:
Arterial disease manifesting as pain upon movement

World War II. Chips's owners probably said something like this: "Let the Army teach him a few manners and if he thinks home is so bad, let him get his butt shot at over in Europe."

Chips went through military training and served with the 3rd Infantry Division in Algeria, Morocco, Tunisia, Sicily, Italy, and France. During one maneuver, Chips "singlehandedly" attacked an Italian machine-gun position and forced the surrender of its crew. He was wounded in action and received the Purple Heart; other acts of heroism earned him the Silver Star.

The Way Dogs Are

Chips and his bravery were the subjects of two speeches in Congress; his exploits were widely publicized and served as the model for many fictitious dog stories. Eventually, because federal regulations prohibit animals from receiving decorations, the awards the famous canine received were revoked.

Decorated or not, it was in Chips's nature to be a fighter, but he had none of the personal attributes for diplomacy. The canine hero reportedly bit General Eisenhower on the hand during the Roosevelt-Churchill Conference in Casablanca in 1943.

What I'm trying to say, using the above example, is that if an animal is bred for one trait such as aggressiveness, the opposite trait of congeniality is missing. (See Table 3.3 for a listing of breeds and special attributes.)

How dogs are today is a direct result of what dogs were bred for originally. For example, terriers that are small whirlwinds of energy, activity, and aggressiveness were bred to chase, ferret out, and kill rodents and other animals, such as badgers and foxes. Some of that same energy and ferociousness is present in modern-day terriers, such as Yorkies and Scotties.

Ease of training is an attribute of retrievers, and dogs like the Labrador make excellent service dogs because of their intelligence and love for learning. A herding dog, the collie, was designed to work sheep, not to attack them, so for the most part collies are not attackers or biters. (Chips was part collie, so there are exceptions.) Dogs such as the bloodhound were brought up to let us know when they found someone or something; therefore, it is only natural for scent hounds to be barkers.

Although some sporting breeds such as cockers and hunters like the Afghan hound were instinctively good at what they were bred to do, they are today not easily trained in areas such as obedience and housebreaking. Dogs listed as excitable in Table 3.3 are energetic—a helpful trait in a dachshund chasing a rabbit, but not so helpful if barking excessively, snapping at children, or demanding attention. In the same way, aggression is desirable in a guard, but not so great in a household of young children or elderly grandparents.

This chapter is not meant to discourage you from adopting a purebred dog, nor is it intended to increase your fear if you already own one. It is meant to kindle your awareness that your dog's inheritance is an important factor, although not the only one, in determining

Table 3.3

Breed Specialty

Breed	Specialty	Attributes
Bloodhound	Scent trailer	Good nose, loud continuous bark, laid-back nature, not aggressive
German shorthaired pointer	Follow, point to birds	Lean, fast, good nose, not aggressive, easily trained
Labrador retriever	Spot and retrieve birds	Excellent senses of sight and smell, easy to train, not aggressive
Fox terrier	Catch and kill fox	Fast, excitable, highly aggressive
Collie	Herd or guard sheep	Gentle, easily trained, not aggressive
Irish setter	"Set" at site of fallen bird	Protective silky hair, aggression medium, excitable
Afghan hound	Hunter	Silent, swift, good eyesight, high aggression, not easily trained
Newfoundland	Water rescue	Webbed feet, swimmer, laid-back, not easily trained, aggressive
Great Dane	Hunt wild boar	Strong, fast, highly aggressive, laid-back, not easily trained

The Way Dogs Are

Table 3.3

Breed Specialty (cont.)

BREED	SPECIALTY	ATTRIBUTES
St. Bernard	Alpine rescue	Good nose, strong, highly aggressive, laid-back, not easily trained
Bullmastiff	Catch and hold poachers	Strong, powerful jaws, independent, highly aggressive
Siberian husky	Pull sleds	Strong, works in packs, highly aggressive, not easily trained
Dachshund	Badger or rabbit hunter	Excitable, highly aggressive, medium trainability
Pekingese	Companion	Small, silky hair, excitable, medium in aggression, not easily trained
Poodle	Retrieve game from water	Curly, oily hair to repel water, soft mouth, excitable, easily trained, aggression medium
Cocker spaniel	Track, flush birds	Short, powerful legs, excitable, not easily trained, medium in aggression

why he is the way he is. In the next chapter I address choosing and raising the best dog or dogs for you.

QUESTION

Dear Dr. Whiteley,

What is your opinion about people keeping pit bulls as pets? I have seen several in my neighborhood, and have never been afraid of them until now. Do we have any local legislation to protect us from these vicious dogs?

Concerned Citizen in Amarillo

Dear Concerned,

I have treated many dogs with this breeding and have found them, for the most part, to be gentle and easy to handle. They can be and usually are vicious with other dogs.

Pit bulls have the genetic predisposition for aggression. They are potentially dangerous to people because of their powerful jaws and because as fighters they hold a quarry to the finish.

I, however, go along with the school of thought that there is a problem in this country with irresponsible dog owners, not with pit bulls. If you breed a mean dog with another mean dog, and throw in a mean owner to boot, you are bound to end up with puppies that rival Stephen King's Cujo in horror-producing talent.

The AVMA supports vicious animal legislation by state, county, or municipal governments, provided the laws do not refer to specific breeds. Your hometown of Amarillo has a good law: "As a public safety requirement, it shall be unlawful for any person in control of any vicious animal to take such a vicious animal out of any secure enclosure unless such animal is securely muzzled or restrained by a leash. 'Vicious animal,' for the purpose of this section, shall mean any animal having a history of unprovoked attacks or any animal having a propensity known to the person in control to do any act which may endanger the person or property of others."

A vicious animal law, such as the above, is more protective and fair than legislation that singles out a particular breed for restrictions. I believe that pit bull owners must be especially vigilant about restraint and training of their animals because of the possible danger and the fear on the part of the public.

Thanks for writing,
H. E. W.

4
Choosing Dogs

Matching Owner and Pet

Have you ever noticed that some dogs mimic the traits—physical, personality, or both—of their owners while others display the opposite attributes? In the first category were the dogs belonging to my radiology professor in veterinary school, a heavyset and scowling man who liked to stroll into class, blow into the microphone, and shout, "I wish I could breathe fire!"

Although we frightened students could picture Dr. Newton B. Tenille with an English bulldog, he bred and raised pugs, whose squashed faces and grimacing expressions made excellent substitutes. I have no idea what the dogs' names were, but I do remember what we students called them: Newt I, Newt II, Newt III, named after you-know-who.

In the second category were the models and animals picked for advertising purposes by the animal vaccine company I worked for in the eighties. In one ad, a nude-to-the-waist male body builder was featured with a tiny, big-eyed kitten. In another, a sophisticated female model clothed in expensive furs was pictured cuddling a scruffy-looking coon dog with torn ears.

The idea was that clients would notice the ads because the person-animal combinations were unusual. The unexpected result was that female staff members at veterinary hospitals wrote asking for enlargements of the male-model ad, and animal rights adherents wrote demanding a retraction of the ad of the model clothed in animal fur.

Results of advertising campaigns aren't always what are hoped for or anticipated. In the real world of animal companionship, the results aren't always what are hoped for or anticipated.

It helps, though, to know what you have to offer a pet and what you expect from that pet. Some questions to ask include the following: What purpose is the dog to fulfill? What are the costs of dog ownership in both money and time? What are the health and make-up of family members, including existing pets, who will share quarters with the dog? What type of pet will these quarters comfortably accommodate?

Role

Let's take the first question: What role or purpose is the dog to fulfill? Are you interested in a guard dog or lap puppy, a hunting dog or

Choosing Dogs

racing canine, a show dog or companion? Some dogs can fulfill more than one role; however, it makes sense to choose a dog who closely matches his job description.

A friend of mine owned a chocolate-colored Labrador retriever named Dan. I was especially fond of this dog because of his sweet disposition; most Labradors are friendly, which allows them to be both hunters and companions. However, Dan's owner bought the dog to guard his new house in the country.

When anyone approached my friend's driveway or yard, Dan, wagging his tail, would run up with a ball or Frisbee in his mouth. As a watchdog, he was a washout. Perhaps the family was at fault in the way they raised him, but more than likely Dan just didn't have it in his nature to be a guard dog. In Table 3.3, Labrador retrievers are listed as "not aggressive."

Monetary Expense

An inquiry into the expense of pet ownership might be approached with additional questions. If you think Dow Jones is an Eastern religion brought to America by a woman named Mother Jones, and if you live paycheck to paycheck and already own five dogs and two cats, adding another pet should be delayed until you win the million-dollar lottery. On the other hand, if you can budget for dog food, supplies, health and grooming care, obedience training, boarding expense, and so on, by all means consider a dog. And if you have a favorable relationship with Dow Jones, buy an expensive one if you want—one that requires monthly trips to the grooming parlor and veterinary hospital.

Time Expense

Time is a commodity as precious or more precious than money to many families today, especially the working mother. A recent survey of 1,100 pet owners conducted by the American Animal Hospital Association found that the female head-of-household is the pet caretaker in 66 percent of families. Only 19 percent of pets are cared for by male head-of-households and 7 percent by the children.

If your obligations are such that you know adding a pet is too much for you at this time, and you are tempted to give in to young children's demands for a dog, resist that guilt trip. When the children are older and have proved themselves responsible enough to care for a dog, reconsider. For now, a lower maintenance pet such as a shorthaired cat or a goldfish might suffice, and there are those who should adopt a cactus, not an animal.

If you are convinced you can handle the training and care of a dog, select a breed compatible with your time reserves. Some dogs have greater requirements for exercise, training, and grooming. I have noticed that owners of shar-peis spend more time in veterinary hospital waiting rooms than owners of same-size mixed breed dogs, and caretakers of Afghans spend a lot of time with comb and brush in hand while Rottweiler owners consume Saturday afternoons attached to a leash at the park.

If you have neither the time nor the inclination to housetrain a new puppy in the dead of winter, consider adopting an adult dog—one who has already been trained.

Alternatives to Ownership

It is not only the busy working mom with young children who might find intimidating a fifteen- to twenty-year commitment to a dog. Those who are elderly or who travel or anticipate moving might wish to defer or postpone dog ownership.

I recently read about a "rent-a-pooch" pet shop in Japan that offers dogs by the hour, ranging in price from $10 per hour for a small dog to $20 for a large one. Sounds pricey, yet in the long-run, it is cheaper than a lifelong commitment. The owner of the pet shop says that customers often rent the same dog each time.

In some areas, pet lending libraries, established in schools and/or animal shelters, offer an alternative to pet ownership. The teacher I knew who created such a library for his school used animals to encourage student responsibility and good conduct. Those who earned the privilege could check out a pet plus supplies for the weekend.

Animal visitation programs for nursing homes and hospitals are multiplying, as we become increasingly aware of the emotional benefits that animals bring to those who cannot interact with pets in their home.

Check with your local humane groups for educational and institutional visitation programs in your area. If you are interested in start-

Choosing Dogs

ing a program, contact the Delta Society, an international resource on the relationships between people, animals, and their environment, at P.O. Box 1080, Renton, WA 98057-1080; telephone (206) 235-1076.

ROOMMATES

The age, health, and activity level of all residents, as well as home size and arrangement, should be factored into the pet selection equation. One of my clients, an older woman who lived in a small duplex with an adult retarded son, asked my advice about selecting a puppy to replace the elderly poodle who had just died. I suggested a small dog such as a Welsh corgi or sheltie. Smaller dogs are usually easier for frail persons to care for and live with than large dogs, who can be clumsy in confined spaces and require more exercise.

The woman must have heard only the part about the small dog, because she chose a Yorkshire terrier puppy. Yorkies are not listed in Table 3.3, but the traits of a fox terrier are close—fast, excitable, highly aggressive—and this particular Yorkie was a terror. In short order, he had destroyed the woman's living room furniture, dug up the small yard, disturbed the neighbors with his barking, and bitten his visiting veterinarian.

I would like to say that behavior modification, to be covered in chapter 10, changed the delinquent's ways, but when I last saw the client, the Yorkie still ruled the household with sharp teeth and a fierce bark. In this case, owner and new pet were mismatched.

The new pet and resident pets can also be mismatched. I have known people who adopted a rambunctious puppy to stimulate an older dog to youth and activity. Although dogs are known as social animals, many are perfectly happy being social with their human family.

My dog Bear, at seventeen, is the equivalent of an eighty-six-year-old person. Like some older individuals, his senses are waning; he sleeps much of the time, and moves around slower than he used to. He seems to resent any intrusion by other dogs, especially active puppies. I believe that adding a new puppy to our household at this time in Bear's life would be stressful to him. A couple of years ago, he looked and acted much younger, and he would have, I believe, accepted a new canine member.

Introductions

dog to dog

When introducing a new canine roommate to your resident dog, arrange the first meeting at a neutral place not associated by either pet as "his territory." This can be a park or a friend's yard.

Although it is helpful if both dogs are on a leash, let the two interact with little interference from you. The dominant dog will act aggressively; it is hoped the less dominant will accept his position as second dog. Although the positions may reverse later, the adult dog is usually "top dog" to a puppy.

When the dogs are placed together at home, it is best that you adhere to the social structure played out in the first meeting. Dogs don't want to be treated equally; they like to know where they fit into the social structure of dogdom. You don't allow this natural relationship to develop if you are always interfering; on the other hand, you don't want one dog beating up the other.

Feed the dogs together in the same room, at the same time, but with separate bowls. If one dog refuses to let the other eat, you may have to separate them at feeding time for a while. This can be done quietly, without loudly chastising the dominant dog; you want him to associate the presence of the new dog or puppy with good things, not constant punishment or verbal admonishments. It takes about two weeks for dogs to establish their social order at home.

dog to cat

Dogs and cats do not establish relationships the same way dogs do among themselves. Much depends upon their early conditioning to the other species. I have known cat-hating dogs who could do away with a cat within a blink of an eye, and I've known some fierce felines.

It's best to have the dog and cat under control—on a leash, in a crate (dog) or cat carrier (cat)—when the two meet for the first time. Don't allow the two to interact without being present to monitor the meeting. Also, provide separate food bowls, sleeping areas, and places where the cat can escape from the dog.

The introductions go much easier if the dog has been obedience trained. If he decides to chase the cat, call him to "come" and "sit." Make sure the cat's claws are trimmed, and if he acts aggressively toward the new dog, remove him quietly to a room of his own.

Choosing Dogs

Shared Rooms

While we're on the topic of selecting roommates, it is appropriate to consider the type of rooms to be shared.

pets in rented premises

My mother-in-law recently moved into a HUD-sponsored housing facility. Her apartment fell under a federal law that stipulates that the owner or manager cannot prohibit or prevent tenants from keeping common household pets in their apartments or from discriminating against pet owners. In this facility, residents with pets live on a particular floor and must heed rules, such as adhering to state laws about vaccination, providing a sanitary method for the collection and disposal of pet waste, ensuring adequate restraint of pets taken off premises, and registering pets with the housing manager.

If you rent a house or apartment owned by a private landlord, there may be a no-pet rule. Although leases that prohibit children or discriminate racially are not legal, private individuals can indeed prohibit the keeping of pets on their property. Exceptions are made for seeing-eye, hearing-ear, and some types of service dogs, if your state has laws governing these canine assistants.

But there are considerations besides legal ones when selecting a pet to join you in your castle. Why is it that people who own expensive tapestries and velvet couches always seem to share quarters with long-haired cats and dogs, such as German shepherds, known for shedding. I suppose it is because you notice the animal hair on the fancy furnishings.

Most of us don't need to be told that a *miniature* pinscher would be a better pinscher choice for a roommate than a doberman if you live in a twentieth-floor efficiency housing your antique windmill collection. However, that's not taking into account what I call the "heart factor."

THE HEART FACTOR

When the heart overrules the brain in a decision, the heart factor has entered the equation. I have allowed the heart factor to color my decisions about pet selection.

Several years ago I dropped by the pound to confer with officials there about a laboratory I was conducting on their premises for my veterinary technology students. My daughter Kimberly, then ten years old, spotted a tiny puppy who was the last of the litter and would be put to sleep in the morning if I didn't say yes to "Oh Mom, can we take her?"

That puppy was Little Bit, a blue-eyed deaf (in some breeds, congenital deafness is associated with white coat and blue eyes) and mentally dumb Australian shepherd. "Act in haste, repent in leisure" is an old adage that comes to mind about my relationship with Little Bit.

I came to regret adopting a dog who couldn't hear and was therefore difficult to train, one that dug out of the yard and slept under neighborhood cars, and one that died at age two under the wheels of an automobile she could not hear. Should I have known better? Of course. Would I do it again, knowing the outcome? Of course.

The heart factor also affects those who have a dream that centers on a dog. Such was a man I call Pierre, a dark-haired native of French New Orleans who was my mailman when I lived in that city.

"What do you know about Siberian huskies?" he asked me one day at my mailbox. He went on to explain, rather shyly, that he had just bought a husky puppy at the local pet store for $500. "It's coming down from up north after the litter's weaned. I've been waiting nearly a year for one with blue eyes, and I'm finally gonna get him," he said excitedly.

A Siberian husky in New Orleans? I didn't have the heart to dampen Pierre's spirits by saying what I was thinking: are you building an air-conditioned doghouse or planning to snow-sled across Lake Pontchartrain? I just encouraged him to bring the puppy in for a checkup and vaccinations as soon as he received him.

A month later, Pierre appeared at the hospital with his puppy. "Ain't he a beaut!" he said proudly, as he set a scraggly, eight-week-old pup on the exam table.

The puppy, whose name was Nikos, was thin with ribs showing and had a pot belly and dry, dull hair. He was the classic picture of parasite infestation.

I raised the puppy's upper lip to examine the color of his gums; they were as white as my lab coat. I did a fecal check, which revealed what I had suspected—hookworm and roundworm eggs crowded together on the slide—and a blood sample revealed a critical lack of red blood cells.

"Pierre," I said, "I'm going to recommend that you take this puppy back to the pet store and either exchange him for another puppy or

Choosing Dogs

get your money back. He is loaded with worms, and it's a wonder he's still alive. His blood count is dangerously low. If I worm him and those hookworms release their hold on the intestinal wall, he could bleed enough to put him over the edge. He'll have to have a blood transfusion before I can risk treating the parasite problem, and even with that, he might not make it."

Pierre looked down at the pup and stroked the shaggy, silver head. "I've waited so long for one with blue eyes. He's just what I want, and there's not another one at the pet store like him. No, I can't take him back," he said, shaking his head.

I tried again. "But, Pierre, the treatment will be expensive; he might need more than one transfusion. If he doesn't make it, you'll be out both the $500 and the medical bill."

"I can't just let him die," my client said. "I've wanted a dog like him all of my life. You just do what you need to do. I'll see to the bill, and God will see to the dog."

I wouldn't have told you this story, which happened over two decades ago, if it didn't have a happy ending. What impressed me at the time, and what has made the incident remain in my memory, was the heart factor.

I came to realize that Nikos, who by six months was a handsome dog with thick, silky hair and a jaunty walk, was a dream fulfilled for Pierre. A descendant of generations of New Orleans residents, this native Louisianian had never traveled far from his "roots." The blue-eyed, silver-haired husky represented an exotic world to the far north and visions of Jack London, Canadian Mounties, snow-covered terrain, and sled dog races. What would life be without dreams, and what would life be if we didn't, at least some of the time, follow our hearts?

WHERE TO FIND A DOG

In Table 4.1 I've listed common sources of dogs and what I consider the pros and cons of each. In earlier examples, I've mentioned obtaining dogs from the animal shelter and pet store. If Pierre and I had gone to a reputable breeder, we would have, I hope, been spared our particular sorrows connected with adopting puppies with inherited defects and parasitism.

Many people adopt puppies from individuals or neighbors who are

Table 4.1

Where to Find a Dog or Puppy

PLACE	PROS	CONS
Shelter or rescue group	Give a needy animal a home. Large selection. May offer low-cost vaccination and neuter programs.	Exposure to other animals, increasing disease potential. Stressed. Background unknown.
Pet store	Contract may allow for return within short period of time.	Exposure to other animals. May be stressed. Background unknown.
Neighbor or individual	You know the mother and father, home environment. Can observe interactions of dog family; ask questions about health care of mother and litter.	Genetic background unknown.
Breeder	Breeder can answer questions about genetic background. You can inspect condition of dogs and facilities, and ask questions about health care of mother and litter. Can meet relatives of dog. Many breeders allow return within short period of time.	It is your responsibility to discern between reputable and disreputable breeders.

giving away or selling them. If you are considering adopting from this source, spend time and ask questions about the behavior, physical problems, and care of the parents and offspring.

Puppies take on the physical and behavioral characteristics of their canine parents. If you are considering a breed susceptible to hip dysplasia or another inherited disorder, find out if either parent has suffered from this problem. Are the canine parents obedience trained? Do they exhibit behavioral problems such as aggression toward strangers? Are the puppies and parents healthy? Have they been vaccinated and dewormed? What type of food do they eat?

Observe the interactions of the canine and human family, and the environment where they live. This is difficult to do if you are tempted by the cute little fellows being given away in the Wal-Mart parking lot.

I am aware that many people experience pet selection in reversed order: the puppy selects the owner. Those prone to the heart factor acquiesce to the dog's good sense in selecting human companions.

Lemon Laws

Under the law, dogs are considered property, much the same as cars or washing machines. Consumer protection laws at the state or local level, designed to protect the public, may apply to dog purchases or may be set up to specifically address canine transactions.

New Jersey has a law that pertains to the purchase of dogs from pet shops or kennels. In essence, the law requires that the dog or cat be examined by a veterinarian within seventy-two hours of date of purchase. If the veterinarian certifies that the animal is unfit for purchase, owing to disease or injury, within fourteen days of sale (within six months in the case of congenital or inherited disorders), or if the animal dies owing to disease or injury within fourteen days, the purchaser has two options: he may return the pet for a refund or for exchange with an animal of equal value, or he may elect to have the animal treated by the veterinarian. The purchaser is also entitled to reimbursement of veterinary fees, not to exceed the purchase price of the animal.

Choosing

I've said much in earlier chapters about purebred animals and potential problems. Yet the case for choosing a purebred dog is that you know what to expect, at least in physical characteristics.

The same holds true for adult dogs. They are already there in terms of looks and behavior. On the other hand, a puppy might be considered pure potential, at least behaviorally. Proper conditioning and socialization can do much to mold him into the type of companion you have always wanted.

I might add that one of the best-natured dogs I ever adopted was an adult when I selected him. Bowser was advertised "free to good home" in the local newspaper, and he proved to be well trained and tolerant with children, plus he was past that chewing and peeing stage.

Gender

What about gender? Unwanted sexual behavior can be alleviated by neutering, yet neutering will not make a dog calmer, less destructive, or less aggressive toward people. If you are considering a breed with high aggressive tendencies and/or excitable nature, give preference to a female who tends to be less aggressive and calmer than most males. In terms of housebreaking ease and general trainability, females rank higher than males; males generally demand more time for play and exercise than females, and are more likely to scent-mark their territorial boundaries.

One of the most famous canine movie stars of all times was and is a female impersonator. That star is Lassie, and there have been a succession of seven Lassies, all male. The reason why males have played the role all these years is that masculine collies are bigger and have fuller coats.

In return for using a male with beautiful hair, Lassie's trainer must contend with other less pleasing male traits. The original Lassie came to Rudd Weatherwax, an animal trainer, to be cured of his habit of chasing motorcycles. Although Weatherwax never broke Lassie I of chasing motorcycles, he did train him to be a great actor, playing in his first movie, *Lassie Come Home*, with Roddy McDowall, Elizabeth Taylor, and Donald Crisp.

Choosing Dogs

In an interview with Bob Weatherwax, Rudd's son and trainer of the current Lassie VII, news reporter Ron Miller writes:

> By the way, I know Lassie is really a boy and so does he. Though he works as a female impersonator, I can guarantee you Lassie doesn't act like a sissy in any way. He regards his confusing sexual identity as just a part of making a living.
>
> In fact, Lassie is so normal that he even gave proof of it by lifting his leg on the sofa in Weatherwax's house. His owner was not overjoyed.
>
> "Lassie," he grumbled, "I hope you realize you've just blown your image for good."

When Two Are Better Than One

If you will be away from home much of the time and want two dogs who can socialize in your absence, I recommend that you adopt two young puppies, littermates preferably, who can form social bonds with each other as they grow up. The desirability of adopting another dog or puppy as a playmate for your resident dog depends upon the social nature, health, and age of your resident dog.

Breeds used to living in packs, such as huskies and malamutes, are often more settled and less destructive when living in a multiple-dog household. If you have the choice, adopt two females or a male and female rather than two males, who are more likely to fight with each other.

Also, it is best not to adopt two "top" dogs who must compete on a regular basis for that position. The behavioral traits associated with dominance and submission are covered in greater detail in chapter 7.

Personality Tests

There are several so-called puppy tests designed to determine the personality traits of individuals within a litter. Basically, you are trying discover if specific puppies are fearful, aggressive, submissive, playful, and so on.

In one test, you pick up a puppy and cradle him on his back in one arm while placing the other hand gently on his chest. If the puppy is a dominant personality, he will show a long period of struggling, twisting, and biting. If fearful, he may act panic-stricken, be stiff, or show other signs of fear, such as crying and whining. A submissive puppy will be subdued or cowed. A people-oriented, confident puppy may initially struggle, but will soon relax in response to your words of encouragement.

Obviously, this is not a foolproof method of determining puppy personalities, especially if you are a stranger and if the puppies are tested in a novel environment or the mother or litter are stressed by the extra noise and confusion of children and other visitors.

Even doing the serious task of selecting a lifelong canine companion, you must use common sense. L. M. Boyd is quoted in the book *Mondo Canine*: "Dog trainers tested various breeds to see how they behaved under various circumstances.... In initiative requiring individual action—firecrackers set off near a litter of puppies—the barkless African Basenji performed the best. Bit the fellow who lit the firecrackers."

I don't recommend testing reactions to firecrackers. It is more sensible to meet a potential canine friend—dog or puppy—in a quiet and familiar place and assess his reaction to the sound of your voice and your offer of friendship—an extended palm. (For more tips, see Table 4.2.)

QUESTION

Dear Dr. Whiteley,

I have a Chinese pug with a very short coat (his hair covering is so thin you can see his skin through his hair on tail, tummy, legs, and feet). We live in western Wisconsin, where our winters can be quite severe. Our pug is two years old and likes to play outside with our blue heeler. We have a nice coat for him, which protects from his neck to his tail, but we know of no way to keep his feet warm and dry when he is out in snow up to his neck. He goes out at 10 to 20 degrees above zero or colder, and plays for a half-hour or so and comes back with his feet red and frostbitten and possibly freezing.

What really happens to his pads and feet in these circumstances? Do his pads and feet have so little circulation that they really freeze? If my toes froze they would fall off.

Choosing Dogs

Table 4.2

Matching Owner and Pet

Pup Personality	Handling Needs	Owner
Timid, shy, fearful	Soft voice, gentle touch and handling	Responds to sensitive owner; unsuitable for dominant adults or loud and rough children
Dominant, aggressive	Firm, immediate, and consistent control	Responds to firm disciplinarian; unsuitable for young children, frail adults
Sociable, easy-going	Social boundaries and training	Responds to consistent owners of all ages

What happens to my pug's pads and toes? Will his feet get tougher and tougher with time, like a callus, so they can take more and more cold without causing damage?

Wisconsin Mom

Dear Mom,

Frostbite causes inflammation and, in extreme cases, destruction of body tissues (human or animal). Minor cases of frostbite result in redness, heat, pain, and swelling. After these signs subside, irritation and itching may occur; the body part is usually sensitive to cold. In severe cases, circulation to the body part is destroyed, and the affected part may shrivel or drop off.

A dog acclimated to your cold Wisconsin winters survives better in ice and snow than a dog from the South or one kept indoors at all times. Your dog might appreciate a pair of booties to go with his winter coat. You may have to experiment to come up with the best water-repellent material. The Eskimos often use sealskin, but I don't know about its availability in Wisconsin. Perhaps heavy denim or leather would suffice. The booties can be fastened to the dog's legs above the dewclaws with Velcro or tape. The booties must fit tightly enough to prevent their coming off, but not tight enough to constrict circulation. Remove the booties when they get wet.

Please check with your pug's veterinarian about his thin hair coat. Certain hormone conditions, which are treatable, can cause thinning of the hair coat.

Best wishes for a fun-filled winter.
H. E. W.

5
Puppies—The First Weeks

The first twelve weeks may be the most important in a dog's life. It is during this time that the puppy acquires the physical and social characteristics that determine future behavior. See Table 5.1 for concise information about the puppy's physical and social development.

BEFORE AND FOLLOWING BIRTH

The physical and emotional health of the pregnant mother influences that of her offspring. As much as 60 percent of the weight of unborn puppies is gained during the last three to four weeks of pregnancy. Not only should the bitch receive more food during these last weeks of gestation, but the food should be highly nutritious and easily digestible (feeding the pregnant dog is covered more extensively in chapter 12).

If the mother is severely malnourished and carrying a large litter, the puppies may be born with compromised immunological systems, making them more susceptible to infection. Even if puppies survive to adulthood, retardation of the immune system has been shown to be passed on to the next generation.

Puppies born to malnourished mothers often exhibit signs of fading puppy syndrome—crying excessively, failure to gain weight, and difficulty keeping warm. If the mother perceives them as unfit, she may ignore them. These pups rarely survive.

During the last few weeks of pregnancy and extending through the first two weeks after birth, puppy brains undergo rapid development. Severe protein deficiency, one-third to one-half of optimum, in the mother's diet can cause stunting of brain growth in the newborn. Even if adequate nutrition is supplied after birth, deprived puppies do not catch up with puppies receiving adequate nutrition in the uterus. These puppies are slow learners.

Laboratory experiments in rats suggest that permanent changes in emotional behavior occur in pups born to malnourished mothers. These changes, which last a lifetime, result in intense excitement and preoccupation with feeding. In dogs, this type of emotional retardation occurs most commonly in runts competing for nutrients and nipples in large litters.

During this same period, just before and after birth, drugs used to treat the mother and/or newborns can cause changes in the vulnera-

Table 5.1

Puppy Development

STAGE	CHARACTERISTICS
Before birth	Vulnerable to physical and emotional health of mother; body movement; pinch reflex (withdraws toe from pinch).
0 to 2 weeks	Primary social relationship is with mother; physical development includes crawling, rooting (pushing head into warm objects), sucking and nursing, whining and yelping; urination and defecation stimulated by mother; responds to sensations of touch, pain, warmth, cold, hunger, and smell.
2 to 4 weeks	Relationship with littermates important; physical development includes growling and barking, tail wagging, teeth near surface of gums; urination and defecation beginning to take place outside nest; behavior includes food seeking (investigative to find food, antagonistic in attacking and protecting food, investigative in eating food), and play-fighting and mounting-clasping littermates; senses of sight and hearing operative.
4 to 12 weeks	Relationships with dogs, other animals, people, and environment important; weaning takes place; learning of pack behavior (dominant-submissive postures directed toward mother, littermates, and people); socialization; fear imprinting.

ble brain cells of immature puppies. Experiments using diazepam (Valium) in rats showed that babies exposed to the drug around birthing time had greater problems with coordination and were more emotional than controls at six months of age. Just as in humans, using drugs in the pregnant and nursing bitch should be avoided.

Another experiment with rats that I find interesting may be applicable to both human and canine behavior. In this study, female rats who were stimulated to fear in late pregnancy produced young who were more fearful and emotional in general as adults than controls from mothers who did not experience fearful emotions during late pregnancy. The lesson here might be to limit fear-inducing stress to the bitch during late pregnancy.

After birth, physical contact between mother and offspring is important for puppy emotional health and survival and for bonding with the mother. Infant puppies from birth to approximately two weeks of age respond to the outside world aided primarily by senses of touch, taste, and smell. It is the smell of the mother's saliva and the stimulation of her touch when she licks puppies that tell the young who she is. When a mother licks her nipples, she lays down a scent trail for pups to follow. If you wash away the saliva from around the bitch's nipples, pups have difficulty finding them.

Studies, again in rats, show that licking and grooming by the mother rat produces chemical changes in the baby. When the baby is taken away from the mother, his growth hormone decreases; this is nature's way of ensuring survival. If the mother's smell and touch are removed for as little as forty-five minutes in newborn rats, the infant lowers his need for food to keep himself alive until the mother returns. If the mother never returns, the pup's lower metabolic rate results in retarded growth.

This phenomenon can be demonstrated in humans. In the case of premature babies, those receiving human touch via massage gain weight as much as 50 percent faster than babies not so stimulated. Eight months later, massaged babies were found to be bigger in general, with larger heads and fewer physical problems.

Do the above experiments have applicability in raising puppies? I believe they do. If a mother falls down on the job of licking, grooming, and other forms of dog-to-dog touching, we must take her place and provide the tactile stimulation that seems to give the body the go-ahead to develop optimally.

Puppies—The First Weeks

Young children, with adult supervision, should be allowed to play for limited periods of time with puppies if the canine mother permits. In one study, kittens who received human handling for ten minutes a day soon after birth opened their eyes sooner, emerged from the nest sooner, and were more active than kittens not interacting with people.

It is believed that handling is a mild form of stress, fine-tuning the adrenal system, which produces the fight or flight hormones. Individuals who receive this early arousal are calmer and less emotional when stressed as adults. An experiment by Dr. Michael Fox of the Humane Society of the United States demonstrated that puppies stimulated by stroking and flashes of light are better problem solvers as adults than puppies left alone.

During the first few days after birth, puppies display what's known as flexor dominance (the puppy will curl his back and legs when held up by the neck), a reflex reflecting his position in the womb. By day 4 or 5 after birth, a puppy will extend his legs when held in the same position. By the second or third week of life, however, the puppy is able to control the position of his limbs.

The newborn puppy spends 30 percent of his time nursing and most of the remainder of time sleeping. His sleep is characterized by muscle tremors and twitches. The mother stimulates the newborn to eliminate by licking the anus and genitals with a warm, wet tongue. During the period from birth to two weeks of age, the bitch is the primary influence on puppy development.

The Helpless Infant

The length of pregnancy in both dogs and cats is relatively short—approximately nine weeks—and offspring are born immature. It is interesting to compare dogs with guinea pigs, who are pregnant a comparable length of time and produce approximately the same size litters, averaging three to four young.

Newborn guinea pigs are born with hair, open eyes, and teeth and weigh one-fifth to one-fourth that of the mother. They begin eating solid food a few days after birth. On the other hand, newborn puppies are small and helpless. They have hair but are toothless; their eyes and ears are sealed until about ten days of age, and they must depend upon the mother to keep them warm and provide food. A day or so before birth guinea pig fetuses react to intense and sudden sound with a startle response, evidenced by eye closure, body curling, and a facial grimace; puppies are eighteen to twenty-five days old before they show a startle response.

Puppies and kittens are born at a relatively immature stage for a reason. Wild canids and cats are hunters. It is easier to hunt, which takes speed and agility, when not pregnant. After the young are advanced enough to maintain their body temperature and have opened their eyes and ears, beginning at about ten days of age, the mother is free to be away from the den much of the time. She is able to hunt and bring back prey, which supplies the food she needs to produce milk, and within a couple of weeks, the nutrition that directly (by regurgitating) nourishes her offspring.

In wolf families, the father and related females help care for pups by bringing back food, which is regurgitated for pups, and by pup-sitting while mom is away hunting. Regurgitating food for pups is rare in domestic dogs, but may be one of the reasons why dogs will sometimes eat regurgitated or vomited food—their own or that of others.

Two to Four Weeks

At this point, vision and hearing become functional. Orientation toward sound and visual objects begins around three weeks of age, and recognition of specific people and depth perception develops by day 28. Regulation of body heat is increasingly self-regulated, and puppies begin to leave the nest and to explore. Lapping liquids and urinating and defecating on their own begins around three weeks of age.

During this time puppies develop surface and location preferences for elimination. Owners should provide puppies an area for elimination located away from, but easily accessible from, the nest. It is also beneficial if the texture of this area is different from that of the nest. If the nest is lined with cloth towels or diapers, use newspaper for the potty area.

Ingestive behavior changes as puppies initiate nursing while the mother withdraws more and more. Puppies now begin to investigate food, protect it by growling, and sample by eating.

Puppies—The First Weeks

Puppies learn to be dogs by interacting with both the mother and their littermates. In a study with German shepherds conducted in Sweden, it was discovered that certain behaviors in pups—whining, for example—are maternally imprinted. This was determined by synchronizing births in bitches and immediately exchanging some pups from each litter. By doing so, experimenters observed that maternal influence on the behavior, in contrast to genetics, was greater than expected. This is another reason to closely observe the behavior of the mother of pups you are considering for adoption. If you value quietness in a pet, limit your selection to silent breeds such as the African basenji and/or observe the mother closely for vocal behavior.

Puppies orphaned soon after delivery, especially those separated from siblings, are deprived of canine modeling; they do not know how dogs are supposed to act.

Orphans

Puppies can become orphaned any time after birth, but it is during the first four weeks after delivery that human intervention is most critical if they are to survive. Recommendations for raising orphans are generally the same, and are covered later in this section. Consensus among experts breaks down, however, concerning the extent of psychological damage experienced by the orphaned youngsters.

Drs. Benjamin and Lynette Hart, who specialize in animal behavior, report their findings in *Canine and Feline Behavioral Therapy*:

> Based on experimental work with maternal deprivation, we would expect such orphans to be excessively cautious, fearful, or aggressive as adults. Unless one can foster orphaned puppies or kittens onto mothers with other young, or at least raise them as a litter together, one would be well-advised to consider having the animals discretely euthanized so that unsuspecting people will not be tempted to adopt them.

The opposing argument about adopting orphaned puppies is made by John C. Wright, a psychology professor at Clemson University, in the *Cornell University Animal Health Letter*: "When puppies are litter-reared, that is, kept with their littermates and with a minimum of handling and human attention, they show less interest in exploring their environment and are less stimulated by new and different objects and scents. This is in dramatic contrast to two-week-old puppies hand-reared in homes away from the kennel, who spent more time investigating novel objects and apparently had better developed perceptual abilities." Dr. Wright suggests that hand-rearing—involving exposure to unfamiliar people, other animals, and other novel stimuli—may be the more effective strategy, "resulting in a puppy that adjusts better and is more easily managed."

I think we can learn from both views. If possible, provide solitary puppies a chance to interact with members of their own species and spend quality time with them, just as you would when nurturing a human baby. Socialization of puppies to animals, humans, and place (covered in the next section) is reported to begin between three and four weeks of age, yet I've found no creature who developed according to a timetable in some book. There is overlapping of all puppy stages. Err on the side of providing too much rather than too little handling and physical care of those who have lost their mother to illness or death.

Tiger, my Chihuahua neighbor, was raised as an orphan. All of us who know Tiger remark that he is almost human; his dog-to-human communication skills are awesome. If he wants go outside, he grasps someone by the finger and pulls the person along to open doors, and he seems to know what each one of us is saying or thinking. When he does not get his way, he sulks in a most humanlike manner. Tiger is more human than dog, and the reasons are obvious. When it was time for the little fellow to learn to be a dog, there were no canine role models; he followed the lead of Louise and Nip, his very attentive and loving human family.

Runts, those puppies who are born more immature or fail to grow at the same rate as the rest of the litter, should be considered similarly unable to fend for themselves. Littermates and mother often respond to the runt with harassment and neglect; dogs for the most part are not altruistic (there are documented exceptions). Although we may elect to step in to render aid to runts, we should be aware that these diminutive puppies are more likely than their larger littermates to suffer both physical and emotional problems.

During the first month of life, puppies maintain body heat by cuddling with their mother and littermates. Orphan or runt pups deprived of this source of heat must be provided for by maintaining environmental heat near 86 degrees Fahrenheit during their first week of life, 80 degrees the following two weeks, and 75 degrees the next two weeks.

Use old blankets and towels placed inside a large cardboard box for bedding. Give the puppies something warm to snuggle against, such as several plastic bottles filled with hot water and covered with dish towels. A heating pad or lamp can be used, but should cover only part of the box so the puppies can move to a cooler spot if they get too hot. A stuffed animal provides company.

Feed puppies four to six times a day for the first few weeks of life. Commercial formulas, such as Esbilac, can be purchased at the pet store or veterinary hospital. In an emergency, use evaporated milk (not skimmed) diluted to contain 20 percent solids (three parts milk to one part water). Warm the formula to room temperature before feeding.

Depending on the size of the puppy, you can use a dropper or doll's bottle for feeding. Commercial bottles are available at the pet store. The puppy will soon graduate to a regular baby bottle and nipple.

After feeding, stimulate each baby to defecate and urinate by rubbing the anus and genitals with a cotton ball saturated with warm water.

Puppies can be introduced to solid food when they are three weeks old. Mix one part dry puppy food with three parts water, or two parts canned puppy food with one part water. The mixture can be smeared around the puppy's mouth so he can lick it off.

I admit that I've never raised a litter of orphans from birth to weaning, but I'm an experienced puppysitter. One of my patients, a large doberman, developed mastitis, an inflammation of the mammary glands, soon after giving birth to a litter of five huge puppies (the dad was a Great Dane).

Easy enough for me to say, but I recommended the pups be supplementally fed, as I feared the mother's milk would be poisonous to them. My client wanted to attend an out-of-town Bison Convention over a long weekend and couldn't find anyone to care for the pups, then two weeks old. I volunteered, but I wanted to renege when I saw the doberman's owner climbing the steps to my house with a playpen, gallon of formula, sack of diapers, and diaper bag overflowing with baby bottles. It took three trips to his car to get the supplies and puppies moved into my kitchen.

My two daughters, both under ten years old at that time, were overjoyed at the prospect of being parents to a litter of puppies and proved helpful. I have a treasured photo showing my girls dressed in their nightgowns, feeding two hungry puppies with baby bottles while the rest of the litter sucked on the edge of their gowns.

Sucking excessively and/or inappropriately is, by the way, a symptom often exhibited by orphans or puppies weaned too early. This nonnutritional sucking often occurs as puppies suck each other's ears and penises, causing irritation to body parts. Suggestions for treatment are covered in chapter 8.

Four to Twelve Weeks

By four weeks, puppies are becoming independent. The mother increasingly avoids and snaps at those intent upon nursing. Weaning takes place, and play and exploratory behavior with siblings continue to occupy much of the pups' day. At around seven weeks, the puppies are adopted by their new families.

This period, between four and twelve weeks of age, is the most impressionable time of a puppy's life; psychological habits imprinted now are difficult to change at a later date.

Socialization

Socialization of puppies to their own species, to other animals, and to people begins between three and four weeks of age and continues to around twelve weeks of age, with the most critical period occurring when they are six to eight weeks old. Attachment to familiar sites and objects occurs also around this time. Keep in mind that every puppy is an individual and may develop earlier or later than his peers in specific arenas of socialization. (See Table 5.2.)

What is socialization? The technical definition is the acquisition of species- or cultural-specific behaviors. It is closely related to attachment (bonding with others and/or place) and with identity (a puppy knowing he is a dog or a child knowing he or she is a member of the human race). Sociologists Bretherten and Ainsworth, contrib-

Table 5.2

Sensitive Periods of Social Development

Socialization to other dogs	Weeks 3 through 8
Socialization to humans	Weeks 5 and 7 through 12
Adaptation to novel experiences	Weeks 5 and 12 through 16
Fear imprinting	Weeks 7 through 14

utors to the book *Species Identity and Attachment*, edited by M. Aaron Roy, write: "The organism is said to have an appropriate species identity if it chooses the correct partner for mating and displays appropriate reproductive, parenting, and other species-typical social behavior."

Dr. J. P. Scott, who experimented with socialization of puppies, reports that pups raised with people but without dogs become attached to humans but not to other dogs. When two puppies raised without canine modeling were introduced to dogs, they reacted by barking and with other threatening behavior. When mature, these two dogs failed to respond sexually to other dogs. One was sexually attracted to the male cat he was raised with and the other to a vacuum cleaner bag. A vacuum cleaner bag? Sorry, Dr. Scott did not give details.

In the cases of these two puppies and of Tiger, the human family treated the canine offspring with kindly care. Yet it does not take tenderness to create the bond. Puppies given human contact of a negative sort (punishment for approaching the scientist) during the socialization period nevertheless became attached to the scientist. As soon as the investigator ceased punishing them, the puppies maintained a closer bond with him than puppies treated with uniform kindness. This scientist concluded that the attachment process takes place in spite of negative reinforcement or punishment.

Similar results were seen in infant monkeys born to orphan mothers who mistreated them; attachment occurred regardless of the abuse.

The puppy becomes socialized to dogs by interacting with the mother and with littermates. It is through play or play-fighting that puppies learn how hard to bite, when to retreat and advance, and how to mount and grasp in a type of sexual play.

Studies of different canids show that the more social species, such as dogs and wolves, play more and earlier in life than do the more solitary species, coyote and red fox. Play, therefore, serves as a teaching mode for pack living.

Play behavior becomes ritualized, and adults use the same body postures that puppies learn during this period. Initiation to play starts with a raised paw and a bow—the dropping of forelimbs while maintaining eye contact. This is followed by tail wagging and jumping until the playmate takes up the chase. The chased partner maintains his tail in a downward curve and grins. The chase ends in a mock fight.

Ritualized play behavior in dogs is not the same as in cats, and this accounts for some of the animosity between the two species. If a dog wants to play, he lifts his forepaw and wags his tail; in cat language this means "I'm going to scratch your eyes out!" If the cat raises his paw to scratch, the dog thinks he wants to play and so on. Cats and dogs who grow up together learn the other's language; they become socialized to each other.

Playing and interacting with children and adults are what socialize the puppy to people. According to J. P. Scott, puppies raised without human contact react "like little wild animals, showing every sign of extreme fear—defecating, urinating, and biting when caught."

We never see puppies raised without human or dog contact, but it is interesting to review the results of social isolation. When isolated puppies were reunited with normal siblings, the isolated puppies became subordinate to the extent of being severely injured by their more aggressive dog-oriented littermates. When puppies who had been isolated were put together, they remained apart, forming no pack or social behavior.

Puppies could be removed from isolation at any time up to seven weeks of age and develop normally. But isolation extending past that period causes the puppies to exhibit an inability to interact normally with others of their species. Isolated puppies tend also to become attached to their physical environment and the objects it contains, experiencing separation anxiety when removed from the familiar setting. Scott says, "We must conclude that separation from a familiar environment produces a long-lasting emotional response which is distressful to the dog. Depending on its genetic disposition, the separated dog will respond either with fearful or aggressive behavior."

The Wolf-Girl

If dogs can think they are human, can humans think they are dogs? It depends, of course, on whether people are socialized and form attachments and identity in the same fashion as dogs.

One of the ways we form a physical identity is by observing ourselves in the mirror. I may inwardly cringe when I see the triple chins and chipmunk cheeks staring back at me, but I never doubt that the reflection is me. Infants and adult humans who have never seen mirrors before react just like animals, responding to the image as if it were another person. After a short period of exposure, however, they begin to recognize the image as themselves. The great apes are the only animals that learn to recognize themselves in mirrors.

What if we had never seen our reflection in the mirror and could not remember ever seeing another member of the human race? If our companions were dogs and wolves, would we know we were different? Would we try our best to fit into the canine culture in which we were raised?

On October 17, 1920, the Reverend Singh, a missionary in Bengal, India, reported the "capture" of a wolf-child of approximately eight years of age, whom he named Kamala. Dr. Aaron Roy, in the book *Species Identity & Attachment*, explains:

> Singh's explanation of wolf-rearing is difficult to believe. [Singh's explanation was that Kamala had been brought to the wolf den as a food source.] Yet it is even more difficult to believe that she had been raised by humans to any extent. At her capture and for many years thereafter, Kamala's behavior was so animal-like [prefers the company of dogs and behaves like them: laps water and eats raw food, walks on all fours, is incontinent and howls at night] that it is incomprehensible to accept the notion that humans had reared her prior to her jungle living. It is difficult to believe that inter-

acting with the wolves or other jungle animals after weaning from her parents could so completely erase her orientation toward people.... One could hypothesize that Kamala had been kept alive early in life by humans, but confined in a hut or pen with dogs or pet wolves (possibly with the "mother" wolf with which she was found) and away from regular human contacts. In this way her reference was canids, a species she identified with and imitated.

In spite of loving care on the part of Reverend and Mrs. Singh, Kamala made progress toward human socialization very slowly. It was only after five years that she would use the bathroom, wear clothes, or walk upright. At her death nine years after she was found in the jungle, Kamala had acquired a few words that she could put together in simple sentences. She was approximately seventeen years old when she died of kidney failure.

This story of a wolf-girl is sad and almost unbelievable, yet in the twenties in Bengal, aboriginal people ran from strangers and lived in remote jungle villages. Unfortunately, female babies were never highly prized, and Kamala was reported to look somewhat different physically from her peers, leading to another theory as to why she may have been abandoned in the jungle.

Although this book is not devoted to understanding humans, I find the comparison between us and our animal brothers too tempting to pass up. Perhaps we do form our identity in the same way as dogs, making it a little easier to understand how dogs can be raised to think they are human. Even though these people-oriented canines may make great surrogate children, I think they are deprived if they miss out on the joys of being with and relating to members of their own species.

Fear Imprinting

Overlapping the socialization period is a window of time, from seven to fourteen weeks, when fear imprints quite readily in the young pup. As this is the time that the puppy is introduced to his new home, his caretakers, trips in the car, and visits to the veterinarian, you should be very careful that these prove to be pleasurable experiences.

Puppies—The First Weeks

The puppy will take his cue from you—not what you say but how you say it and your body language. If you have a needle phobia, let someone else accompany the puppy to the vet's office for his vaccinations. I use this example, for it is something I know about firsthand. My mother is needle phobic; when I was a child and went to the doctor for shots, she would scream and run out of the room. Naturally, I grew up to hate receiving injections (it's better to give than to receive), and I've had to fight the phobia all my life.

Thunderstorm phobias are common in dogs, and one can only guess that some develop during this impressionable time in the young puppy's life. In certain cases, it is noise in general that is frightening to the dog; in others, it is specifically thunderstorms. One phobic dog is a champion gun dog; he enjoys the excitement of the hunt and the sound of guns firing around him, yet he becomes a quivering coward at the very hint of a storm. Thunderstorm phobias are covered more extensively in chapter 11.

Recommendations

I recommend that puppy adoptions occur between the ages of seven and eight weeks. Adoption before seven weeks may hamper the puppy's relationships with other dogs; adoption after eight weeks interferes with socialization to his new human family. (Refer to Table 5.2.)

Exceptions might be made in adopting puppies earlier from extremely aggressive mothers or mothers with other bad habits, in an attempt to prevent the mother's influence. Also, you might want to adopt puppies later from a household with children if you want to socialize puppies to human kids.

Before the puppy is brought into your home, prepare an appropriate bed for him, locate a potty area distant to his bed, and obtain such supplies as puppy food and toys. Be aware that everything you do or say, and the manner in which you do it, influences his behavior at this age. Make sure that the impression you make is the intended one.

The impressions you make and the handling method you choose are different for specific personality types. If your puppy is extremely shy and submissive, you must take care to use a soft voice and gentle handling. This type of puppy becomes even more fearful and withdrawn when confronted with harsh voices and jerking or with other rough maneuvers. If your puppy is aggressive (you'll know because he growls and/or bites when you do something he doesn't like), he must be treated with consistent firmness from the first day of your relationship.

Dr. Bonnie Beaver, a nationally recognized expert on animal behavior, suggests in "Potential Brat to Perfect Pet," *Veterinary Medicine/Small Animal Clinician*, the following for "potential brats": "A puppy must also learn to accept dominant behavior from all his/her owners. For this, the process involves doing anything the puppy does not like until the puppy tolerates it. Have the owners lay it on its back and hold it by the sternum [chest] until it quits struggling. Hold the muzzle shut gently but firmly until there is no resistance."

Dominant puppies are aggressive with their eating behaviors. Dr. Beaver urges owners to train the puppy to allow family members to take food from him. Again, you are trying to establish in the puppy's mind that family members are the "top dogs," not the other way around. She writes: "While the puppy is eating, have the owners take the food bowl away. If the puppy growls or bites, the dish is not returned for at least five minutes, otherwise it is given right back. This process is repeated until the puppy no longer reacts hostilely. Children in the family should practice this procedure under supervision, before the puppy becomes large enough to harm the child." This same technique can be used when the puppy becomes possessive of any item.

I have emphasized that the ages of four to twelve weeks are prime for socializing a puppy to other dogs, other animals, people, and place. After the puppy has been given a few days to adjust to his new home, introduce him to old people, children, loud teenagers, and railroad porters if you want him to be well adjusted around all sorts of people.

I mentioned in my book about cat behavior that sometimes a single person will adopt a cat and fail to introduce that pet to human members of the opposite sex. Later, if the owner's dating status changes, the pet may have a difficult time adjusting to the new girlfriend or boyfriend and may react with fear or aggression. So it is with dogs.

If the puppy is to share his environment with cats, birds, or other

Puppies—The First Weeks

animal companions, introduce them to him now (introducing a new dog or puppy to a resident dog or cat is covered in chapter 4).

If you anticipate adding these pets later on, borrow a few representatives or provide sensory initiation—sounds via recordings, smells, and so on. (Use the same techniques as for babies, addressed below.)

Take the puppy for walks in the park, rides in the car, and trips on the yacht. Introduce bathing, brushing hair, trimming nails, cleaning ears, and brushing teeth so that the puppy will learn to tolerate these necessary grooming procedures.

A secure place is important to all of us, and the canine species is no different. If a crate is to be the puppy's new home, make it comfortable and free from distractions and noise. This is a place the puppy can go when he needs to rest. There should be a balance between providing novelty and new experiences and regularity and security.

QUESTION

Dear Dr. Whiteley,

I am expecting our first child in a few months, and am worried about our dachshund. Skipper, a three-year-old neutered male, is very possessive of the house and both my husband and me. I'm not sure how he'll respond to sharing our time and attention with the baby. Any suggestions?

Pregnant in Athens

Dear Pregnant,

Dogs assess their environment with their senses. Therefore, it will help to introduce babies before the birth of your own through smell, sound, and vision. Expose Skipper to the scent of baby powder, baby oil, formula, and diapers, and the sound of rattles, as well as a baby crying through recordings (start with volume low, gradually increasing the sound until at any level there is no reaction from the dog). Let your pet see and smell the new equipment, changing table, crib, diaper bag, and so on.

You might also borrow a baby from a friend, so that Skipper can observe you cuddling and cooing with the infant. At the same time, have your spouse hold and cuddle

Skipper. Change places with your husband—you hold and cuddle your pet while your husband interacts with the baby. The goal is to have your dog associate the baby with more, not less, attention from family members. Reward good behavior with praise and treats; ignore misbehavior.

After your own baby arrives, try to spend quality time, even if for a short period, with your pet. When visitors arrive to fuss over the baby, provide them with new pet toys and treats so that Skipper can also receive attention and gifts.

Baby's safety should be the primary consideration. Ensure that your pet is healthy by taking him to his veterinarian for a physical examination, parasite check, and vaccinations before the baby arrives. And most important, never leave baby and dog together unsupervised.

Congratulations!
H. E. W.

6
The Dog Senses

Hearing

The dog's ability to hear is better than ours, especially when it comes to hearing high-pitched sounds. We can hear in the range of 20,000 cycles per second (cps); a dog's range is more like 34,000 to 40,000 cps, and a cat's is even higher, up to 60,000 cps.

All three of us—people, dogs, and cats—have about the same ability to hear low-pitched sounds. The ear is generally least sensitive in the low frequency range; otherwise, we would hear all our body vibrations.

Because dogs hear at higher frequencies than we do, they may respond to certain gadgets, such as electronic pest-control collars and remote devices to change television channels. If your pet reacts with anxiety by moving away or vocally protesting when you activate one of these devices, be aware that you may be sacrificing your pet's comfort for yours.

A veterinary journal recently cited the case of a dog exposed to the low-battery warning sound from a smoke detector; the low-battery sound is a high-frequency beep emitted every few seconds. The dog was confined to a downstairs room in which the smoke detector was located, and neither his barking nor the warning sound were heard by the owner, who was sleeping upstairs. The poor dog was so disturbed by this constant noise that he destroyed the room and finally broke out of an exterior door. It took a week for the dog to recover from this distressing episode.

Some animals hear even higher pitched sounds than dogs and cats; bats, for example, hear up to 98,000 cps and dolphins up to 130,000 cps. Yet the bat doesn't hear those low sounds that we hear; he can hear only the high-pitched sounds we can't hear. It's the same with dolphins; their hearing starts at 100,000 cps. Animals have their own lanes of sound—ones in which they communicate and ones to which their ears are the most sensitive. If we all heard the same sounds, the bombardment to our hearing sense would be overwhelming.

Nature writer Diane Ackerman, in her book *A Natural History of the Senses*, describes auditory niches: "Nature allows an animal a little decorum and privacy when it comes to its own species. Otherwise, a warning to its brethren would also signal a predator." There is, however, overlay. A vocal mouse is inviting the interest of an astute dog or cat.

The Dog Senses

In the same way, perhaps, a loud car will invite the interest of dogs who chase cars. Years ago, when I wrote a pet-care column for the *Saturday Evening Post*, readers wrote in to describe their pets' strange behavior concerning Volkswagens. That was in the days when you saw and heard more VW Beetles on the road. It seems that some dogs are discriminating in the cars they chase, opting only for Beetles. I've asked several automobile mechanics, and they've confirmed that the car makes a distinct sound.

There is a particular distance range, as well as pitch range, within which animals hear. If you are calling children and dogs for mealtime, dogs can hear from a distance four times farther away than kids. The mobility of a dog's outer ear allows him to rotate toward and pinpoint the direction that sound waves are traveling; dogs can locate the source of a sound in six-hundredths of a second.

It would seem that a cup-shaped erect ear would be advantageous over floppy ears for sound sensitivity. In contrast, dogs who hunt by scent—bloodhounds, for example—usually have long, floppy ears. The drooping ears are advantageous to the tracker, for they tend to screen out distracting sounds and allow the dog to concentrate on his superior sense of smell.

There is, of course, an overlapping of senses; smell and hearing are both useful in pinpointing the location of a quarry. Vibrations that trigger our sense of touch are intimately involved in our ability to hear low sounds; taste and smell combine for food appreciation. But Dr. Dare Miller, a Beverly Hills animal behaviorist, says, "Hearing is by far a dog's keenest learning sense, without doubt, the fastest route to his mind."

Some years ago, Dr. Miller developed a method of training dogs that relies on their ability to perceive high-frequency sounds. His invention is simply a chain that sends out a sound just out of the upper range of the average dog's hearing. The sound, heard subliminally, interrupts the dog's behavior—whether the dog is chewing your bedroom slippers or digging up a flower bed—and causes him to prick up his ears and listen. Dr. Miller used the chain to reinforce the teaching of appropriate behaviors, as well as such commands as come, sit, heel, and stay.

Bringing as many of the dog's senses as possible into the learning situation is helpful. Teach the dog to respond to both voice and visual cues (hand signals). If a dog's hearing sense is later compromised by age or disease, he can compensate with his visual sense.

Deafness

The hearing sense of puppies is immature at birth. Hearing approaches adult level after the ear canals open, but mature hearing is delayed for most individuals until weaning, at six to eight weeks of age. For this reason, breeders of dogs prone to inherited deafness should delay hearing tests until puppies are six weeks old.

I have already mentioned my experience with a blue-eyed deaf Australian shepherd. Color influences inherited deafness. Predominantly white, merle, or piebald coat color, as well as blue eye color owing to lack of pigmentation of the iris, predisposes to inherited deafness. Affected breeds include dalmatians, English setters, Australian shepherds, border collies, and Shetland sheepdogs.

Spaniels and hounds have an abnormal susceptibility to ear infections because their long ears prevent evaporation of moisture from the ear canals. Poodles and other breeds with hair growing inside the ear canals may develop infections when moisture is trapped in plugs of hair and ear wax. All dogs are prone to infections from foreign objects, particularly foxtail grass awns, which are found in the Southwest, and from ear mites that cause inflammation of ear canals. If you see your dog tilting or shaking his head frequently, ear infection may be the problem; an infected ear may also give off a detectable odor. Regardless of the cause, an untreated ear infection can compromise a dog's hearing sense.

Hearing loss in dogs may also be caused by tumors, injuries, or damage from certain antibiotics, and may be related to the aging process. Exposure to high-decibel levels impairs hearing ability; dogs subjected over time to sounds such as those produced by heavy-metal rock groups might suffer the consequences. My husband, a retired military sergeant, is borderline deaf owing to years on the rifle range without earplugs; gun dogs probably suffer a similar job hazard.

Until recently, little could be done to help dogs with severe hearing impairment; however, Dr. Patricia J. Luttgen, a veterinary neurologist, has been experimenting with canine hearing aids. She has fitted several hearing-impaired dogs with a molded device inserted into the vertical ear canal. The problem, she says, is getting the dog accustomed to the hearing aid. Dogs are trained to wear the aid for short periods as the volume is gradually increased. Dogs with large, thick matted ears, such as cocker spaniels, experience more problems wearing the aid because of sound interference.

Not every dog is a candidate for this type of therapy. If deafness is caused by nerve damage, a hearing aid will not help the problem. Even if the hearing deficit is ameliorated by a hearing aid, training of the dog will be intense and time-consuming.

Dr. Luttgen administers a BAER (Brainstem Auditory Evoked Response) test to access the level of hearing in each ear. If she determines that the dog is a candidate for an aid, she suggests that owners buy a package of foam earplugs sold at drugstores; if the dog can be taught to endure the earplugs, he might be trained to tolerate a hearing aid. Working with audiologists, Dr. Luttgen designs and fits an aid molded specifically for each patient. She attempts to enhance the hearing in one ear only.

The tests, fitting, and technology involved in designing hearing aids for dogs are the same as for people, yet the costs may be greater—$1,200 to $1,500 for a dog—because of the difficulty in fitting and training. Several years ago, a universal-type hearing aid for dogs was available; Dr. Luttgen describes her experience with this type of aid as a "dismal failure."

The BAER test is an extremely helpful diagnostic tool for deafness; because of expense, however, it is found primarily in the offices of veterinary specialists. Dr. Luttgen has kindly consented to refer veterinarians and clients interested in having the test performed to specialists in their area. Write or call Dr. Patricia Luttgen, Neurological Center for Animals, 7261 W. Hampden, Lakewood, Colorado; telephone 303-989-4656.

Before the BAER test, we—clients and veterinarians—relied primarily upon behavioral clues for a diagnosis of severe hearing loss. Sometimes we used the response of the dog to a hand clap or tuning fork to make a determination. Interestingly, some dogs with severe hearing loss will respond—they "feel" or "see" what is happening. Others with no hearing deficit fail to respond—they are frightened or stressed or become acclimated to certain repeated sounds.

After talking with Dr. Luttgen, I am convinced that few dogs are candidates for hearing aids, and that other means of preventing and treating hearing loss are more practical. Frequent physical examinations by your pet's veterinarian ensures that treatable conditions leading to deafness are detected promptly and handled aggressively. Dogs with inherited deafness should be neutered to prevent propagation of the condition. Hearing-impaired dogs should be taught to respond to hand signals and be kept in a fenced yard or house for their protection. Raise deaf puppies in homes with other dogs who can act as role models from which they can take their "cues."

BALANCE

The inner ear functions as the organ for balance as well as for hearing. When the head is turned in any direction, fluid moves within the inner ear's semicircular canals and sends information to the brain. Changes in gravity and linear motion are detected by two other fluid-filled sacs within the inner ear.

When a running dog turns, the head moves first. This stimulates the balance system before the body falls, and the animal adjusts his muscles to prevent falling. Motion sickness often occurs because the sensation of movement occurs without accompanying muscle activity.

The primary physical signs of motion sickness are vomiting and salivation. Emotional signs may include uneasiness and fear. Treatment is aimed at alleviating the fear by conditioning the dog to the car, boat, or airplane and/or by the temporary use of tranquilizers and antimotion drugs.

VISION

Most humans, I believe, are visually oriented, as evidenced by the axiom "a picture is worth a thousand words." Not so with dogs; their senses of hearing and smell play a much larger part in painting the sensory picture of their world.

To those who are visually oriented, color plays a prominent role in enjoyment and assessment of the environment. For an animal who hunts at twilight and blends into the brush for protection, color is not a prerequisite. There are two kinds of visual receptors in the eye's retina—rods and cones. Rods are important for seeing in dim light while cones function in bright light and in color vision. Cats see

The Dog Senses

better in the dark than do dogs because they have more rods in their retinas.

Dogs probably have a limited ability to see color, primarily in the long wavelengths of light (reds). The majority of objects are seen by dogs as a washed-out gray, such as our world appears at dusk. (Ruminants such as cattle detect medium and long wavelengths of light—yellow, orange, and red—better than short wavelengths—green, blue, and violet—so, yes, the bull does see "red" when the matador flashes his cape.) The animals reported to have the best color vision are our cousins, the primates, with the chimpanzee coming in as "top dog" in the arena of color detection.

A dog's eyes look and see differently from ours. Although not as far as wolves, a dog's eyes are placed farther to the side of the head than ours, one of the reasons why dogs are about ten times more sensitive than people to peripheral movement. This eye placement varies by breed—the so-called sight hounds, such as borzois and Afghans, have frontally placed eyes more like us, while guard dogs, like the German shepherd and akita, have more laterally placed eyes. Prey animals—rabbits, for instance—need to observe their surroundings so that foxes or other hunters don't catch them unaware; they literally see from both sides of the head (periscopic vision).

We have binocular vision: the field of vision from each eye overlaps. Dogs have poorer binocular vision (only a small area of vision overlap) than us, therefore they see less well close up, have poorer depth of field, and are less adapted to see detail. Cats, by the way, are between dogs and people in terms of overlapping visual fields.

Dogs see better than people in dim light, but not as good as cats. Cats are considered nocturnal—active at night—versus dogs, who are diurnal—active during daylight.

The dog sees better at lower light levels than people do because his pupil opens wider and because he possesses a tapetum lucidum, a layer in the back of the eye that reflects light; this reflection gives the animal's eyes a second chance to absorb light rays. The tapetum is responsible for the glistening of animals' eyes in the dark in response to a shined light; a tapetum is present in the eyes of most domestic and wild animals but is missing in pigs and humans.

Along the inner corner of each eye of the dog and cat is an extra eyelid, called the nictitating membrane, or third eyelid; this structure, which serves to protect and move tears across the eye, is a remnant of the complete third eyelid seen in lower animals such as chickens.

The lymphatic tissue of the third eyelid may enlarge and "pop up" into view in the medial corner of the lower lid in a condition commonly called "cherry eye"; this ailment may affect one or both eyes. Certain breeds, such as the beagle, American cocker spaniel, St. Bernard, weimaraner, and English bulldog are predisposed to cherry eye, a common problem which is cured by surgery.

The third eyelid has no muscles of its own, but it spreads across the eye in response to contraction of muscles surrounding the eye. Protrusion of the third eyelid is a prominent sign of diseases causing contraction of striated muscles, such as strychnine poisoning and tetanus (lockjaw).

Blindness

Although the eyes are the primary organs of light reception, sensitivity to light may not always correlate with vision. Many blind animals respond to photic stimuli—electromagnetic radiation in wavelengths that include the visible spectrum and rays that stimulate movement toward or away from light in plants. It is believed that this sensitivity to light not related to feel or touch is derived from the pigmented areas of the skin.

The inability to see can be congenital—the animal is born blind—or acquired. There are numerous inherited conditions for which there is breed predisposition; a few are listed in Table 6.1. Sight can be impaired by physical trauma, and for this there may be a breed propensity. For example, corneal ulcers (a break or tear in the surface of the eye) are seen commonly in dogs with protruding eyes, like the Pekingese.

Eyesight can be lost or impaired also by disease, tumors, and dietary deficiency. In the old days, when canine hepatitis was a frequent problem, the diagnosis was a given if the dog, usually young, came into the office with a sudden-appearing "blue" cast to one or both eyes. I usually gave a sigh of relief when presented with this strange phenomenon, for I knew the diagnosis and knew that the pup, except on rare occasions, was on his way to recovery. The bluish ocular cloud was due to an immunological response to the disease and would soon disappear.

Table 6.1

Breed Disposition of Inherited Ocular Disease

MICROPHTHALMOUS (SMALL EYE)

Collie
Doberman
Australian shepherd
Miniature schnauzer
Old English sheepdog

CONGENITAL CATARACTS

Miniature schnauzer
American cocker spaniel
Boston bull terrier
German shepherd
Standard poodle
Golden retriever
Old English sheepdog
Staffordshire bull terrier

COLLIE EYE ANOMALY

Collie
Shetland sheepdog
Border collie

ENTROPION (TURNING IN OF EYELIDS)

Chow chow
English bulldog
Shar-pei

PROGRESSIVE RETINAL ATROPHY

Irish setter
Collie
Norwegian elkhound
Miniature long-haired dachshund
English cocker spaniel
Toy or miniature poodle
Tibetan terrier

CENTRAL RETINAL ATROPHY

Labrador retriever
Golden retriever
Border collie
Collie
Shetland sheepdog
English springer spaniel
Cardigan corgi
Briard

CONGENITAL GLAUCOMA

Doberman

PERSISTENT PUPILLARY MEMBRANE

Basenji

Another example of a disease affecting sight is that of diabetes, which causes cataracts in both dogs and people; altered glucose metabolism changes the lens of the eye.

Regardless of cause, cataract surgery for dogs is becoming increasingly common; most veterinarians refer patients needing cataract surgery to a veterinary ophthalmologist. I have a colleague who owns a specialty ophthalmology practice in Dallas; this veterinarian offers surgeries such as the placement of glass eyes selected for esthetics, as well as surgery and treatment performed for medical reasons. My acquaintance can empathize with his patients, for he has worn a glass eye since a childhood accident rendered one of his eyes blind.

Both people and dogs can function well with one eye, so it may be difficult to detect unilateral blindness. In other instances, blind dogs become so adept at compensating for visual loss with their superior senses of smell, hearing, and feel that they get along almost normally in a familiar environment. Maneuvering of obstacle courses (in both light and dark), response to menace (blinking at quickly moving hand or penlight), and tracking of moving objects are procedures sometimes helpful in determining blindness. It takes an expert to make a definitive diagnosis.

As mentioned, the senses of smell, hearing, and feel can compensate for loss of visual ability. Training your dog to respond to sound cues, maintaining a familiar environment, and offering yourself as guideperson are helpful for the blind dog.

I read several years ago about a man who devised a sort of cane for his blind dog. The dog, a short breed like a dachshund, was fitted with a collar-head harness contraption to which were attached several four-inch canes. The canes functioned like a cat's whiskers—feelers that gave information back to the dog about his surroundings.

SMELL

To me, the sense of smell is the most exciting to research and write about; it is a sense that is subjective at best—what smells great to one person or species turns another completely off. Although we lag behind our four-footed friends in this ability, we join them in the mostly unconscious way our bodies respond to smell.

In response to a question from a reader about why people like and dislike certain smells, Marilyn Vos Savant writes in *Parade* magazine:

The Dog Senses

There are innate likings and dislikings for smells based on the consequences of interacting with them. For example, the smell of ripe fruit, which is healthy to eat, is appealing; but the smell of rotten meat, which can be dangerous to eat, is revolting.

The other school of thought is that odors are pleasant or unpleasant depending on your past experiences with them. For example, flowers would smell bad if you've had negative experiences with them, such as associating them with sickrooms; but skunks would smell good if you've had positive experiences with them.

The sense of smell is physically located in the olfactory region of the nasal cavity. This region is yellowish in color; ours are light yellow, while animals that far surpass us in smelling ability have dark-yellow olfactory regions—the fox's is reddish brown and the cat's is a rich, dark mustard brown.

The sense of smell is present at birth; puppies find the way to the mother's nipples by following the path of saliva she has laid down around her mammary glands. Smell plays a vital part in the recognition of and bonding between parents and offspring.

The sense of smell peaks in middle age and then declines; this aging of the senses takes place in people and animals. Certain drugs, trauma to the head, radiation, and medical conditions such as diabetes and epilepsy can interfere with the capability to smell. Viral infections, the common cold in humans, and distemper in dogs, for example, can damage the nasal mucosa, interfering with an individual's sense of smell. This is one of the reasons why nothing "tastes" good when we're in bed with a cold.

Heating food to volatilize odors is sometimes helpful to entice the reluctant eater to appreciate the food's aroma and to take the first bite. Other nursing tips include humidification of the air and saline nose drops to clear the nasal passages. Most of us, people and dogs, suffering from viral diseases recover completely our sense of smell within a few weeks.

Within the nose of the dog are over 200 million scent receptors; we have a mere 5 million. And the dog has fourteen times more nasal membrane over which to filter air than do we. The dog's mobile nostrils bring inspired air over the subethmoidal shelf within the nose (a structure missing in people) to the nasal membranes mentioned above. The air molecules trapped above the shelf accumulate rather than wash out with expired air, the way ours do.

The sensation of odor arises through small particles of material dispersed in the inspired air. Dogs are good at sniffing, usually in cycles of three to seven sniffs, which brings these particles into the nasal cavity and stores them. Although it is not socially acceptable to sit in a gourmet restaurant sniffing, we do something similar. If we taste—a sense intimately associated with sense of smell—something delicious, we inhale or exhale, driving the air in our mouths across the olfactory region so we can smell it better. For something to be tasted, it must be dissolved in liquid (saliva) and for something to be smelled it must be airborne.

Tracking

Writer Diane Ackerman says that the animals with the keenest sense of smell walk on all fours, their heads directly over the ground, where the damp, heavy, fragrant molecules of odor lie. Dogs like bloodhounds are better at following a ground scent, while other breeds—the collie, for example—track above-ground air scents. Air-scenting dogs hold their head high, sniffing the odor contained in the breeze. If they lose the scent, they travel in ever-widening circles in an attempt to pick it up again.

Bloodhounds can smell a person's scent even if the quarry has been absent several hours; the dog tracks the few odor molecules that seep through shoe soles and land on the ground as the individual walks. Dogs determine the direction of tracks by comparing the scents of consecutive prints and following the prints in the direction of increasing intensity. The best time for a dog to follow a ground scent is when the soil temperature is a little higher than air temperature. This phenomenon occurs primarily in early evening, the time when most carnivores are out and about in search of dinner.

Dogs can be trained to follow scents. Skill is enhanced by exposure to the scent they are to track. Males are reported to be better at it than females, supposedly because they use this sense to a greater degree in territorial and sexual behavior. In humans, females score higher in sensitivity to odors.

Inheritance has much to do with the ability to track. In an experi-

The Dog Senses

ment performed in the sixties, Drs. J. P. Scott and J. L. Fuller placed three breeds on different occasions in a one-acre field with a mouse. Beagles found the mouse in about a minute, fox terriers in fifteen minutes, and Scotties not at all, even though one dog accidentally stepped on the mouse.

We have capitalized upon the dog's superior sense of smell to find lost people, contraband, bombs and mines, mold, drugs, natural gas leaks, truffles, and termites. Dogs are used, also, to detect heat in cows and to determine whether human twins are identical or not (identicals have the same scent while fraternal twins do not).

Individual Scent

Although biologically related humans and dogs smell more alike than those not related, scent is individual; we—animals and people—give off different odors. Dogs are not self-conscious about meeting a fellow canine and smelling his anus, genitals, and mouth, reading from the scent the individual's sex, social status, and food preferences. Dogs also claim territory by leaving calling cards of scent—urine, anal sac secretions, and feces.

Studies show that mice can determine genetic differences between potential mates by smell alone. In some way, individual scent gives an indication of the mouse's immune system; mice who choose a mate offering genetic diversity and a hardy immune system give birth to offspring more likely to survive and propagate under the old "survival of the fittest" principle.

Roger Caras, in his book *A Celebration of Dogs*, describes how tracking dogs follow a specific human scent: "On the trail the scent hound is seeking particulate matter, bits of dead skin that have scraped off the fleeing or wandering youngster. It scrapes away with every movement and floats to the ground, which is in fact the scent trail. The areas where the limbs meet the torso create unique smells, apparently, in every human being. So the running person, even the walking person, acts like a bellows spraying the ground with microscopic bits of self."

Although we can't do with our sniffers what dogs and mice can do, we are pretty good at scent detection. Children and adults can by scent alone determine if a piece of clothing was worn by a female or male. New human mothers can select their own infant's smell (from newborn T-shirts) from other infants at greater than chance odds; babies can pick out their own mothers.

Scent and Sex

The female dog advertises her receptiveness to males by urine marking and by drops of vaginal secretions. After reading the clues left on bushes and other inanimate objects, the male dog smells her up, so to speak, and makes a more direct assessment of her availability. It is reported that male and female wild dogs urine-mark one after the other on exactly the same blades of grass or leaves of bushes to inform all interested parties that they are a pair.

We're not so different from dogs. Smell plays a part in both the physiology and the behavior of human sexuality. Pheromones (chemical secretions) in women's sweat glands affect the menstrual cycle. This is the reason why women living closely together—sharing a dormitory, a barracks—find that their menstrual cycles synchronize. Young women cloistered from men reach puberty later than those who are around men on a daily basis.

The perfume industry capitalizes upon the idea that the "right" scent will attract the opposite sex. I suppose love potions work the same way. There is some scientific basis that perfume works as an aphrodisiac. Many fragrances contain musk, harvested from the anal sacs of wild animals. We can detect musk when diluted to minute amounts, and are affected in some way by it, because it is close in chemical makeup to human testosterone. In this case, more is not better; undiluted civet or musk is extremely repugnant.

According to research at the Center for Sensory Disorders at Georgetown University, approximately 25 percent of people with smell disorders lose their sex drive. Conditions that impair a dog's sense of smell would have an even more devastating effect on the individual, because the ability to smell not only impacts canine sexual behavior but also parenting, territorial behavior, and social activity.

TASTE

Dogs have approximately 1,700 taste buds, compared to 9,000 for humans, located on the tongue. As mentioned earlier, taste and smell are senses intimately associated with each other. What smells good usually tastes good.

The Dog Senses

Dogs are attracted to food initially through the sense of smell. Texture and taste influence palatability after the dog is eating.

Taste is reported to influence the selection of a diet containing elements for which the animal is deficient. For example, vitamin-deficient rats will select foods high in the missing vitamin. Salt-deprived rats will select saline over water when given a drinking choice. I am often asked if dietary deficiency is a factor in dogs suffering from pica (the eating of unusual things), but I have failed to find lack of nutrients the basis for pet dogs who eat pantyhose, feces, and garden hoses. However, dogs deprived nutritionally may "know" on a physiological basis what they need and choose accordingly if given a choice of food.

In humans, the four specific tastes are sweet, salt, bitter, and sour (acid). Other taste sensations include combinations of these four and/or smell. Dogs prefer diets containing sucrose (sugar) over bland diets; however, it is unkind to encourage your dog with sweets, which contribute to gum and tooth decay and obesity.

In a study conducted by researcher Dr. Katherine Houpt and her colleagues, diets containing low levels of sucrose were found to be more attractive to female than to male dogs. In general, females have a stronger preference for sweet foods than do males, regardless of species. For example, Adam Drewnowski, director of the Human Nutrition Program at the University of Michigan, said in a *Parade* magazine article that "Women tend to crave fat-sugar combinations like chocolate and ice cream; men prefer fat-protein or fat-salt mixtures such as steak, pizza, and french fries." There's no hope for me; I love all the above.

Many of the same disease and trauma conditions that affect the sense of smell impair the sense of taste. These include liver and kidney disease, diabetes, cancer, radiation, and influenza. Ever wonder why airline food is tasteless? One reason is that high altitude and cabin pressure dull the sense of taste. I guess that's one reason Tang was an acceptable substitute for fresh orange juice for astronauts and astro-monkeys.

TOUCH

Touch, as described in chapter 5, is closely associated with thriving, in both people and animals. It is by touch, as well as scent, that newborns are cared for and about. The mother curls her body around the young to bring warmth and nurturance; she licks the genitals to stimulate elimination. Touch is important in adults, too. Stroking and petting your dog reduces his heart rate, blood pressure, and temperature; the same act lowers your heart rate, blood pressure, cholesterol, and temperature.

Changes in the electromagnetic current in the atmosphere just before an earthquake produces static electricity, which triggers the sense of touch by making the pet's hair stand up and quiver. This is one theory as to why some animals can predict quakes.

Whiskers, which occur around the muzzle and elsewhere on the dog's body, are especially well furnished with nerve endings, making them touch receptors; whiskers can be moved voluntarily by the dog.

Pain

The sensation of pain is the body's natural protection against injury; it is primarily a warning system. The reaction threshold for pain varies from animal to animal within the same species. Animals who tend to be high-strung and excitable are less able to endure pain.

Anticipation also seems to stimulate the pain response. I have had dogs yelp and scream, for the owner's benefit usually, before I touched them. If the owner steps out of the room, the little fellow will often calm down and behave nicely for the examination or vaccination. Others mimic pain by holding up the injured paw long after recovery; in this case, the animal has been trained, usually by a well-meaning owner, that he will receive sympathy, petting, or treats in response to his pain.

Diversion can help alleviate pain; mild pain can, also, create a diversion. This is the basis of biting the bullet, slipping a rubber band around the ears of a cat, and twitching a horse.

In the case of the twitch, a chain is placed over the nose of the horse and twisted, causing a certain amount of pain. The horse is preoccupied with the pain on his nose and will presumably miss the fact that the veterinarian has bandaged his leg. The cat is stunned by the rubber band, giving a few seconds to administer the vaccination. Apparently, medical doctors don't take the same oath about tempering pain with anesthesia as we dog doctors do, for my last personal medical procedure, which I considered quite painful, was done without benefit of Valium or bullet.

Pain sensation is immature in the puppy. This is the reason we can dock tails and remove dewclaws without using anesthesia; these procedures are performed when pups are less than a week old. Pain sensation is at adult level by four weeks of age. Pain is discussed also in chapter 11.

Heat

The newborn puppy is unable to maintain his body heat and will exhibit rooting behavior—burrowing into warm objects. This attraction to heat lasts until the puppy is eight to ten days old. An older animal experiencing cold will fluff his hair to increase its insulating qualities and will shiver (shiver reflex begins at six days of age) to produce heat.

Receptors, which register sensations of warmth and cold, are present throughout canine skin, but are not as well developed in dogs as in humans. Small dogs, as mentioned in chapter 3, are unable to maintain body heat as well as larger dogs; in winter Tiger, my Chihuahua neighbor, spends much of his time lying on a blanket on the hearth of the wood-burning stove. While I'm on the topic of touch and heat, I'd like to mention a critter closely involved with canine life—the flea.

Flea pupae lie dormant in the environment—house carpeting, for example—until they feel the faint vibrations of a dog, cat, or person passing. Then, they rapidly emerge from the immature state and hop on their host, guided by the victim's body heat and breath. The pupae can remain dormant for months, even years, waiting for the right stimulus, which is why the dog or you can move into a previously vacant house and suffer a plague of fleas.

OTHER SENSES

I have described the physical senses—hearing, balancing, seeing, smelling, tasting, and touching—by which people and animals assess and interact with their environment. The body rhythms, homing, and aesthetic senses are faculties that also influence the way dogs live

Body Rhythms

How does your pet know that you return home from the office every day at 6 P.M.? How do you know it's time to get up, awaking moments before the alarm clock goes off? That sense of knowing time is termed the biological clock or circadian rhythm; it's related to the twenty-four-hour day and with the cycles of the moon.

It seems like something out of a werewolf tale that we humans, or even our canine friends, would be controlled by moon cycles. Yet my neighbor says that he is affected by the full moon, experiencing migraine headaches that do not go away until the moon phase changes. Admissions of both men and women to mental hospitals increase at the time of a full moon.

How does it work? Light and moon phases impact in some way on the body's pineal gland, located at the base of the brain, which in turn triggers the biological clock in the brain's hypothalamus.

Biologists cannot define circadian behavior in terms of molecular mechanism; they have, however, found a genetic basis for the biological clock. Specific genes that control circadian behavior—different for each species—have been isolated in both the golden hamster and the mouse. The mouse gene is appropriately named "clock." A mutation of the clock gene changes an animal's perception of the twenty-four-hour day to one with more or fewer hours.

It is through genetic manipulation that we have changed the heat cycle in most breeds of female dogs from that of once yearly, as in the wolf, to every six months. The heat cycle of wolves might appropriately fall under the category of circannual rhythms, which is defined as physiological or behavioral events occurring annually.

Circannual rhythms occur in animals and people who experience seasonal changes. Those animals who hibernate during the winter are responding to this rhythm, as are people who suffer seasonal affective disorder (SAD), characterized by prolonged periods of depression in response to the low light levels of fall and winter.

The pattern of activity during the twenty-four-hour day, controlled by the circadian rhythm or biological clock, is much the same for wild and domestic canids. Dogs and wolves are most active during the early morning—foraging, investigating, marking territories—and rest later. There is a trio of neighborhood dogs who follow that pattern here; every morning Chow, Tramp, and D.D. (Dump Dog) get together for a communal romp and roam.

sleep

In the wild, sleeping conserves energy needed for hunting; in pet dogs, sleeping conserves energy for playing, exercising, and other activities.

There are two types of sleep: slow wave or quiet sleep (SWS) and rapid-eye-movement sleep (REM). It is during REM sleep that dreaming occurs, and dogs do dream; the REM sleep is the most critical. Pet dogs sleep about 50 percent of the time in short and frequent sleep-wake cycles.

Dogs denied adequate sleep, especially REM sleep, may suffer physical and behavioral problems and impaired learning ability. Experiments show that sleep-deprived dogs will rebound by sleeping more until they have caught up with the sleep deficit.

Narcolepsy is a sleep problem characterized by attacks of inappropriate sleep. The affected dog collapses or falls asleep within seconds or minutes after playing or eating. It is an inherited disorder in dobermans.

Waking owners during the night is a sleep dilemma, but the dog, who has usually napped all afternoon, considers it the owner's problem. The dog may initially wake the owner to go out to do his business, and then finds a nightly stroll through the neighborhood to his liking. Treatment suggestions include exercising the dog prior to bedtime, free-choice food left for the dog's midnight snack, teaching the dog to respond to "quiet" and "stay" commands when he disturbs you, installing a dog door, and ignoring his pleas.

Sleep disturbances of shift workers and jet lag are two conditions in people who experience abnormal switches in the sleep-activity cycles. Biological time is out of synch with local time, and they feel unwell until their bodies adjust to the new time. Dogs also travel by jet and work in shifts. One study revealed that drug-detector canines cope well with variable working hours. This is because dogs sleep naturally in brief and frequent sleep-wake cycles, which allow them sufficient and easy adjustment to changing routines.

In spite of the above study, change a dog's schedule only gradually.

Dogs and cats are creatures of habit and ritual, and an hour's delay in feeding to accommodate fall time change, for example, is stressful to dogs conditioned to expect dinner at a specific time.

Homing Sense

When I lived in Amarillo, Texas, a story about Tippy, a dog belonging to Bob and Lorrayne Vogel, appeared in the *Amarillo Globe News*. Tippy, a female mixed terrier, moved with the Vogels' son, Rob, to Mesa, Arizona, where the homesick dog dug under the fence and disappeared. Sixteen months later, Bob and Lorrayne Vogel found Tippy—thin, matted, and covered with ticks—on the road leading to Amarillo's Tradewinds Airport where they hangered their private plane.

The Vogels were, of course, overjoyed to find Tippy and puzzled about how the little dog had traveled the 750 miles, crossing three mountain ranges and the desert, to arrive home; on the original move to Arizona, Tippy and Rob flew.

The Vogels revealed this about Tippy: the dog was obedience trained, imaginative, and curious; she used to climb a ladder to the house roof and check out the neighborhood; and the little dog loved to copilot the Vogels' private plane, leading to the theory that Tippy was heading toward the beloved plane's hangar when found.

The above characteristics may paint the picture of a loyal and intelligent animal, but they do little to explain how Tippy found her distant home after an absence of over a year, when others of her species get lost crossing the street to grandmother's house. I have found some explanations by reading the scientific literature, but none that tells specifically how Tippy found Amarillo.

For one, the homing instinct is not learned. Young deer mice with no experience will return to the home nest. Other animals that home take the shortest route, not one they've had experience with. And, as previously mentioned, some are better at it than others.

Aesthetic Sense

Aesthetics is the study of beauty and of the psychological responses to it; beauty as defined here is usually associated with art.

The Dog Senses

Specieism is a school of thought that attributes aesthetic intent for the movements, marks, or sounds of another species.

Heather Busch and Burton Silver, authors of *Why Cats Paint: A Theory of Feline Aesthetics*, are proponents of specieism, as they set about in their book to prove that cats paint to create an interpretation of their environment and to create beauty, just as human artists do.

Zoologists argue that feline art is mere territorial behavior, similar to when the cat, using secretions from the sweat glands between his paws and using claws instead of paints, marks on trees and other vertical surfaces, including couches.

There are examples in *Why Cats Paint* of feline-produced abstract paintings and of fabric sculptures, accompanied by highly detailed interpretations from expert art critics. Although I am no expert, the fabric art, anyway, looks to me like the claw markings of a misbehaving cat.

Nevertheless, certain cat paintings—for the most part acrylics on canvas—are fetching prices in the neighborhood of $20,000 per painting. Misty, a cat in Toronto, painted "Interring the Terrier," which critics claim depicts a small headless terrier being stuffed inside a red armchair by two frogs and a sardine; this painting sold at auction for $21,000. I am beginning to see the beauty associated with cat paintings.

Critics have thus far rejected the artistic renderings of canine painters. But an 8,400-pound elephant in the Burnet Park Zoo in Syracuse, New York, has produced art that has drawn the following comment from Jerome Witkin, an expert on abstract expressionism: "I consider these drawings to be very good drawings by any artist, whatever her race, origin—or weight."

Aesthetic sense in animals is not reserved for the visual arts. Music is art, and I find that dogs are sensitive to and appreciate the soothing musical strains of the great masters. The New Guinea singing dog produces the melodic-sounding howls for which he is named.

Dr. Michael W. Fox, an authority on canine behavior, writes in *Superdog* about canine aesthetics:

> One of the most obnoxious behaviors for many dog owners is that of the dog when it finds some foul-smelling material. Dogs love to roll in obnoxious organic material because they

have a highly evolved sense of smell, probably a million times better than ours, and I believe that they have an aesthetic sense in this modality: they like to wear odors much as we, a more visually oriented species, like to wear bright clothes or something different for awhile. Wolves enjoy rolling in meat or some other food they particularly like before they actually eat it. This again may mean that "wearing" certain odors is an aesthetic experience, the aroma remaining to be savored long after the meal has been eaten.

Some experts propose that wild dogs or wolves roll in organic material to camouflage their scent from prey or other predators. It may be that some dogs wear scent for aesthetic reasons and others for camouflage, and still others for motivations we have yet to discover.

Aesthetics may be more a component of intelligence and communication, covered in the next chapter, than a true sense like hearing or sight; yet it is an ingredient that makes living richer for all of us. Perhaps, evolution will favor those who create and appreciate beauty.

QUESTION

Dear Dr. Whiteley,

We had a mother dog abandon a puppy on our doorstep. We tried to get the mother to take the baby back, but she refused and kept shoving him aside.

My wife and I finally took the puppy, who was smaller than his littermates, and bottle-fed him. Within a day, we noticed that the puppy's abdomen was distended, and that he wasn't having bowel movements. On closer inspection, we discovered that the puppy had a small pink spot but no opening through which to have bowel movements. We were heartbroken, because the puppy had to be destroyed after all our efforts. The mother dog rejected the puppy because he was different. How do they know?

Heartbroken in Canyon

Dear Heartbroken,

Survival of the fittest seems a cruel law of nature. Yet bitches deliver more puppies than can be supported in the

The Dog Senses

wild or adopted by responsible human parents. Only the strongest are destined to live to propagate the species.

A mother dog uses all her senses—vision, hearing, smell, touch—when interacting with her offspring. She probably senses that a puppy is defective and has a poor chance of surviving. It is also possible that the mother knows on a more innate level, the way a bird knows which way is south and a salmon knows which way to swim. The universe in its overall design is perfect.

You are to be commended for your efforts to save the puppy. The congenital deformity that you describe is called atresia ani—the puppy was born without an anus. The condition can sometimes be surgically corrected.

H. E. W.

7
Intelligence and Communication

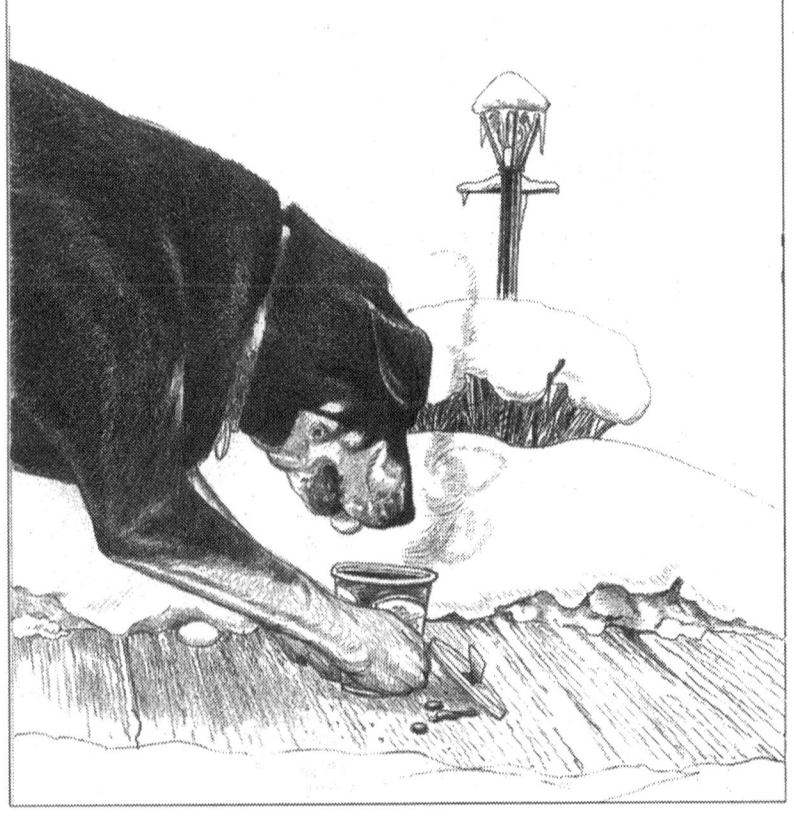

INTELLIGENCE

There is a selective component for animals with larger brains. Unless we interfere, survival of the fittest and smartest propagates the species. Those animals with the best senses are attuned to subtle events in the environment, allowing them to find dinner and avoid danger. Better motor systems in the brain allow improved locomotion for hunting, escape, territorial defense, reproduction, parental care, and manipulation of objects.

Intelligence, for all of us, involves behavior that is genetically determined and behavior that is learned. For the most part, the behavior necessary for survival is innate or inherited, while learning is reserved for less critical information. Yet over generations, behavior that is learned can become innate.

Morphogenetic resonance, also known as the "hundredth monkey" phenomenon, can be used to explain how behavior that is learned becomes innate. In the 1950s, on the small island of Koshima in Japan, a group of Japanese scientists air-dropped sweet potatoes onto the beach to ensure the survival of a colony of isolated monkeys. An eighteen-month-old female monkey, called Imo by the scientists, carried her sweet potatoes to the ocean to wash them free of sand and grit. Within seven years, all the young monkeys and those few adults who imitated their children had learned the behavior of washing food.

According to Lyall Watson, author of *Lifetide*:

> In the autumn of that year an unspecified number of monkeys on Koshima were washing sweet potatoes in the sea, because Imo had made the further discovery that salt water not only cleaned their food but gave it an interesting new flavor. Let us say, for argument's sake, that the number was ninety-nine and that at eleven o'clock on a Tuesday morning, one further convert was added to the fold in the usual way. But the addition of the hundredth monkey apparently carried the number across some sort of threshold, pushing it through a kind of critical mass, because that evening almost everyone in the colony was doing it. Not only that, but the habit seems to have jumped natural barriers and to have appeared spontaneously, like glycerine crystals in a

Intelligence and Communication

sealed laboratory jar, in colonies on other islands and on the mainland.

Although the number 100 is used arbitrarily in this instance, the hundredth-monkey phenomenon is one way of explaining evolution and why inventions and ideas occur almost simultaneously in different parts of the world. It is also how wild canids became domesticated all around the world at approximately the same time, 12,000 years ago.

Problem Solving

The ability to make independent decisions and solve problems is an indication of intelligence. Are dogs good problem solvers? You bet they are, although sometimes we wish they'd wait and let us make those independent decisions for them.

In her book *The Hidden Life of Dogs*, anthropologist Elizabeth Marshall Thomas uses the example of a dog's weighing alternatives and making a decision. The female dog in question routinely joined her owner and two other dogs on a daily walk and swim. One day the female was distracted and missed the daily swim. When she caught up with the pack, they were on the way home. Thomas explains:

> Poised beside the trail, she first looked to the right after the group, then looked to the left at the river, then looked to the right a second time, then looked once more at the water, made an instant decision, rushed full speed up the trail to the river, plunged in, quickly swam a few strokes, then turned back to the bank, leaped out, and tore after her group, not stopping to shake until she had caught up to them.

Charlie Waterman, in *Gun Dogs and Bird Guns*, gives an example of canine problem solving:

> Joe's pointer, Lady, was one of those reliable, conscientious dogs who takes work seriously. She was retrieving a quail for Joe when he hauled off with his old Fox and shot another one, which she encountered on the way back in. Now there

are stories of dogs pointing birds with others in their mouths and there are stories of dogs bringing in two at once, but Lady had never studied those programs and she was confronted with what the military experts might term a problem in logistics. Here she was with one bird in her mouth and another bird that she wanted to take to Joe too.

After a brief survey of the situation with several changes of expression, Lady gulped hard, swallowing bird number one, and triumphantly turned toward Joe with bird number two in her mouth. But halfway in, while mentally reviewing the situation, Lady concluded she had done wrong. A look of canine consternation came to her face and she apologetically crawled the last twenty feet on her stomach.

How human is the above example. Many times I've made a snap decision and then realized the full impact of what I had done, crawling, at least figuratively, back on my belly.

What Makes Us Different?

In the article "What Makes Us Different?" in *Parade* magazine, scientists Carl Sagan and Ann Druyan discuss intelligence: "The uniqueness of humans has been claimed on many grounds, but most often because of our tool-making, culture, language, reason, and morality. [Other experts include spontaneous production of art in their list of intelligence traits.] We have them, the other animals don't, and—so the argument goes—that's that."

Sagan and Druyan systemically show that animals exhibit attributes that we formerly ascribed only to humans. I found the example of primate morality particularly fascinating.

In a set of experiments, macaques received food if they pulled the chain that would electrically shock their fellow monkeys; the reaction of the shocked monkeys was plainly visible to those who had to make a decision about pulling the chain. If the macaques refused to pull the chain, they went hungry. "After learning the ropes, the monkeys frequently refused to pull the chain; in one experiment, only 13 percent would do so—87 percent preferred to go hungry."

Do dogs and wolves display altruism, one so-called attribute of in-

Intelligence and Communication

telligence? I believe that they occasionally put the interests of others before their own. In August 1984, eleven-year-old Sean Callahan was playing when he came across a coiled rattlesnake. Leo, a standard poodle, jumped between the boy and the snake, suffering in the process six bites to the face. The dog recovered, to be inducted into the Texas Pet Hall of Fame.

Was the dog responding instinctively or did he deliberately save his master at his own expense? What about the wolf mother who raised the human child cited in chapter 5? Was the decision to nurture rationally contemplated or a hormonally driven response, at least initially? I like to think that we—human and animal—occasionally see the interests of our neighbor as no different from our own.

There is a scientific theory that holds that a species has the entire behavioral repertoire of his ancestors and of the more advanced members of his kind within his genes. Times of stress can cause an individual to revert behaviorally to more primitive means or to more advanced ways to deal with the threat. Maybe an act of altruism is the result of tapping into an advanced intelligence of which we are all capable if the need is great enough.

Sagan and Druyan say this about the responsibilities of human intelligence:

> We live at a moment when our relationships to each other, and to all the other beings with whom we share this planet, are up for grabs. . . . If intelligence is our only edge, we must learn to use it better, to sharpen it, to understand its limitations and deficiencies—to use it as cats use stealth, as katydids use camouflage—to make it the tool of our survival.

COMMUNICATION

Communication is defined as the "giving and receiving of information," and it is an attribute of intelligence. Dogs communicate by assessing visual and scent messages, by facial expressions and body language, and by vocalization.

Humans use facial expressions and body language to communicate, but the language means different things in human and canine communication, and human facial expressions and body language vary according to culture and location.

People living in Arab nations stand close and look intently into each other's eyes when talking; in the United States, this type of closeness is reserved for lovers only. In Hispanic cultures, a young woman avoids direct eye contact with a man, while this evasion of the eyes is considered indicative of deception in America. In Israel, people engage in public staring, while in the Orient staring is considered rude behavior.

Staring in canine culture means dominance. If you stare at an aggressive dog while approaching what he considers his territory, you are inviting a confrontation.

A confrontational problem with which we veterinarians are all familiar is the fear-biting caged dog. In this instance, a canine patient, who has acted rather submissively on the exam table, becomes a fighting demon when you go to retrieve him from the back of the treatment cage. The dog is stressed and fearful; he is unsure of the situation and responds with mixed body language. The biting end may show dominance and aggression—stare, dilated pupils, raised hair, erect ears, bared teeth—while the rear end shows submission—crouched body posture.

Dr. Bonnie Beaver, an animal behavioral expert from Texas A & M, recommends that the human handler back into the cage, avoiding direct face and eye contact while snaking an arm around the reluctant patient. When submissive body language, slow movements, and sweet talk fail, I recommend a thick glove or full body armor, depending on the dog. Fear biting is covered more extensively in chapter 10.

Sometimes we ascribe human emotions to dog behavior. We say that the dog acts guilty when he slinks back in a submissive way to our admonishments. Dogs are fortunately spared that most wasted of human emotions, guilt. If the dog slinks back, as in the example of the confused bird dog, he is responding submissively to our dominant verbal or body language.

The canine grin or smile has an element of submission to it; an aggressive dog does not smile. Jean Craighead George, in *How to Talk to Your Dog*, equates the human smile with the dog tail wag: "The dog wags its tail only at living things. A tail wag, the equivalent of a human smile, is bestowed upon people, dogs, cats, squirrels, even

Intelligence and Communication

mice and butterflies—but no lifeless things. A dog won't wag its tail to its dinner or to a bed, car, stick, or even a bone."

Scent Messages

Chemicals called pheromones are present in canine body secretions—saliva, feces, urine, ear wax secretions, anal sac secretions, vaginal and prepucial secretions, and secretions of the perianal and dorsal glands. When dogs meet, they sniff each other's face, mouth, ears, tail, anus, and genitals to decode from these secretions the other's sex, social status, food preferences, age, and emotional state.

When a dog smells another dog's mouth, he is reading the saliva message. It tells the dog's food history, as does anus sniffing. Feces are also used by some animals as a calling card, marking the depositor's territory when seen, as well as smelled, by others. Urine is used in the same way to mark territory, provide a familiar smell, and tell social rank and sexual responsiveness.

When urine and feces are left as calling cards, the ground surrounding the message is often scratched by the depositor. This serves to stir up the scent and to draw a visual arrow to the odorous calling card. The dog may also be adding another scent clue to the area by depositing secretions from the sweat glands between the toes.

Urine-marking ability in dogs is quite impressive—up to eighty times in a four-hour period. Placement of the urine mark is important. It makes sense to place the mark close to nose level. That's one reason why male dogs cock their legs and urinate as high as possible on trees and bushes and other vertical surfaces.

Both males and females can cock their leg or squat to urinate; one set of statistics says that males use the raised-leg position 97.5 percent of the time while females squat to urinate 67.6 percent of the time. And dogs often go through the motions without urinating. As males are more likely to use this phony behavior in the presence of other dogs, the behavior is likely a flashing action rather than an indication of an empty bladder.

Dogs like to cover another's scent markings with their own. One veterinary hospital where I worked placed a plastic fireplug in the side yard for the purpose of collecting urine specimens. The pet's owner, technician, or veterinarian led the patient past the urine-impregnated fireplug, with the hope that the dog would take the hint and offer a sample. The trick was being fast and agile with the specimen cup.

In situations where a dog feels anxious—separation anxiety, for example—depositing feces or urine on the owner's clothes and bed may be a way of covering a familiar scent with his own. The behavior is not intended for spite or a loss of housebreaking knowledge; it is an attempt to relieve the extreme anxiety that these dogs are feeling when separated from a beloved owner. Separation anxiety is covered in chapter 11.

inappropriate urine marking

One of the most interesting cases of urine marking I've viewed was at my favorite spring fete—the annual rabies vaccination drive. One of the rules of the event was that all owners adhere to local canine leash laws. As we know, though, laws are meant to be broken.

A matron arrived with five Pomeranians, whom she released without collars and leashes from her car into the parking garage, where I was waiting at one end with my syringe. I watched with some consternation as the male dog visited each of the four or five people bent over the Ping-Pong table, writing out checks and certificate information. The Pomeranian urine-marked the pant legs of everyone at the table. No one noticed the sprinkling except me; and being a coward, I said nothing. After all, it's the smells and yells and other sensory stimulation that add to the excitement of the rabies drive.

I observed another interesting case of urine marking within my own family of grandpets. My son and daughter-in-law's dogs are Max, a nine-year-old setter, and Ted, an active one-year-old Lhasa apso. Max lives, for the most part, in the fenced backyard, which he considers his territory, while Ted resides in the house, except when entering Max's yard to do his business. Max follows Ted around the yard, remarking every spot that Ted has sprinkled. Sometimes, tall Max appears to grow weary of the effort and just straddles short Ted and sprays the intruder himself. It is an ultimate display of dominance and territoriality.

Dogs are more apt to urine-mark in novel places than at home. The presence of a new dog inside or outside the house may, however, stimulate the activity within a dog's home domain. If the dog chooses a particular spot to mark, clean this area of urine smell with an enzy-

Intelligence and Communication

matic cleaner advertised to eliminate urine odor and declare the favorite area off-limits by using barricades or booby traps, such as loaded mousetraps.

As this type of marking is most frequently seen in intact males, castration is the treatment of choice. Castration is curative in approximately 50 percent of cases involving male dogs; the unwanted behavior should be eliminated either immediately or in approximately three months. Spaying female dogs also eliminates the urine-marking used to advertise her sexual readiness. When neutering fails to remove the incentive to urine-mark, hormonal treatment may alleviate the problem.

While we're on the subject of sex and smell, I should mention that dogs can determine a lot about a cohort's sexual status from prepucial and vaginal secretions. Genital sniffing is normal behavior in dogs, but becomes rather disgusting when transferred to humans in what is commonly called "crotch sniffing."

crotch sniffing

Brian Kilcommons, a dog trainer in New York, suggests that you move boldly and bodily into the dog participating in nosing under skirts and around crotches. If you jump back in horror, most dogs will interpret this retreat as submissive behavior on your part. Make the dog back away while you are sharply admonishing him with "No!" Diverting the dog's attention or bringing him under an obedience command will rescue the visitor being sniffed up.

anal sacs

What about my favorite of canine calling cards—anal sac secretions? The fragrance of anal sacs may be Chanel No. 5 to dogs, but it's the social kiss of death to people. After a day of expressing anal sacs, my nose rebels by going to sleep. Forgetting that my clothes carried odorous clues to my activities, I often drop by the dry cleaners or grocery on my way home from work. After a while, I noticed that people clear the way for me to check out first. And they say that courtesy is dead.

Anal sacs, for those lucky few who have no firsthand knowledge, are two balloonlike sacs located on either side of the anus. They become filled with smelly material that ranges in consistency and color from a straw-colored liquid to a pasty black. The dog may express

Understanding and Training Your Dog or Puppy

the glands during a bowel movement or by scooting his rear along the ground. During times of excitement, including sex and fear, the dog may also express the glands. These are some of the emotions that other dogs read from the anal gland droppings deposited in the environment.

Infection or impaction of the glands, with symptoms of scooting, pain on sitting, and licking and biting at the anal region, are seen more frequently in smaller breeds of dogs and in obese dogs with poor muscle tone. A visit to the veterinarian is indicated if your pet displays the above symptoms.

other glands

Perianal glands are located in the skin surrounding the anus. Secretions from these glands are most obvious in older intact males, and these secretions impart to other dogs the information that an older, male dog was here. Problems with these glands, most often tumors, are more frequent in cocker spaniels, English bulldogs, samoyeds, and beagles.

The dorsal tail gland, a small elliptical gland absent or small in most dogs, is a scent gland found in wild canids. Secretions contain a pheromone used for scent-marking trails.

Facial Expressions and Body Language

dominance and submission

The study of the facial expressions and body language of wolves gives insight into dog behavior. Wolves live for the most part in packs of two to twenty animals, and communication is designed to keep the group together and reduce friction among members. For example, if a weaker individual defers to the more dominant wolf with appropriate body language, a fight is averted, everyone knows his place, and harmonious relations are maintained. Dominance hierarchies exist for both males and females in the pack.

A dominant, or alpha, wolf uses body language to maintain status over the group. The dominant wolf stands tall with legs stiff, hair and tail raised, ears erect and pointed forward, teeth bared, and eyes narrowed to slits; it maintains eye contact with a stare. Weaker

Intelligence and Communication

wolves usually respond with passive submission. The submissive individual crouches low, tucks the tail, flattens the ears along the head, pulls the lips back into a grin, looks away, rolls over on the back, and may urinate.

Active submission occurs when the submissive wolf approaches the dominant wolf and tries to lick and nuzzle his face. The language is friendly submissive—crouched body posture, flattened ears, grinning facial expression, and avoidance of eye contact, while wagging the tail.

Wolves hunt together to bring down prey larger than themselves. One wolf-hunting behavior—the nose bite—used to bring down a moose is similar to that used by early English bulldogs and bull terriers in the sport of bullbaiting. The pariahs discussed in chapter 3 are the only domestic dogs who hunt and live like wolves in packs. Our dogs may congregate for morning excursions, like the canine trio of Tramp, Chow, and D.D. mentioned in the previous chapter, but they are not dependent upon hunting for a living.

Dominance and submission in dogs are expressed in much the same body language as that used by wolves. Table 7.1 addresses these traits.

Dominance over owner—Most behavioral experts suggest that the human family is the equivalent of the dog's canine pack. It is important that every member of the human family be dominant to the dog. How do dogs display dominance over the owner? They exhibit many of the traits covered in Table 7.1.

Biting and other aggressive behavior, body slamming, mounting and some cases of jumping up are ways that dogs display dominance over people. The dog may rush the door, pushing you aside, to be "first." This behavior should not be tolerated. The dog must be admonished and brought immediately under obedience commands. See chapter 9 for teaching of commands.

One of the worst cases of dominance over the owner that I've experienced was that of an aggressive male basset hound owned by a little old lady. This was a gross case of mismatched owner and pet. The dog was originally owned by the woman's son, and he may have been able to discipline the dog. The present owner, however, was totally intimidated by the dog.

The woman called me to come to the house to vaccinate the basset because she was unable to load him into the car to take him to a

Table 7.1

Traits of Dominance and Submission

FACE, EYES, EARS	TAIL, HAIR	POSTURE
Dominance		
Head erect; ears erect or laid back; direct stare; dilated pupils; shows teeth	Tail erect or straight; wags tail tip; piloerection	Posture erect; stiff-legged; mounting; hip slams; shoulder slams; head or paw over adversary
Submission		
Head low; eyes averted; ears depressed; grin	Tail low or between legs; no piloerection	Rolls on back; urinates: exposes genitals

veterinary hospital. As I entered the client's house, the dog stood just inside the hallway barking at me. With the owner's help, I was eventually able to place a muzzle around his nose, and I quickly administered the shots. When I removed the muzzle, however, the dog lunged at me, missing my hand by a fraction of an inch; catching my lab coat sleeve instead, he ripped it to tatters. Then the dog stood his ground, barking at me until I retreated from "his" house.

Dominance aggression has both inherited and learned components. Bassets are generally nonaggressive, and I suspect that this representative of the breed became a tyrant because his owner let him get away with it. I think that a more dominant owner could have, at least early in the dog's life, brought him under control rather easily. This type of aggression occurs in both males and females. The breeds known for dominance aggression include English springer and cocker spaniels, Rottweilers, dobermans, chows, and diminutive Lhasa apsos.

Drs. Benjamin and Lynette Hart, authors of *Canine and Feline Be-*

Intelligence and Communication

havioral Therapy, recommend two approaches for treating dominance aggression. The first is direct, aimed at proving to the dog that you are dominant over him. As wolves within a pack use force, this approach utilizes physical force and punishment for dominant actions on the part of the dog. Examples of force are shaking the small dog by the scruff of the neck when he misbehaves or "choking" with a choke chain the larger dog.

Timing is important, and must coincide with the misbehavior. You must also win each encounter; if the dog is able to prove himself dominant during the interaction, the behavior is reinforced and the next confrontation becomes even harder to win. Also, the choking approach can prove dangerous; in a fight to the finish, you or your pet might be injured. We see in veterinary hospitals dogs who have been hung or choked as punishment, suffering from ruptured blood vessels of the eye, as well as tracheal and esophageal damage. Treatment of dominance aggression, especially of a large dog, should be undertaken with direction from a veterinary behaviorist or animal trainer.

A more indirect approach to treating dominance aggression depends upon the dog being obedience trained. Attention, petting, and food rewards are withdrawn, while actions likely to prompt aggressiveness on the part of the dog are avoided. When the dog wants attention, give him an obedience command such as "sit." If the dog performs, give a reward in the form of petting, praise, or food. The dog is never rewarded unless he obeys, thereby reinforcing the dominance of the owner. All members of the family must use the same tactics.

One method for treating a dog who shows dominance traits such as rushing the door, jumping up to "kiss" visitors, and pulling you along to produce "dog-walker's elbow" is the Promise system, available through veterinarians. The Promise halter is a double collar, with one loop around the neck and another around the muzzle; at the bottom is the control ring for attaching a leash or ten-foot control lead. If you pull on the lead or leash, you control the dog's head.

Dr. Robert K. Anderson and Ruth E. Foster, developers of the control collar, say that the halter is based on a dog's natural instinct to pull against pressure, but unlike regular collars it puts the pressure on the back of the neck and away from the front of the throat. The halter provides control in a way similar to a pack leader who encircles the nose and lower jaws of a subordinate canine, and to a mother dog who brings a puppy under control by picking up or putting pressure on the scruff.

When the dog misbehaves, you tug on the lead and bring him to a stop. I know a large English sheepdog who loved to greet strangers by jumping up, placing his paws on the visitor's shoulders, and giving a big slurp of a kiss. This type of behavior was cute when Alfie was a pup but rather intimidating when he grew to eighty pounds. It was also dominant behavior on the part of the dog—a way of saying "I'm bigger and taller than you."

I think the Promise system is indicated for retraining Alfie to greet strangers by sitting and extending a paw. As Alfie makes the rush toward the door, his owner grabs the lead while admonishing him to stop. Good behavior of sitting and extending a paw are rewarded.

Ask your pet's veterinarian about the Promise system or call 1-800-333-8363, or 303-279-2326 in Colorado.

Other types of aggressive behavior are covered in chapter 10.

Dominance over other dogs—Many people think in terms of fairness, discouraging displays of dominance within their family of dogs. Yet dogs are confused when you rush in to make sure the submissive dog has his turn at eating first, being petted first, and ensuring other social amenities befitting the "top" dog. It is better that you acknowledge the dominant dog and treat him accordingly. In most cases, the resident dog is dominant to the new dog; the older dog is dominant to the younger, the stronger to the weaker, and so on. Later, the status may change.

As I mentioned, mounting other animals is a dominance trait. Although mounting is a necessary part of the canine sexual act, dogs who mount others of the same sex are engaged in dominance behavior, not homosexuality.

Submissive urination—The act of urinating submissively begins early in a pup's life. After the mother nurses her puppies, she nudges them over onto their backs and licks them to stimulate urination and defecation. Later, the mother merely looks at him and the puppy rolls over and urinates.

When an adult dog performs the same behavior, he is responding to dominant signals from his human parents or to the excitement of a stimulating event. Dominant signals may include such innocent behavior on your part as walking toward, reaching for, or leaning over the dog and staring at or speaking to him.

Intelligence and Communication

If you raise your voice or act aggressively by your body language (rubbing his nose in it or hitting with a newspaper) to the urinating act, you are exacerbating the problem. The dog will act even more submissive—perhaps urinating when you enter the room next time.

Avoid signals of dominance and punishment. Let the dog come to you instead of approaching him directly. Walk slowly, speak softly, avoid looking directly into the dog's eyes, and squat to the dog's level when interacting with him. Do not pet the dog by touching the top of his head, shoulder, or back, as this is perceived as a dominant gesture on your part; you may pet him by rubbing his chest or under his chin.

Often a submissive puppy will outgrow the extreme symptom of urinating if he is handled with kindness and calmness. Avoid stimulating the puppy who urinates during excitement. Socializing the puppy to strangers and novel situations (addressed in chapter 4) will do much to relieve his anxiety later.

left-pawed, right-pawed, or ambidextrous

Which paw a dog leads with or extends to be shaken has nothing to do with dominance or submission, but it is a part of body language that influences the dog's behavior if you try to change it. If a dog has learned, for example, to extend one forepaw in greeting, he becomes confused and stressed when you expect him to perform the trick with the other forepaw.

There is a pattern of left and right in nature, and this goes for paws, flippers, claws, and hands. Flat fish, such as flounder and sole, begin life as symmetrical, vertical-swimming animals, but they turn over and commit to one side early in life and remain horizontal from that time forward. Elephants use one tusk more than the other, and the favored tusk becomes worn down while the other remains larger. Of 200 parrots observed in one zoo, the majority were right-footed while only two were ambidextrous.

Humans are more often right-handed, so going against the majority proves complicated for those who are natural lefties. A statistical study of children entering Arkansas Children's Hospital in Little Rock showed that left-handed kids had more accidents, and were perceived by parents and other caretakers as more clumsy than right-handed children. It could be a self-fulfilling prophecy: those expected to behave in an awkward manner do so.

It is okay for your dog to be left-pawed or your child to be left-handed. Perhaps, they'll both become outstanding athletes, like those famous southpaws of baseball.

Vocalization

Dogs are more vocal than wolves, who howl to communicate with others of their species but rarely bark. Coyotes, which I hear frequently here on the mountain, are similar to wolves in the way they use vocalizations. Biologist Raymond Coppinger and linguist Mark Feinstein write in the article " 'Hark! Hark! The Dogs Do Bark...' and Bark and Bark," in *Smithsonian* magazine: "When we raised coyotes from puppyhood along with dogs in our lab, the coyotes remained silent and wary even when their kennelmates joined in frenzied, raucous bouts of group barking."

Animal behaviorist J. P. Scott once counted a cocker spaniel's 907 barks in a ten-minute period. Dog barks are in long, rhythmic stanzas, in contrast to adult wolf and coyote barks, which tend to be isolated and brief.

Coppinger and Feinstein document the barking habits of modern wild dogs—the New Guinea singing dog, the Asian pariah, the Australian dingo, and the African basenji—as dogs who can bark but rarely do, opting instead to howl. They disagree with those who suggest that we have domesticated dogs to be barkers: "We think that the wild ancestor of the dog may have largely domesticated itself, entering into a mutually beneficial symbiosis with humans—and is not a product of conscious human selection."

Coppinger and Feinstein believe instead that the extensive barking behavior of adult dogs, in contrast to wild canids, is the result of the adult dog's retaining infantile behaviors: "Stuck in adolescence, the dog barks so much because barking is what a *juvenile* canid does." They explain that all wild canine pups are noisier than adults, but that excessive puppy vocalizations are lost as the individual matures. But whether we did it through selective breeding or it came about by natural selection, today's domestic dogs are very vocal, retaining into adulthood juvenile traits such as whining and crying, as well as extensive barking.

Not only do domestic dogs differ from wild canids in their use of vocalization, but individuals and breeds differ in their use of voice. If you are in the market for a watchdog, the following breeds are

Intelligence and Communication

known for their watchdog barking. The barking frequency is the same for males and females:

> Rottweiler
> German shepherd
> Doberman pinscher
> Scottish terrier
> West Highland white terrier
> Miniature schnauzer
> Standard poodle
> Airedale terrier
> Cairn terrier
> Chihuahua
> Yorkshire terrier

Arctic breeds and hounds are known for their howling. Susan Butcher, veterinary technician and winning sled-dog racer, is quoted in *Mondo Canine:* "Dogs have a lot to communicate to a person who's willing to listen. My dogs have five or six different howls, happy howls, sad howls, change-in-the weather howls. Bitches in heat have incredible flirtatious howls."

Smokey, my malamute neighbor, has a most mournful howl, heard easily a mile up the mountain from where he resides. My granddog Sarge, a chit (mixture of chow and pit bull), howls in reply to emergency sirens heard quite well from his house a mere two blocks from an interstate highway. Does Sarge howl because the sound hurts his ears? I don't think so. I think he mimics a sound that triggers some ancient communication instinct.

There are other dogs who offer a sort of high-pitched howl in response to music; perhaps it's a sing-along reaction. The baying of hounds is a natural behavior in response to finding a sought-after individual or object. Other dogs respond to their environment by barking, whining, growling, yelping, crying, and moaning.

My dog Bear barks at certain foods—fresh bones and tallow—but not at others, such as dog food or table scraps. Okay, so I adhere to the old adage "Do as I say, not as I do" about feeding with non-dog-food items. Regardless, I think the barking behavior has something to do with Bear's perceiving the fresh goodies as "live bait." He also moans in response to biting and scratching an itch. I suppose that's as close to ecstasy as an old neutered dog can get.

While I'm telling Bear tales, I might as well admit to aiding and abetting his barking proclivities. He and I take a walk together almost every afternoon. Along the way I may sit on a rock or fallen tree trunk to rest, think, or just enjoy the view. I must speed through my meditations, though, for Bear comes back and barks right into my face as if to say, "Get up you lazy. . . ; no loitering on the trail." The fact that I do his bidding is proof that dumb is another description of me.

The vocalizations of dogs—and mammals in general—fall into two classes of vocal signals: low-pitched signals that signify aggression, hostility, or dominance and high-pitched tones conveying appeasement and submission. In a similar way, low, deep vocalizations are associated with large adult animals who are dangerous and competitive, while high sounds suggest small or young animals. It is, of course, the tone and the way you say it that means more to your dog than actual words. See Table 7.2 for the meanings of canine vocalizations.

barking dogs

Why do dogs do it—bark their heads off? Dogs bark to communicate, to alleviate boredom, to define space or territory, and to train you. If the dog is rewarded by your letting him inside the house when he barks excessively, he has trained you to let him inside.

If you want to change that training, you are going to have to change the reward system. When the dog barks, he must never be let inside; only when he is quiet should he be rewarded by letting him join you inside. Of course, this approach takes nerves of steel and good relations with your neighbors. Again, gaining the diagnostic skills and advice of an expert is always a good idea before treating a behavioral problem.

Then there is remote punishment, which comes with a warning. If the dog barks, as a sign of separation anxiety, when you leave the house, punishment will make the anxiety to which he is responding even worse. Remote punishment occurs in conjunction with or immediately (within seconds) after the dog starts barking, but is not associated by the dog with the person administering the punishment. One method might be to position the water hose directly over the

Table 7.2

Vocal Communication

VERBALIZATION	MEANING
Bark	Warning Greeting Attention seeking Excitement
Howl or bay	Assemble pack Greeting Alarm Location marker Celebration Mimic sound
Growl	Threat Play (teeth hidden)
Yelp	Hurt
Cry or whimper	Fright Hurt
Whine	Attention seeking
Moan	Pleasure

dog's kennel. When the barking begins, the water is turned on from a position you can monitor from nearby.

The Promise collar is also useful for administering remote punishment (from the end of the ten-foot control lead) in response to barking behavior. There are lots of electronic devices designed for correcting the excessive barker. Some depend on microphones, which pick up the sound and emit a loud noise in response. Ultrasonic bark collars emit a high-frequency sound, inaudible to humans, when the dog barks. One report suggests a 60 percent success rate for breaking excessive barking with ultrasonic collars. A more harsh and drastic method is the electronic shock collar, which administers a shock in response to barking behavior. It is my belief that electric shock collars should be reserved for experts at treating canine behavioral problems.

whining dogs

Whining is vocalization heard frequently from puppies, especially when you and the kids leave for work and school. If you rush to pick up the puppy while saying "Oh, my poor baby" when the pup whines, you are reinforcing a vocal response. Better to ignore the protestations and reward silence with attention.

The case that comes to mind is human rather than canine, but the behavior works the same. As a working mother, I was overcome with guilt every time I left Susan, my firstborn, at the nursery or babysitter's. Susan, now a grown-up professional woman, was a smart kid who reinforced my torn emotions by screaming, crying, whining, and yelling each day as I left her.

One morning after Susan had been extremely vocal, I went around the outside of the day-care center and peered in the window, only to find that the baby who had been inconsolable just moments before was now playing happily with another child; the entire performance had been for my benefit. I hope she's just half as convincing as a lawyer.

QUESTION

Dear Dr. Whiteley,

My three-month-old male chow chow is becoming aggressive to family members and strangers. He bites at my ankles when I am working in the yard and has started growling and snapping at the mailman. Is there anything I can do?

Concerned in Boise

Dear Concerned,

The chow chow is classified as a breed with high aggressive tendencies, and males usually show more dominant personality traits than females. Your puppy is beginning to think of himself as the "top dog" in your family.

Never stimulate the puppy with tug-of-war or other rough games. When the puppy snaps at you, freeze; don't pull back when he bites at your pants legs. Distract the pup

Intelligence and Communication

with a loud noise such as a hand clap or a tin can filled with pennies, or throw him a chew bone. Teach your puppy the basic commands of come, sit, heel, and stay. When he starts to misbehave, direct him to "come" and "sit."

Your puppy is still in the socialization period (roughly four to twelve weeks). During this time he will establish a pattern for relationships with other animals and people. I suggest that you introduce the pup to visitors, children, and the mail deliverer. Make each visit an upbeat and friendly encounter. Give the puppy special attention or a treat while the mailman is present; later, ask the mail deliverer to give the puppy a treat, which you supply. Praise the puppy for good behavior.

Good Luck!

H. E. W.

8
The Essentials

Air

The quality of air affects all of us, plants as well as animals. Air filled with smog, tobacco smoke, toxins, allergens, and viral or bacterial agents contributes to disease conditions, especially in stressed individuals.

Industrial-size air purifiers that clear the air of dander, dust, molds, and other airborne irritants are helpful household items for families with pets suffering from a compromised immunological system or respiratory distress. Some units plug into a standard electrical outlet while others fit into the home heating system.

Humidity impacts breathing comfort and susceptibility to respiratory infections. If the air is extremely dry, as it is here in the mountains during winter, humidifiers are indicated.

Barometric or atmospheric pressure changes also influence our emotional and physical health. For example, mice are more active when barometric pressure is rising, and horses run and whinny before storms. I mentioned in *Understanding and Training Your Cat or Kitten* a patient who developed a condition commonly called rolling skin disease, triggered by thunderstorms. Weather change also affects human behavior; psychotic episodes, depression, and aggressive criminal behavior, as well as certain physical disorders such as headaches, occur more frequently during shifts in atmospheric pressure.

Altitude affects atmospheric pressure. The lower barometric pressure at 8,000 feet above sea level where I live makes baking a cake difficult. Air here on the mountain is literally thinner or less dense than at lower altitudes; people and animals visiting from the lowlands can experience breathing difficulties until they adjust to breathing thinner air.

The experience of breathing air, the most essential element, is the same for all living things. I like the way Diane Ackerman describes breathing in her book *A Natural History of the Senses*: "A breath is not neutral or bland—it's *cooked* air; we live in a constant simmering. There is a furnace in our cells, and when we breathe we pass the world through our bodies, brew it lightly, and turn it loose again, gently altered for having known us."

The Essentials

WATER

Drinking and water have the same relationship as breathing and air. Most drinking in dogs occurs in conjunction with meals—during, right before, or after. Fresh water should be made available to the dog at frequent intervals or at all times.

Water intake is influenced by environmental conditions and activity levels. Dogs drink more when it's hot, replacing water lost primarily by evaporation from the tongue during panting and from respiratory surfaces.

Dogs also drink more when exercising. Racing sled dogs performing in competition were found to average 6.57 quarts of water each per day, in comparison to nonracers at 1.17 quarts daily; this extra water is needed to cool the canine athlete, who generates excessive body temperature during exercise.

Working animals should be encouraged to drink early in the exercise period, and cold water (40 to 50 degrees F.) is preferable, as it empties from the stomach more rapidly and cools the body faster than warm water.

Although melting ice and snow are certainly cold-water sources, the dog living outside in winter freezing conditions should be provided with fresh water several times a day. Electric water bowls, which keep water thawed, are available from pet stores.

One water source is food. Canned food contains more water than semimoist brands, which in turn contain more water than dry food. Increased salt content stimulates dogs to drink; one treatment for the older dog with compromised kidney function is to salt his dog food to encourage the consumption of water to flush out his urinary system. Although we all know that water is a poor substitute for food when we're hungry, animals deprived of food will drink more.

FOOD

Selection

Since domestic dogs no longer catch and kill their food, they have developed into animals with smaller teeth and shorter jaws than wolves. When given a choice, the domestic dog prefers canned dog food to fresh meat, especially raw. The call of the wild just doesn't appeal to most dogs nowadays.

Dr. Katherine Houpt, an animal behaviorist at Cornell University, found that dogs more often select canned or semimoist food over dry, and meat over nonmeat protein sources. Meats in order of preference are beef, pork, lamb, chicken, and horsemeat.

Unlike cats, who are true carnivores and cannot survive healthily without eating meat, dogs have adapted over the years to eating nonmeat foods. Prepared diets free of animal tissue are available or can be prepared for vegetarian owners who are opposed to feeding their dogs meat. It takes an expert to prepare a balanced vegetarian diet for dogs, and I refer you to the numerous books devoted to the topic available at bookstores and libraries.

One of the advantages of dry food is its dental tartar-reducing quality, and one of the disadvantages of canned food is that it cannot be left out for long without spoiling, especially in hot climates. Good diets are available in all three forms—dry, semimoist, and canned—and it is more important to select the correct diet for the animal's life stage or nutritional needs than to worry about form.

Dogs eat for physiological and psychological reasons, just as we do. Putting two dogs together at dinnertime will usually stimulate both to eat more, unless one is so submissive that he is too intimidated to touch the food. Wild canids tend to eat in a feast-or-famine mode and some dogs do the same, overeating as long as you continue the feast.

Increase the palatability or good taste of the food, and the dog will eat more. Although there is a limit, adding some fat and protein will increase palatability. As puppy foods contain more fat and protein than adult foods, dogs will usually choose the puppy food first. And cat food contains more protein than dog food, prompting an occasional dog to steal his feline companion's food. Fat contains 2.25 times the energy of an equal weight of carbohydrate or protein; therefore, diets high in fat are high in calories, too.

Cold weather brings forth an increase in appetite as the dog puts on extra fat for the winter; pregnancy and lactation are also a stimulus for the mother. Drugs such as tranquilizers have an appetite-stimulating effect. Conversely, dogs eat less when the weather is hot, females eat less when in heat, and dogs receiving central nervous system stimulants such as amphetamines eat less.

The Essentials

Most dogs, according to Dr. Houpt, if given free access to food will eat many small meals throughout the daylight hours. If your adult dog does not overeat, he may be given free-choice food, or meals supplied two or three times daily.

Dogs are attracted to food by its smell first, then the feel or texture of the food in their mouths, and finally by taste. When switching your dog's diet, try to duplicate the familiar smell and texture as closely as possible for a smooth transition. When the dog is particularly resistant to the new food, add it in small quantities to the old diet until the change is completed.

Dogs prefer warm to cold food, and one of the reasons is that heat volatilizes the odor. Watering a food will serve to entice some dogs to eat, but use only a little—just enough to moisten the food. When nursing a reluctant canine eater, add a little water to his food and heat it to body temperature in the microwave.

Our own food prejudices and lifestyles influence the way our pets eat. Obese owners are more likely than thin owners to own obese dogs, and middle-aged or older owners more likely to own obese dogs than young owners.

Nutritional Needs

The nutritional needs of dogs vary according to individual, breed, and life stage. After weaning, the puppy should be fed a balanced growth diet, which contains more calories and higher levels of protein and minerals, such as calcium and phosphorus, than maintenance diets, in amounts sufficient for him to attain average growth for his breed.

Overfeeding during the growth period will cause obesity, owing to an increase in both size and number of fat cells. Obesity in adults is due primarily to an increase in fat-cell size rather than number. As adults, you and the dog can shrink the size of the cells through dieting, but, alas, little can be done to reduce the number of fat cells. Oh well, more about my favorite New Year's resolution—losing weight—later.

Overfeeding the large-breed puppy may accelerate growth, predisposing the puppy to certain skeletal diseases. On the other side of the feeding scale is severe underfeeding, which stunts growth, causes poor hair coat, and compromises the immune system.

If your puppy is always eating or is a member of a breed prone to obesity—Labradors, cairn terriers, cocker spaniels, dachshunds, shelties, bassets, and beagles—control the amount of food available. Toy breeds might be fed three to four times daily while larger puppies can be fed twice a day for fifteen- to twenty-minute feeding periods.

Free-choice feeding can commence when the puppy has reached 80 to 90 percent of his anticipated adult weight, which usually is between nine and twelve months of age. The food can be switched from a growth to a maintenance diet about the time of his first birthday. Giant-breed puppies reach physical maturity at a later date; delay the switch to adult food until they are eighteen to twenty-four months old.

Adult dogs are fed a maintenance dog food, with high-protein, light, performance, and senior formulation variations. Suggestions for feeding the pregnant or lactating bitch and the elderly dog are covered in chapters 12 and 13, respectively.

The energy requirements for maintenance vary with breed. Generally, the smaller the breed, the greater the calories needed per unit of body weight. Even within the same breed, there is great individual variation in energy or caloric requirements. When scientists at the Purina Pet Care Center working with obese Labrador retrievers decreased their caloric intake by 27 percent, it took from thirteen to thirty-five weeks for the dogs to reach ideal weight. Those with higher energy requirements lost weight more rapidly.

The energy needed to maintain human body weight varies in much the same way. Carol Percy, a nurse and diabetes coordinator at the Shiprock Indian Health Services Hospital in New Mexico, says that American Indians tend to have a "thrifty gene" that causes them to store fat. It is a survival adaptation allowing them to endure when times are hard and food supplies are low. Percy says that the thrifty gene is nonadaptive now that Native Americans have a constant food supply and get less exercise. This tendency to store fat is often deadly, because obesity increases an individual's propensity for Type II diabetes, the eighth-leading cause of death on Navajo reservations. Although my ancestors came from the British Isles and Switzerland, I have a thrifty gene, too. I commiserate with my Indian friends and neighbors.

Scientists reported in the journal *Nature* that a gene in mice, which they named ob, is responsible for overeating. When normal mice gorge themselves with food, a protein controlled by the ob gene signals the brain to halt food intake and increases the metabolic rate to utilize the extra calories. Mice with defective ob genes eat with abandon and become obese. People have genes similar to the mouse ob gene, and researchers are studying a population of obese people on the island of Kosrae in Micronesia, looking for gene mutations responsible for overeating.

Women, by the way, have a greater percentage of body fat than men, and in general store fat easier. Several years ago, the Arctic and Antarctic explorer Will Steger told me that the female expedition member who accompanied him on one of his Arctic missions fared much better maintaining her body heat and body weight than did the male expedition members. See, that extra fat isn't all bad.

In a study of eighteen Labrador retriever puppies at the Waltham Centre for Pet Nutrition, males were determined to have a significantly higher body weight at five months of age than females. This extra weight in males was caused by a higher lean tissue mass and higher bone mineral content.

The caloric and nutrient needs of an animal vary greatly depending upon such factors as weather, work or exercise, life stage (growth, pregnancy, lactation, old age), stress, and illness. In a new study released by the Iams Company, racing sled dogs were found to burn an average of 11,220 calories of energy per day, in contrast to 2,490 calories needed by nonracing sled dogs from the same kennel and 700 calories needed by the sedentary twenty-pound pooch. This is a huge difference in maintenance needs. The racing dogs were fed a specially formulated diet with extremely high fat and protein levels.

Prescription diets are prescribed by veterinarians for disease conditions, and include those used to treat heart disease, kidney and urinary tract problems, food allergies, obesity, and intestinal disease.

New food products to help prevent dental problems include Hill's Pet Nutrition Prescription Diet t/d and Heinz Pet Products' Tartar Check. The diet, which is advertised as nutritionally adequate for long-term adult maintenance, is oversized kibble designed to form a fiber pattern of transverse striations that mechanically clean the teeth. Tartar Check is a biscuit advertised to reduce tartar buildup. Both food products are designed to be used on clean teeth to prevent tartar accumulation. Dogs suffering from gum and periodontal disease should first have their teeth examined and treated by a veterinarian.

Every day entrepreneurs find ways to enter the billion-dollar pet food industry. I noticed recently an article about a dog restaurant. It makes sense that a pooch might want to step out for a bite after spending the night at the pet motel or shopping in a boutique offering doggy fashions. And what about Frosty Paws, an ice cream substitute for dogs? All in the fun, I suppose, but it's hard to keep Rover down on the farm eating dog chow when the big lights of places like Paris, Texas, might offer Frosty Paws at the local A & P.

Feeding Problems

obesity

Obesity is the most common nutritional disease of dogs (affecting 25 to 44 percent of pet dogs). It occurs when the dog's intake of dietary energy in the form of calories exceeds the body's energy needs and the surplus is stored as fat. An animal is considered obese if his body weight is more than 20 to 25 percent over his ideal weight.

One way of accessing ideal weight is to compare your dog's current weight with his weight as a young adult. Of course, when I apply that formula to myself—current weight compared to my weight when I graduated from veterinary school or married—I get terribly depressed.

Here is another way to test fatness: Stand behind your dog and run your fingers down his ribs. If the bones are easily felt, the dog may be too thin; if the bones cannot be felt because a layer of fat covers them, he is probably too fat. A waddling gait, protruding abdomen, and fat pads over the hips are other signs of obesity.

When I was a member of the Army Reserve, I once exceeded the military weight limit for my age and height, but passed the skin-fold thickness test for obesity. Skin-fold thickness does not correlate to obesity in dogs as it does in people, because the dog's skin is loosely attached and easily lifted from underlying tissue.

Obesity is a health hazard; overweight dogs have an increased risk of developing traumatic and degenerative orthopedic disorders, heart disease, diabetes, heat stroke, anesthetic accidents, and certain types of bladder cancer. Factors contributing to a dog becoming overweight include inherited propensity, hormonal imbalances, old age, neutering, lack of exercise, and overeating.

As mentioned earlier, some dogs and people have what could be called a thrifty gene. Based on lean body mass, not body weight, food intake is less for obese individuals than for lean ones. Even after weight loss, previously obese individuals require 27 percent fewer calories to maintain optimal body weight than those who have never been obese. In other words, an obese individual's metabolism becomes very efficient, and the tendency to put on weight is ever-present.

As we age, human and dog, we tend to put on weight. Most individuals lose muscle mass and add fat at the same time as physical activity lessens. Neutering doubles the chances that a dog will become overweight. A neutered animal expends less energy roaming in search of romance and feeding demanding puppies. Related to this reduction of sexual energy is perhaps a tendency to boredom eating. Neutered animals also put on more weight than their intact neighbors because the sexual hormones that depress appetite are absent. An owner can counterbalance this tendency toward obesity by monitoring the dog's calories and increasing his exercise.

A sluggish thyroid gland and other medical problems can also lead to obesity, but these conditions are rare in comparison to the psychological factors that contribute to an animal's becoming overweight. Both obese people and animals have certain emotional habits in common. For one, we are great plate cleaners, eating for all the starving dogs and people in China. We're more attentive and responsive to external food stimuli than are our thin friends, succumbing without a fight to guacamole dip or Milk-Bone treat. Fat humans and dogs tend to eat more rapidly than normal-weight ones, and in tests, obese individuals tend to be more temperamental or excitable than controls. Obese people and animals who have lost weight tend to act just like fat ones; therefore, weight reduction is often short-lived.

For some animals, exercise alone is sufficient to lose weight; for others, a diet is needed. When calories are restricted during dieting, the body compensates by lowering the metabolism in an effort to conserve energy; exercise prevents this expected drop in metabolic rate from occurring, thus providing another benefit.

Dieting for dogs can be approached in several ways. Because of the health risks involved, I do not recommend surgery, drugs, or fasting. What I do suggest is limiting the amount of food or placing the animal on a reducing diet. See Table 8.1 for some weight-control recommendations.

Prescription reducing diets offer low-fat, high-fiber formulas. Lowering the fat content reduces the caloric density of the ration; fiber, for the most part indigestible, increases stool bulk and prolongs eating time. The dog will feel full and consume fewer calories, even if he is eating the same amount on the reducing diet as he was on his old food.

When attempting to restrict the amount of the dog's standard diet, reduce caloric intake to approximately 60 to 70 percent of that required for maintaining optimum weight. To do this, it is necessary to know the pet's optimum weight and the caloric density of the diet. Since most owners are not adept at making these calculations, and because every diet and exercise program should be designed for the individual pet's physical condition, I recommend that you consult your veterinarian before instituting a treatment program for obesity.

anorexia

Anorexia is diminished appetite, and can have medical and behavioral origins. When the cause is medical, appetite-stimulating drugs and good nursing care are treatment options. When the origin is behavioral, treatment consists of offering a highly palatable diet and enticing environment. The sight of another dog chowing down will do it for some reluctant eaters.

I had a client whose dog Gretchen, a slightly obese schnauzer, ate only Vienna sausages and Kentucky Fried Chicken (the original recipe). The dog belonged to an elderly widow who resided a block away from the Colonel's place. When the two favorite foods were withdrawn, Gretchen refused to eat, and she could afford to be picky since her body weight was sufficient.

Dr. Katherine Houpt, the behaviorist mentioned earlier, cites a similar case in the article "Feeding and Drinking Behavior Problems," which appeared in *Veterinary Clinics of North America*. Dr. Houpt's suggestions include gradual removal of the favored food while providing a balanced dog food for a limited period of time every twelve hours. This method should work because dogs eat to maintain a set point of body weight controlled by the body's stored

The Essentials

Table 8.1

Weight-Control Recommendations

1. Get a physical examination of dog by a veterinarian.

2. Weigh pet, estimate ideal weight and goal weight, and set time limit for achieving goal weight.

3. Figure the amount of regular or reducing diet to be fed per day. Divide that amount into three small meals.

4. Keep dog out of room when you are preparing food and family members are eating.

5. Prohibit between-meal snacks. Use nonfood reward for behavior training or offer small portions of day's ration.

6. Design two ten- to fifteen-minute exercise periods per day for dog.

7. Offer dog a stimulating new environment so he will not be tempted to eat from boredom—new toys, chew bones, car trips.

8. Offer dog extra attention in the form of walking, petting, training, and play so that he will not focus on food deprivation.

9. Weigh dog every week and record his weight.

10. After dog reaches goal weight, feed the amount of food needed to maintain that weight. Continue to weigh dog weekly.

---

fat. If an animal is starved for a few days, he will eat more when the appropriate food is supplied to regain the lost weight.

My client had not the resolve or willpower to change her pet's eating habits. It was easy to get rid of the Vienna sausages, but the Kentucky Fried Chicken was another matter entirely. The dog was exposed to its smells when she went outside in the yard or for a walk on her leash. The widow was used to bringing home a chicken meal for her own supper. The last I heard, the suggested dog food had gone stale and had been thrown out, while Gretchen had expanded her Kentucky Fried Chicken diet to include roasted and extra-crispy.

excessive sucking

Puppies, particularly those who are undernourished or orphaned, may suck the bodies of littermates or themselves to satisfy a natural nursing desire. Body parts offering nipplelike projections are most vulnerable—ears, tails, vulvae, and scrotums. Treatment is separation or offering a substitute object, such as a rubber toy or chew bone.

In dobermans, there is an inherited tendency in some individuals to suckle their own flanks or to suckle the bedding. The dog indulges in this behavior before going to sleep, similar to the child who sucks his thumb or twists the satin edges of a blanket. Treatment is unnecessary unless skin and hair loss is extensive, or the dog sucks your imported Persian rug. In the latter case, buy him a cheap rug from Wal-Mart, and hide the expensive one.

eating grass

When dogs caught large prey for food, they first ingested the organs, which contained partially digested vegetable matter. If house pets develop a craving for this type of vegetable matter, they eat grass. Unlike cows and other ruminants, dogs do not have a digestive tract adapted to digesting raw plant material. Although partly digested or cooked plant material may be well tolerated, raw vegetables are usually vomited.

Certain dogs learn to associate ingestion of grass with vomiting, and seek out plants to eat when they feel nauseous. Limiting access to large amounts of grass or offering small amounts of fine fresh grass might limit the behavior.

coprophagia

Coprophagia is the eating of feces, and involves two types: the ingesting of the dog's own feces and the ingesting of feces of other animals. As mentioned in chapter 5, the consumption of feces and urine of puppies is normal behavior of mother dogs. The behavior serves to keep the nest clean until puppies can travel outside the nest area to eliminate; a clean nest is less likely to attract predators. In adult dogs, however, the behavior may subject the dog to increased exposure to parasites, and most owners find the habit repugnant.

Ways to deal with the behavior include walking the dog on a leash, removing feces as soon as it is deposited, and muzzling the dog when he is alone outside. Training the dog to defecate on command or to return to the house immediately after defecating are other methods that work for the dedicated owner.

Although dietary deficiency is not usually the cause of coprophagia, some experts recommend a dietary change to twice-a-day feeding of a good-quality ration high in fat and protein and low in carbohydrate. If dietary change fails to correct the behavior, manipulating the food and, hence, the feces is another alternative. Adding pancreatic enzymes to the food renders it distasteful; the commercial product Forbid contains these enzymes and is designed to treat coprophagia. If the stool is made soft, the fun of eating a poopsicle is diminished; this change in stool consistency is accomplished with drugs such as stool softeners.

Another technique is adding Tabasco or other hot pepper sauce to the stool; this may be worth a trial period, but most authors report failure, as the dog is rewarded when he finds an undoctored stool. There is no easy answer for preventing this unwanted behavior, and often a series or combination of methods must be used before the dog stops the behavior.

begging

Rich Hall, in his *Sniglets* cartoon, coins a new term for begging: "Fooview (*foo'·view*) n. The ability of a dog to inflict guilt from any angle in the room while he watches his master eat." My dog Bear is an expert, as are most dogs, at fooview. I occasionally succumb and give him a bite of my snack, thus rewarding the begging with intermittent reinforcement.

Intermittent reinforcement ensures that Bear is going to continue to sit at my feet and stare at me each time I pop food into my mouth in his presence. The correct behavior on my part is, of course, to never reward his begging with a tidbit.

The best feeding policy is to offer the dog high-quality dog food twice a day, in his own bowl, away from the family dining area.

Shelter

Dens and Territory

We share with dogs and wolves a desire for a den—a place of our own where we can feel safe, snug, and protected from the outside world. I suppose this is why we call the family room in our home a den.

It is our sense of territorial rights, which we share with canids, that justifies defending our dens from outsiders. Anthropologist Elizabeth Marshall Thomas writes, in *The Hidden Life of Dogs*, "Wolves are well known to be territorial, which is to say that they lay claim to certain areas, which they defend as best they can from other wolves.... Dominance and ownership were surely very closely tied.... The dominant female gets to give birth inside the den. Thus ownership and dominance are life itself to wolves, and dogs remember this, and act accordingly."

Technically, there's difference between territory, which is the space guarded from intruders, and home range, where an animal normally lives and ranges. Most domestic dogs have a range that consists of the house, if they are inside dogs, and the yard. In many instances, range and territory are the same.

My dog Bear, an outside dog, considers the wrap-around porch his territory. It is here that he eats, drinks, and sleeps; he tries his best to keep other dogs and critters off his porch. His range is a little larger, extending to the garage with its deck, the building we call the bunkhouse, and a short distance along the dirt road coming and going past our property. This corresponds with the findings of behavioral scientist Alan Beck, who found that urban strays established tiny ranges of 0.1 to .06 square mile.

Elizabeth Marshall Thomas, however, decided to conduct her own research about home range by following her dog Misha: "Misha's range more closely resembled the 200- to 500-square-mile territories roamed by wolves...." Other investigators found that large dogs travel over twice the distance from home that small dogs do; rural dogs travel much greater distances than city or suburban dogs;

and certain breeds—Arctic dogs like the samoyed, for example—have very large ranges.

Dogs, like people, have different needs to explore and expand their range or to stay closely associated with home, and the inclination has innate, sexual, and learned components. Take Blacky, for instance, who had learned that life on the street offered more excitement than life in a comfortable backyard.

A small stray terrier, Blacky was brought to the veterinary hospital where I worked to be put to sleep, and I adopted her instead. In spite of the good medical care, food, companionship, doghouse, and fenced yard that I provided, Blacky would not stay at home. She dug under, through, and over any barrier to walk the streets, as must have been her habit for years. Although she returned for the goodies I provided, Blacky nonetheless insisted on maintaining her free lifestyle.

Contrasting with Blacky are dogs suffering from what is known as kennel-dog syndrome. In this instance, a dog who is raised in a kennel for six months or more is unable to cope with any environment other than the familiar kennel or den. Even when placed in what we would consider happy homes, dogs suffering from kennel-dog syndrome become very stressed. These dogs might be compared with people suffering agoraphobia, an anxiety disorder in which the fearful person refuses to leave home. Symptoms in dogs include extreme submission, fear-biting, and anorexia.

Roaming

Dogs leave home for a number of reasons, including sex, food, fellowship, and excitement. To prevent roaming, the incentives for leaving must be taken away while the rewards for staying are enhanced.

Neuter the intact dog; in one study, castration was curative in preventing roaming in 90 percent of male dogs. Reduce boredom by supplying chew toys and knuckle bones, and providing routine times for play, exercise, and other interactions with members of the family. Offer eatable treats for staying home.

One method of rewarding with food is to withhold the dog's dinner for twenty-four hours. Then provide the wanderer with tidbits of a food reward (small piece of chicken or weeny) every fifteen to twenty minutes for the first two days; extend the time between snacks to every fifteen to forty-five minutes on a variable basis for the next three days, and continue the reward system on an intermittent basis.

If the roamer has a favorite place or person he visits for food and companionship, use remote punishment to reduce the allure. A garden hose turned on Rover just as he is entering Mrs. Greengrass's yard might be effective.

Escaping

If Rover is rewarded during a breakout by family hoopla, riding in the family car (if he likes the car), or being placed inside the house while the fence is repaired, he is going to repeat the behavior.

Intermittent reinforcement—he is able to break out some of the time—is a great incentive for him to keep trying to escape by climbing over, under, or through the gate or fence. In other words, you must make sure that he never escapes again after that first time. Escape-proofing your yard may mean a new fence—chain-link, electric, or invisible.

The Invisible Fence system consists of a boundary wire installed a few inches underground, a radio-receiver dog collar, and a radio transmitter that plugs into an electrical outlet. As the dog wearing the collar approaches a set distance from the boundary, he receives a warning sound; if he proceeds, he receives an electrical shock.

High-Rise Syndrome

The Department of Surgery at the Animal Medical Center in New York City evaluated dogs and cats treated at their facility who fell from high-rise buildings. Naturally, there are more cases of high-rise syndrome in New York City than here in Mora County, where I live.

The Animal Medical Center staff compared dogs falling out of high buildings with similar events involving cats and humans. The range of heights fallen by surviving dogs was one to six stories, while cats fell two to thirty-two stories and lived to meow about it. Humans are like dogs in that they do not survive falls greater than six stories. The shorter the distance a dog falls, the greater his chances of recovery.

The Essentials

Cats fare better when falling from extreme heights because of their air-righting reflex ability, which allows them to reach terminal velocity at about five stories and to orient their bodies like flying squirrels. This position decreases falling velocity by increasing drag, and allows the landing impact to be distributed over a greater portion of the cat's body.

Most dogs who fell did so through windows, with the roof being the next most common origin. In most cases the dog jumped, and I am reminded of the Chevy Chase movie *European Vacation*, in which the poodle jumps off the Eiffel Tower in pursuit of a Frisbee. Dogs who didn't jump fell accidentally or, in one case, were pushed. Dogs and cats who fall from high buildings tend to be young and tend to do so during summer, when windows are open and outdoor play is occurring.

The best protection against high-rise syndrome is prevention. Keep windows screened, closed, and locked. Balconies, ledges, roofs, and the Eiffel Tower should be off-limits to dogs.

Homes Away from Home

Accommodations for dogs are getting fancy. The Steigenberger Frankfurter Hof, a hotel in Frankfurt, Germany, provides a doggy bar offering dog biscuits, cocktail sausages, and other canine cuisine to dogs staying with their owners at the hotel. Amusement parks such as Six Flags Over Texas provide a home away from home for your canine traveling companions.

Whether you are traveling with your dog out of necessity or for the pleasure of his company, make reservations at hotels and motels well in advance. Make sure your dog's vaccinations are current and that you have the necessary health certificates and prescription drugs such as antimotion pills. Identification tags with your name, address, and telephone number are a necessity for the stay-at-home or the traveling dog.

Automobiles

For some dogs an automobile is an extension of his home territory; for others, it is a hated monster.

Protecting the car comes naturally to aggressive breeds. I'm often asked at Rabies Drives to vaccinate old Shep in the car seat or pickup bed; when I'm smart, I refuse because a dog I can handle in a new environment such as a fire station garage will often bite me when I enter his perceived home territory.

Even macho dogs, like those shepherds and Rottweilers at the Rabies Drive, need certain constraints when traveling in the car or pickup. I doctored the cuts and abrasions that my granddog Sarge suffered after falling from the back of a pickup traveling sixty miles per hour, and Sarge is a pit bull mixed with chow; no telling what would have happened to a poodle.

It is a law in some states that dogs traveling in a pickup bed be restrained, and commercial restraints are available at pet stores. Some dogs are more comfortable confined to a familiar crate or carrier when traveling via car. Others can be bridled in a canine safety belt, available at pet stores. And don't leave dogs unattended in a closed car in the summer; dogs are much more susceptible to heat stroke than we are because they don't sweat.

While we're on the topic of dogs and cars, I'd like to mention an ultrasonic device called Animal Lover, which is marketed by Winner International, the company which makes The Club antitheft car system. Animal Lover, which is installed on your car's front bumper, emits a high-frequency sound, inaudible to humans, when the engine is started, and is audible to animals up to 250 feet away when the car is traveling sixty-five miles an hour. The goal is to alert an animal who might not hear the car engine, such as an older dog, or a wild animal in the car's path, such as deer. For more information, call 1-800-527-3345.

Chasing prey is instinctive in wild canids. That instinct is triggered in many domestic dogs by anything that runs away—cats, cars, joggers, and bicycles. Because the joy of the chase is rewarding, it is a very difficult behavior to change. The best method is prevention, such as restraining the dog within a fenced yard. Retraining dogs not to chase cars is at best 40 percent successful; retraining using negative reinforcement is discussed in the next chapter.

QUESTION

Dear Dr. Whiteley,

My dog Pepper, a spayed female poodle, has a breathing problem that I find distressing. She will do this snorting

The Essentials

thing like she can't catch her breath. It will continue for a period of several seconds, and she might do it three or four times a week. Is this a condition I should be concerned about?

Anxious in Lexington

Dear Anxious,

I believe you are describing what some veterinarians term reverse sneeze syndrome, characterized by paroxysms of inspiratory snorting lasting sometimes up to a minute. The cause is unknown, although some experts attribute it to what is known as postnasal drip in people. There is no treatment, and the condition is harmless. However, since an allergic condition or foreign body in the nasal cavity might trigger similar symptoms, you should have the dog examined by his veterinarian.

Best wishes!
H. E. W.

9
Teaching

Puppies begin learning within the first few days of birth, and learning continues throughout life. Electroencephalograph measurements of brain waves determine a relatively mature pattern for puppies six to eight weeks of age. You can teach an old dog new tricks, but it is easier to teach a puppy in that critical period from six to fourteen weeks, approximately the same as the socialization period.

In the old days, veterinarians and animal trainers recommended that obedience training be delayed until the puppy was an adolescent of six months. Today, most experts urge that training start soon after adoption to take advantage of this impressionable period in a pup's development. Puppy classes and kindergarten classes are now offered in preparation for or in lieu of adult obedience classes.

An equally important time span exists for developing children. Joan Beck, syndicated columnist for the *Chicago Tribune*, found this a worthy topic for her column:

> Three decades of research show clearly that factors in the environment—especially appropriate learning stimuli, abundant language and loving, one-on-one attention—actually help shape the neurological structure of the brain so it becomes more "intelligent" for the rest of its life.
>
> These influences are greatest when the brain is growing most rapidly—the first years of life. Providing appropriate learning opportunities in the first three years of life helps more to form basic intelligence than a similar amount of schooling later on.

The first three years in human life correspond well to the first three months in the life of a puppy. This is the reason why puppy classes and positive learning experiences during this stage of development are so important and why isolated puppies almost never catch up socially or intellectually with their stimulated peers.

Behavior is influenced by inherited patterns and by learning. The larger the learning component of the behavior, the easier the behavior is to influence or to change. Dogs learn from you and their environment. Make sure that the lessons they are picking up are those you intend and that their home or den is conducive to good behavior. Teaching your dog behavior favorable to his designated role in

Teaching

your family is the purpose of this chapter, and the section that immediately follows defines some of the ways that dogs learn from you and their environment.

How Dogs Learn

Observational Learning

Dogs learn by observation and imitation, just like you and I do. Experiments show that animals watching another species press a bar or jump over a barrier for food will learn this behavior much faster than those without teachers.

One of my favorite dogs was a long-haired, short-legged mongrel named Shag, abandoned at the veterinary hospital where I worked as a summer intern in the olden days, as my children like to say. Shag soon became my grandfather's dog, and they were often seen planting trees, gardening, and performing other farm chores together.

Once we had the bush hog (mower) attached to the tractor because my grandfather planned to mow the remains of the garden in preparation for next year. I jumped on the back of the bush hog for a ride to the gate as my grandfather drove the tractor by me. Shag observed my actions and imitated them by jumping up beside me for a free ride. Whenever my grandfather drove the tractor, Shag rode on the back of the bush hog. When the mower was in operation, however, the little dog knew not to jump on the machine; if my grandfather lowered the mower to the ground with the admonishment "Shag, off," the dog obeyed good naturedly.

Trial and Error Learning

Dogs learn also by trial and error. Suppose, for example, that Rover escaped from the backyard to play soccer with the neighborhood children in the field across the street. The first time he found freedom by chewing a hole in the wooden back gate. During the next attempt to join the athletes, he found that you had patched the hole with chicken wire. Chewing chicken wire isn't as easy as wood. However, Rover soon learned, via trial and error, that he could loosen the wire by butting it with his head; grasping the wire in his teeth, he shook it loose from the nails fastening it to the gate. He has solved the escape problem, at least until you find something to create a barrier from which he can't escape.

Livestock learn by trial and error to avoid electric fences and to access automatic feeders; the behavior is augmented by negative reinforcement in the case of the electric fence and positive reinforcement in the case of the feeder. Reinforcement training is covered later in this chapter.

Habituation Learning

Habituation is also called extinction. If your new puppy is exposed to your teenager's hard rock music on his first weekend in your home, he is startled or perhaps disturbed by it. Eventually, however, it becomes part of the background noise of the new family to which he is bonding; the loud music becomes less noticeable until it gets no reaction from the puppy.

I worked once in a veterinary hospital where I was the only staff member with small children. When a client came in with active and loud children, the assistants were ready for tranquilizers by the time the kids left. I, on the other hand, was habituated to the inquisitiveness, activity, and noise of children, and their presence failed to disturb me.

Habituation to noise is one way to differentiate between the normal dog who is not getting enough exercise and a truly hyperactive or hyperkinetic one. A hyperactive individual does not show a diminished response to noise over time.

Latent Learning

Latent learning is knowledge acquired at an earlier period that lies dormant until needed. A puppy exposed to young children during the socialization period might not be confronted by these small people again until his owner's grandchildren come for a visit. The dog can relate now because his earlier learning made children a known factor.

Children, by the way, might as well be a species separate from adult humans, when seen from the dog's viewpoint. Children are smaller, some of them crawl on the floor and smell like pablum and

Teaching

spit-up, and they have larger heads in proportion to the body and different voice timbre.

Imprint Learning

Imprinting was discussed extensively in chapter 5; the puppy raised with humans but not dogs, who became sexually responsive to the vacuum cleaner bag, is an example of imprint learning. Imprint learning occurs early in the pup's life during specific critical periods in development.

Insight Learning

This type of learning might be termed rational thinking. Although there is debate about whether animals think, I believe in the mental ability of animals. Take the sheepdog and his enemy, the coyote, for example. They both use insight learning to their advantage.

Growing in number since antipredator poisons were outlawed twenty-three years ago, coyotes are working in groups of four to eight, deploying decoys to lure away guard dogs while others move in on the flocks.

What is the answer? Increasing the sheep dog force. Sheep ranchers are depending more on dogs, and are employing dogs in greater numbers. The choice for protecting sheep is the Akbash, a breed from Turkey ranging in weight from 90 to 140 pounds and looking like a slim version of the Great Pyrenees. He has the size, speed, and rational thinking ability to anticipate and counter the diversionary and other tactics of the wiliest coyote.

Classical Conditioning

Classical conditioning studies date back to the Pavlov experiments: the researcher rang a bell or vibrated a tuning fork when he fed the dogs, and later the mere ringing of the bell elicited a salivation response. We see this all the time. The dog drools when we open the kitchen cabinet where his dog food is stored; the puppy shows fearful body language when we load him in the car because the only place he goes in the car is to the hated veterinary hospital or grooming parlor.

Classical conditioning consists of pairing a stimulus that produces a certain response with a second, neutral stimulus; after a while either stimulus will evoke the response. In the example of the salivating dog, offering the dog food (stimulus) or opening the appropriate kitchen cabinet (neutral stimulus) will evoke the response (salivation).

Training Methods

A dog learns by trial and error that an action will bring pleasure or pain, reward or punishment. Training involves manipulating this system of reward and punishment to facilitate the dog's learning of actions conducive to life in your household.

Positive Reinforcement

By definition, positive reinforcement is something that occurs in conjunction with a specific action, which tends to increase the probability that the action will occur again. The something that positively reinforces can be an object or action that the dog wants, such as food, petting, or praise.

Positive reinforcement can be used to teach a puppy to come when you call his name. Use your puppy's name each time you feed him, even if he's standing at your feet waiting. Call the puppy to dinner when he is in another room. Say pleasantly, "Rover, come." Be consistent and use the same words and tone of voice each time you summon your puppy. If the puppy fails to respond, go get him. Put him down beside the food bowl, say "Rover, come," and place the food in his bowl.

After Rover is accomplished at responding to the meal summons, call him to come on other occasions, but avoid using this command to call the puppy for an event that he might perceive as painful or negative. If you must summon the puppy to administer medication, for instance, go get him.

Reward the correct response to "come" with a food treat; eventually replace the food treat with petting, praise, or other nonfood rewards. Karen Pryor, author of *Don't Shoot the Dog: The New Art of Teaching and Training*, suggests having a variety of reinforcements for

Teaching

any training situation; the little surprises keep learning interesting to the pet.

Correct timing is vital for the success of reinforcement training. If you reinforce too early, you are bribing rather than reinforcing. You are encouraging whatever is occurring at the time you offer the reward.

If you are teaching your puppy to sit, for example, give the command "Rover, sit." If the puppy remains standing, gently push down on his hindquarters while giving the command. Reward the sitting position. If the puppy returns to standing posture before you give the reward, you've reinforced too late; you've rewarded standing instead of sitting.

When using a food reward to teach a beginner, reinforce the desired behavior each time it occurs. If you are training your puppy to retrieve a ball, you must offer him a treat such as a tidbit of weeny and praise each time he performs correctly. After he has mastered the trick, however, the food reward can be used intermittently and eventually phased out so that the puppy will perform for praise alone.

Do not use rewards indiscriminately. Don't use the praise "Good Puppy" to express affection if you intend to use it as a positive reinforcer for training the puppy to perform a trick. When using food as a positive reinforcer, keep the size of the reinforcement as small as possible—a quarter-inch cube of meat. If the puppy is particularly fond of the treat, you can go even smaller. The smaller the reward, the greater the number of reinforcements per training session that can be accomplished before the puppy or dog becomes full or bored.

Animal trainer Karen Pryor says that reward selection should be based on the difficulty of the task. If your puppy retrieves the ball in midair, he should receive more than a bite of weeny.

The jackpot, according to Pryor, is a reward much bigger, as much as ten times bigger, than the normal reinforcement, and should come as a surprise to the recipient. She uses the jackpot to reinforce a sudden breakthrough in the super pupil and to relieve resentment or tension in the reluctant or fearful student. Pryor emphasizes the need for random rewards to keep the student from getting lazy and to keep him working to "hit the jackpot."

Since we are discussing using food as a reward, I'd better add a disclaimer. Take care to select treats that are harmless to the pet. Dogs suffering from a heart condition should avoid salty foods, and those who are obese should not be given high-caloric treats. It may be helpful to change from free-choice feeding to twice-a-day meals during the training period or to schedule training before feeding time to ensure that the pet is hungry enough to trade tricks for treats. Some suggested food treats are:

Vitamin or mineral tablet
Bite of regular ration
Small cube of cheese
Commercial treat
Quarter-inch piece of weeny, Vienna sausage
Tidbit of cooked liver
Ground meatball
Fraction of hard-boiled egg
Bite of cooked, boneless fish
Tidbit of cooked, boneless and skinless chicken breast

Work with your dog for short periods—five to ten minutes at most for an adult and less for a puppy, whose attention span is shorter, so neither of you becomes bored with the process. Stop on a positive performance if possible. Stress, drowsiness, and excitability hinder the learning process. Most dogs do not learn well during the first training period because they are distracted and excited.

I recently saw a documentary about the making of the movie *Lassie Come Home*. Lassie did not like children, and he had to be trained (in this case, *bribed* may be the correct word) to respond to the then-young actors Elizabeth Taylor and Roddy McDowall. The trainer hid a steak under the covers when it came time for Lassie to jump up on Elizabeth's bed, and painted Roddy's face with ice cream to encourage Lassie to lick him.

Negative Reinforcement

Negative reinforcement is something the dog will work to avoid. Pulling on the dog's leash and kicking a horse to make him go are examples of negative reinforcement. As soon as the dog follows along or the horse goes faster, the pulling or kicking ceases.

Dr. Bonnie Beaver, animal behaviorist at Texas A & M, uses negative reinforcement when retraining the car-chasing dog. "The key to success (when it is possible) is to provide the dog with only negative experiences when it chases cars," Dr. Beaver writes in the article "Why Dogs Chase Cars," which appeared in *Veterinary Medicine/ Small Animal Clinician*. Dr. Beaver suggests that the owner make a trip around the block in the passenger seat of a car. When the dog chases the car, the automobile is abruptly stopped, and the owner gets out and chases after the dog while yelling, throwing things— water-filled balloons, pails of water, tin cans filled with noisy objects—or spraying him with Mace.

Another method is to have the dog wear a Promise collar to which a long lead is attached. When the dog chases a car, the lead is jerked continually until the dog stops running after the car. The difficult part, besides balancing the pail of water in your lap and tackling that lead, is that you are negatively reinforcing the car-chasing behavior every time it occurs. If the dog chases a car successfully—the car is chased away and the dog has a good time doing it—the behavior is reinforced positively, which provides a tremendous incentive for the dog to keep chasing cars, especially in your absence.

Punishment

Suppose you come home from work and discover that the dog has turned over the kitchen trash in your absence. You scream at the dog and whack him with your purse before cleaning up the mess. This verbal and acting punishment may help you let off steam, but it will do little to train the dog to refrain from misbehavior that occurred hours earlier.

If the above scenario happens often enough, the dog may learn to associate your return from work with yelling and whacking with the purse. You say, "But, he looks guilty; he must know he's done wrong." The dog is responding with fear or submission to what he has learned to expect from you when you come home from work.

For punishment to be an effective training method it must be administered during or within one second of the misbehavior. The longer the period that passes between the undesired behavior and punishment, the less likely that punishment will change the behavior effectively and the more likely that other behavioral problems will manifest in response to your action. If you catch the dog in the act of turning over or riffling through the trash, yelling and whacking with your purse might be effective punishment.

Remote punishment follows the criterion of applying retribution at the time of unwanted behavior. You might place spring-loaded mousetraps upside down inside the trash; when the dog jumps on the trash can, the movement will cause the traps to snap and pop, scaring the dog away from the can. Another method is a motion detector that emits a loud noise when the dog gets near the trash can.

Contech Electronics, the creator of Scat Mat, makes a circular mat for placing around garbage cans, planters, and Christmas trees. It emits unpleasant static electricity when the pet steps on it. Scat Mat is advertised to keep pets off furniture, cars, kitchen counters, and so on. For more information, call 1-800-767-8658.

Regardless of the method chosen, punishment must continue until the dog has been retrained to avoid the trash can. As you have probably discerned by now, some methods cited of retraining the car-chasing dog might more correctly be termed punishment. The technicalities are less important than the lesson; misbehavior isn't fun and doesn't pay.

NAMING

One of the first acts of ownership and teaching is naming your dog. It is easier for the dog to learn his name if you select a short one- or two-syllable name, such as Ralph or Rover. Sir Winston the Sixth of Huntington Farms is difficult to learn. Nor should you add nicknames or expressions of endearment, such as Sweetums, Snookums or Damn Dog, if those are not his name, for too many names are just as confusing as too long a name.

The American Kennel Club (AKC) prohibits registered names with more than twenty-five letters, names of prominent people (living or recently deceased), words that imply AKC titles, breed names, and obscene names. Although the word *sex* is not normally considered obscene, the pet owner who wrote to Ann Landers about his dog named Sex would probably be barred from using that word as part of the dog's registered name.

I should refrain from suggesting names, as my dogs have had the

Teaching

noncreative monikers of Bear, Little Bit, Spotty, Blacky, Shag, Angel, and Tippy. Bear, however, is rather appropriate. After hearing the story of a black bear breaking through our neighbor's kitchen window, my husband and I were sitting at the dining table when shaggy-headed Bear jumped up and peered into the window next to us. George and I both screamed; for a few seconds we thought our neighbor's bear had joined us for lunch.

Of the 230,810 licensed canines registered with the Los Angeles Department of Animal Regulation in 1989, the ten most popular dog names in order are: Lady, Max, Brandy, Duke, Rocky, Princess, Ginger, Pepper, Blacky, and Lucky.

Patrick McManus, author of humorous books about hunting and fishing, is perhaps more creative than I and my California neighbors. He writes in "A Dog for All Seasons": "We had called the dog Stranger out of the faint hope that he was just passing through. As it turned out, the name was most inappropriate since he stayed on for nearly a score of years, all the while biting the hands that fed him and making snide remarks about my grandmother's cooking. Eventually the name was abbreviated to 'strange,' which was shorter and much more descriptive."

I suggest that you pick a name you like and one you can live with for the rest of the dog's life. Use the dog's name before speaking to him and before giving an obedience command, to get his attention.

HOUSETRAINING

Keeping his den clean is innate behavior in the dog. Cleanliness reduces the incidence of parasites and disease, and nature smiles upon the offspring of sanitary mothers—those who clean young puppies and those who teach appropriate elimination behavior to older pups.

When you adopt a new puppy, you are teacher and your home or apartment becomes the puppy's den. Most adoptions occur around seven weeks, and this is a good time to start housetraining.

Breeds differ in their ability to learn housetraining. Those known for their resistance to potty training include the basset hound, dachshund, fox terrier, Dalmatian, Pekingese, and beagle. Those receiving high marks in this type of training include the bichon frise, miniature and standard poodle, Welsh corgi, Australian shepherd, and doberman pinscher. Females are usually easier to housetrain than males; therefore, if you are adopting a breed known for his potty-training resistance, opt for a girl.

Substrate preferences develop early in the pup's life, and the surface you select as the puppy's elimination site will remain his choice for elimination. Newspaper, grass, concrete, or asphalt commonly become the preferred surface. If you expect the puppy to eliminate on paper, do not select paper for lining his crate or bed.

It is helpful to select an appropriate den and potty area before you bring the puppy home; it is also easier for the puppy to keep his den clean if you limit the size, at least at first, to one room rather than the entire house. Let's say that you've decided that the grassy knoll beside the fence is the best place for Rover's potty; it is a straight shot from the kitchen, where puppy's bed is located, and not far away from the back door.

A puppy normally eliminates when he awakens, after eating and drinking, after play or other activity, and before bedding down at night; these are the times he should be taken to his potty. A young puppy eats three or four times daily, takes several naps, and is often engaged in play activity. This means that you need to be available to take the puppy outside to the designated potty area many times a day, and you may need to stay outside, if that's where the potty is located, for five to ten minutes. Try to provide the puppy with an elimination routine.

In some areas of the country, winter is a difficult time to housetrain a puppy to eliminate outside. It makes more sense to adopt a puppy for Fourth of July than for Christmas if you live in an area where inclement weather is a problem.

If the puppy cannot be taken outside frequently, he can be trained to eliminate on newspapers placed inside a small area opposite his bed and feeding and drinking dishes. When the puppy uses the appropriate potty area, his territory within the house can be gradually expanded. Keep the newspapers in the same location, and place the bottom papers on top of the new ones to provide an odor clue that this is indeed the bathroom.

Accidents happen for many reasons—the inability of the puppy's bladder to hold a large capacity of urine for one—and are not a purposeful event timed to aggravate you. Do you yell at the puppy and rub his nose in it when you find the evidence of an accident? Of course not. You place the puppy outside or in his crate while you quietly clean up the mess. If you catch the puppy in the act, you might forcefully say "no," but that's as far as you should go with the punishment routine. Instead, you positively and quickly reinforce each and every act of appropriate urination and defecation. The puppy's attention span at adoption age is less than a minute. If praise is your positive reinforcer, it should be given as the puppy is actually eliminating.

CRATE TRAINING

A crate or kennel (wire or plastic) can become the puppy's den within your home. Place comfortable bedding (not newspaper if that's what he's going to eliminate on) inside the crate. Leave the door open, and allow the puppy to investigate the crate on his own. A few toys and goodies in the crate might be an incentive for the puppy to take a closer look.

Next, place the puppy's food inside the crate; if the puppy is hesitant to go inside, locate the feeding bowl where he can reach in from outside and take a bite.

After the puppy has accepted the crate by fearlessly coming and going within its confines, place him inside when it's time for a nap or for feeding. You can let him out again as soon as he awakens or completes his meal. If he makes a fuss, ignore him; you don't want to reward barking and scratching by letting him out of the cage. When the puppy accepts the crate quietly, lavish him with praise or offer a treat.

The puppy will soon accept the crate as his room where he can go for naps and rest. If he is left inside for too long, he will be forced to eliminate there. If this happens often enough, he may disregard his natural revulsion against soiling his den. Therefore, taking the puppy from the cage routinely for elimination is imperative. Dog trainer Brian Kilcommons advises, in *Good Owners, Great Dogs*, "Puppies should not be crated for more hours than they are months old plus one. Meaning a three-month-old pup should not be crated for more than four hours; a four-month-old pup for five hours. The self-control of puppies varies; let your puppy guide you."

OBEDIENCE TRAINING

Obedience training consists of teaching your dog the correct response to certain words or hand signals. Ted Baer, author of *Communicating with Your Dog*, writes that his dog Tundra knows over two hundred verbal commands and over seventy hand signals. Other dogs react to verbal commands, like those belonging to humorist Dave Barry, who says in *Yellow Journalism*, "I own two dogs, and they both have been trained to respond immediately to my voice. For example, when we're outside, all I have to do is issue the following standard dog command: 'Here Earnest! Here Zippy! C'mon! Here! You dogs COME HERE RIGHT NOW! ARE YOU DOGS LISTENING TO ME? HEY!!!' And instantly both dogs, in unison, like a precision drill team, will continue trotting in random directions sniffing the ground."

Dogs who rank tops in ease of obedience training include the shepherding breeds, such as collie, Australian shepherd, and Shetland sheepdog; the miniature poodle, German shepherd, and doberman also get good marks in obedience training. Those breeds who have to try harder to become accomplished at obedience commands are the chow, basset, beagle, Afghan, fox terrier, and bulldog.

As mentioned earlier, obedience-training classes for young dogs are sponsored by Obedience and 4H Clubs, veterinary hospitals, humane societies, colleges, and other organizations. A formal class with other participants socializes the pup to dogs and people. But introducing the pup to other dogs has the disadvantage of increasing his exposure to parasites and infectious diseases. Make sure that your pup is properly immunized, and that the class instructor requires that all participating dogs are vaccinated and certified free of parasites by a veterinarian.

The following section about obedience training is an introduction. You and your pet may want to break Ted Baer and Tundra's records of two hundred verbal commands and seventy hand signals. Go to it!

Collar and Lead

Select a flat nylon or leather buckle collar for your puppy; the collar should fit tight enough that it doesn't slip over the pup's head but loose enough that you can fit a couple of fingers between his neck

Teaching

and collar. Ignore protestation on the part of the puppy; after a few days he will become habituated to wearing it. Now attach a lead to his collar; the lead should be connected in such a manner that it comes under the pup's chin.

Squat on the floor, offer your open palm while holding the lead with the other hand, and give the command "Rover, come." If the pup makes an advance toward you, praise him lavishly. If the puppy freezes, bucks, or pulls away, stay where you are and ignore him; when he stops protesting, put him in his crate.

After the puppy responds favorably to "come," stand and take a few steps away with the lead taut; if the puppy follows, give him a treat and praise.

Heel

After the puppy adjusts to the collar and lead, place him on your left side while you hold the lead in your right hand. Say "Rover, heel" as you step forward with your left leg and continue at a leisurely pace with the lead held loosely in the right hand (if you are right handed); pat your left leg encouragingly. If the pup fails to follow, jerk the lead firmly. When the pup follows, stop jerking and offer a treat and/or praise.

Sit, Down, Stay

After Rover has mastered the command "sit" (discussed on page 153), teach this command while the pup is on lead. Gather the excess lead in your right hand so there is little slack; the dog should be positioned on your left side. As you say "Rover, sit," pull up on the lead slightly. When Rover sits, give him a reward and praise. Now you are ready to introduce the command "stay."

After the pup sits, raise the lead above his head and walk slowly around him in a circle while repeating the word *stay*. If he gets up or turns around for a look, jerk on the lead and return him to the sitting position. When the pup stays on command, reward him.

The down position differs from sit in that the dog is lying down. You say "Rover, down" while tipping or pushing him firmly but gently into proper position. Repeat "down" and reward him. The down command is valuable for correcting the dog who jumps up on people or rushes the door. Work to teach the dog to stay after he is in the lying position.

Exercise Training

The benefits of exercise on human emotional and physical health are touted in almost every issue of the popular magazines. Dogs, too, profit from exercise, as active dogs are usually more alert, trimmer, and less stressed than sedentary ones. Many behavior problems in dogs, such as car chasing, destructive digging, chewing, and excessive barking, are alleviated when the dog is given a vocation involving physical exercise.

Mountain living has improved the attitude and activity level of many dogs. My neighbor who is companion to Christy, a fourteen-year-old spayed German shepherd, says that here on the mountain Christy is alert, tracks new scents, chases rabbits, and loves going for a walk. When Christy is at her primary home in Albuquerque, she is lackadaisical and reluctant to leave her air-conditioned or heated house.

Providing a more stimulating environment for your canine companions is possible wherever you live. Expand your dog's range with walks in the park or farmer's field, and swimming excursions to the lake, pond, or seashore. You can teach your pet an exciting new game, such as Frisbee catching or flyball.

Before you drastically change the activity level of your dog or yourself, however, check with your veterinarian and physician. Regardless of the activity chosen, short training sessions are preferable to longer ones, especially for beginners. Beware of taking your pet into areas with physical barriers and other dangers, such as automobiles and boats.

Swimming

Certain dogs such as Ralph, a year-old Labrador belonging to one of my neighbors, take naturally to water. Others abhor water, and have to be trained or coaxed to get their feet wet. If you want your canine companion to join you in the pool, lake, or ocean, start his initiation into water sports early, when he is still an impressionable pup.

Begin at home by introducing your puppy to the sounds, taste, and

Teaching

feel of water. Playing tapes of oceans and streams and running water in the sink give auditory lessons about water. Wet the puppy's face. Fill the sink with a small amount of water, and entice the puppy to put his feet in. Praise every step he takes toward accepting and playing in the water. If the puppy becomes frightened, begin again at a later time.

When your puppy has progressed to the point of sitting and playing in a sink, basin, or bathtub of water, it is time to introduce him to the pool, lake, or ocean. Place a secure collar and leash on the puppy, and take care that the environment is free of distractions and dangers and that the weather is conducive to a carefree outing. Let the pet sense the terrain by feeling, hearing, seeing, and tasting the new surroundings. On the next visit, he will be willing, perhaps, to get his feet damp.

Once your puppy feels confident about getting his paws wet, lead him into shallow water, taking care that he can touch bottom. Introduce a ball or other play item. When your pet is comfortable playing in the water, pick him up and take him into deeper water. Support his weight so that he won't experience an unexpected dunking. As you release your hold, the puppy should begin paddling with his feet. Once the pet is actually swimming, move a couple of feet away from him while still holding his leash. Give him a command to "come." Reward each training step.

Supervise all water excursions, and protect your pet from insects, animals, children, boats, sharp shells, and inclement weather.

TRICKS

Teaching tricks is a great way to spend stimulating time with your dog. He receives attention from you, the reward of performing well, and health-enhancing exercise.

When deciding which tricks to teach your dog, observe his natural inclinations and disinclinations, and plan your training accordingly. If you have a puppy who likes to stand up on his hind legs, you can reinforce that movement to teach him to beg or perhaps stand up and turn around when you give the command "Rover, dance!"

Other folks my age brag about grandchildren; I brag about my grandpets. Granddog Sarge plays dead and spins on cue, looks for squirrels when my son-in-law makes a chattering sound, runs to the back fence in response to "back," jumps in the pickup bed in response to "hup," pricks up his ears when told "watch um," and responds to "no" and other commands. It helps to have a Texas accent like my son-in-law, Bubba, when ordering Sarge to perform.

Roll over and Bow

Give the command "Rover, down." After your pet is lying down, gently turn him over by grasping a front and hind leg and tugging him over while offering a new command, "Rover, over." Reward his performance.

Bowing is another extension of the "down" command. As your dog is responding to "Rover, down," support the groin area with your hand and hold up his rear as he lowers his front to the floor. After the two of you have performed the modified "down" a few times, change the command to "Rover, down—bow." Each time he accomplishes the assisted bow, offer a reward.

Eventually, you will change the command from "Rover, down—bow" to "Rover, bow."

Play Dead

Bubba taught Sarge to play dead by teaching the following commands in progression: sit, down, and roll over. This system of training is called shaping. Shaping consists of taking a small tendency in the right direction and shifting it, one step at a time, toward an ultimate goal.

Once Sarge was lying on his side in response to roll over, Bubba says "bang," and Sarge lies flat on the floor as if dead. Sarge will now play dead when he hears the word *bang*. Bubba used pizza toppings such as pepperoni for positive reinforcement.

QUESTION

Dear Dr. Whiteley,

I am a single working woman who lives alone in a rented duplex in a suburb of a large city. Numerous burglaries have occurred in my neighborhood in recent months, and I am

Teaching

thinking about adopting a dog for protection. The dog will, for the most part, be an inside dog, so a Great Dane is out. Do you have suggestions?

Frightened in Edmond

Dear Frightened,

There is a difference between dogs trained to bark in response to strangers and those trained to attack. I don't recommend an attack dog.

If you want a small dog with breed tendencies to watchdog bark, I suggest a miniature schnauzer, Scottie, or Westie. Standard poodle and airedale, followed in size by German shepherd, doberman, and Rottweiler, are larger dogs known for their guarding abilities.

Males are usually more territorial and aggressive toward strangers; when selecting a pup to be a watchdog, you might give preference to this gender.

During training you will want to encourage and reward your puppy or dog when he barks in response to someone's knocking at the door or a stranger walking outside. To start things off, you might have a neighbor ring the doorbell, knock at the door, and pass outside the front window of your home. You can demonstrate by barking in response to the intrusion. When your canine companion imitates you, reward him. Do not reprimand your dog for barking at your best friend or postman; it is asking too much of most dogs to expect them to distinguish between good guys and bad ones.

After your dog becomes proficient at barking in response to intruders, train him to respond to a "quiet" command. You will use this command after you have been summoned by barking and assessed the situation as safe. For training this command, catch your dog in silence and reinforce the behavior with the words "Rover, quiet" and a food reward. If the dog is overenthusiastic about his job as watchdog, tap him lightly on the nose while giving the verbal command.

Best of luck for finding and training a companionable watchdog.

H. E. W.

10
Aggression and Other Misbehavior

Misbehavior is the primary reason why the bond between people and their canine companions is broken. Early recognition of and treatment of behavioral problems often save a relationship destined for divorce either through euthanasia or abandonment.

CONTRIBUTING FACTORS

Several factors contribute to what we call canine misbehavior. Genetics predisposes to certain conditions. The English springer spaniel is, for instance, one of the leading breeds seen in behavioral clinics for treatment of dominance aggression. It is in the nature of the excitable Yorkshire terrier to snap at children and bark excessively.

If an inherited tendency for emotional or mental disorder is present, stress or perceived stress on the part of the affected animal may trigger misbehavior for coping with the stress. Obsessive-compulsive behavior such as excessive licking, covered in the next chapter, is an example.

Improper socialization when the dog was young contributes to his lack of tolerance for new situations, locations, and people. In other cases, dogs who bond too closely to their owners lack self-reliance and are prone to separation anxiety; the resulting destruction is labeled misbehavior.

Frustration adds its effects for the dog who is bored, confined, or overcrowded, leading to misbehavior such as destructiveness and excessive barking. Medical conditions—epilepsy and lead poisoning, for example—create their own behavioral signs. Anecdotal reports suggest that in some cases high-protein diets exacerbate misbehavior.

Not least in causation are the dog's natural acts that become behavioral problems when the dog's living conditions change. A feral female in heat attracts mates by urinating on bushes; she is misbehaving if she sprinkles the back door. Digging a hole to stay cool in the summer is acceptable when Rover lives on the farm, but becomes unacceptable when Rover moves to a duplex with a miniature patio yard.

Because many factors contribute to canine misbehavior, treatment is rarely straightforward or easy. In most cases, it is going to take

Aggression and Other Misbehavior

more than a brief telephone call to your veterinarian to resolve problems. Initially, schedule two appointments—one for your pet's physical examination and one for consultation about the dog's behavioral problem. The first examination is necessary to rule out physical conditions contributing to or causing the misbehavior. If your veterinarian is uncomfortable discussing canine behavior, ask for a referral to someone who specializes in this discipline.

TYPES OF AGGRESSION

Aggression is the foremost reason why dogs are presented to veterinary behavioral services for treatment. Yet diagnosing a dog as overly aggressive is like saying he is suffering from cancer. There are many different forms of cancer, and so it is with aggressive misbehavior.

A determination of aggressive type must be made before a treatment regime can be recommended or prognosis given; because canine aggression is potentially dangerous to humans, consultation with a behavioral expert is recommended.

Aggressive misbehavior has many origins, encompassing aggressive behavior owing to a dog's dominant traits, possessiveness, territoriality, hunting behavior, fear- or pain-induced hostility, protective behavior toward the young, redirected and play animosity, fighting between members of the same sex, and aggression owing to disease. Sometimes two or more of these factors lead to the aggressive behavior.

Dominance Aggression

Dominance aggression is the most common form of aggressive misbehavior. Although I covered the topic in chapter 7, here I add to or reiterate some of those points.

The most common culprit of dominance aggression is a young adult, intact, purebred male. There is a particularly high incidence in spaniels, both English springer spaniels and cocker spaniels.

The signs or symptoms are aggressive and dominant behavior—growling, snapping, biting, rushing the door, standing over or placing paws on shoulder or lap of owner—which is often perceived by the owner as unpredictable or unprovoked. Yet the astute owner will notice that one or more of these behaviors is triggered by one or more of the following events: the dog is disturbed while resting, sleeping, playing, protecting a coveted object or person; restrained or pulled on a leash; disciplined; groomed; medicated; lifted; and petted, hugged, stared at, or bent over (dominant gestures by owner). If you have a dog who reacts to all of the above stimuli, your dog is a tyrant.

The dog may be aggressive to one or all family members, although typically he will choose those closest to him in dominance in the family pack or those he perceives as challenging him. He is less likely to confront visitors than family members and less likely to challenge family members who are clearly dominant or clearly submissive.

Treatment options include castration, Prozac and other drugs, and behavioral modification. Not long ago, Prozac received much publicity as a wonder drug for changing behavior in both animals and people. At the risk of sounding like your mother, I want to say that there are no wonder drugs, just as there is no free lunch. Specific drugs are prescribed by veterinarians for specific conditions after an accurate diagnosis has been ascertained. If drug therapy is part of your veterinarian's treatment regime, it is usually short-lived. Lasting behavioral changes on the part of the dominantly aggressive dog will be achieved with behavioral modification.

What is behavioral modification? It includes treatment suggested in chapter 7. The "no free lunch" approach is recommended over direct punishment; confronting an aggressive dog is dangerous. This approach means that the dog must obey an obedience command before receiving his reward, which might be lunch, petting, or playing. All behavior on your part, such as bending over, direct eye contact, and petting on top of the head, which might elicit dominance aggression by the dog, is avoided. Indirect punishment is administered by way of a lead and the Promise collar, discussed on page 117.

If the dog's aggressive behavior has persisted, treatment is less likely to be effective. Most experts give a guarded prognosis because the likelihood of eliminating all aggressive behavior is nil. If the actions of the dog are dangerous, euthanasia rather than treatment should be considered, especially if your household includes vulnerable family members such as small children or physically fragile mem-

Aggression and Other Misbehavior

bers. The rub is knowing what constitutes truly dangerous behavior. Perhaps the decision of others gives a clue.

Dr. Ilana Reisner and colleagues at the New York State College of Veterinary Medicine report in "Risk Factors for Behavior Related Euthanasia Among Dominant-Aggressive Dogs: 110 Cases," in the *Journal of the American Veterinary Medical Association*:

> A dog weighing greater than 18.2 kg [40 pounds] was more likely to be euthanized for its behavior than a dog weighing less than 18.2 kg. Alternatively, regardless of body weight, a dog that was aggressive in response to benign dominance challenges [bending over, direct eye contact, etc., by owner] was more likely to be euthanized than a dog that was not aggressive in response to benign dominance challenges. Intuitively, this makes sense. Dogs that react aggressively to benign challenges pose an obvious danger to owners and their families because, so often, the attack appears unprovoked.

Fear-Induced Aggression

For the fearful animal, the first choice of action is likely to be fleeing the situation or hiding from the threat. For many dogs who closely share our homes, these solutions are not available. When submissive body language does not make the threat go away, the fearful dog reacts with aggression.

The fear-biting caged dog was discussed in chapter 7. In this case, the dog cannot escape and he will bite the person retrieving him. The same thing can happen at home. The dog is crouched under the bed, and you peer at him (the dog sees a large face with staring eyes) and perhaps pull him out by a paw, sometimes hurting him, thus adding a painful stimulus to the fearful one. He may lash out and bite you. If you then leave him alone, you have reinforced his behavior; he knows that if he tries to bite, you will do what he wants—leave him alone. On the other hand, punishment will make the fearful dog even more fearful.

Solutions depend, of course, on what makes the dog fearful. Genetics, by the way, plays a part here. A dog can be predisposed to fearful aggression. According to Dr. Bonnie Beaver, of Texas A & M, a dog reacting with fearful aggression is often one who is both timid and dominant. Perhaps a breeder mated an extremely shy dog with an aggressive one. Some of the puppies inherit both traits; they don't know how to act when threatened, their body language contains elements of both submission and dominance, and they bite when threatened.

In the case of the dog crouched under the bed, avoid confrontation—eye contact and loud admonishments—and offer distractions, such as toys, food, or games. Long-term treatment involves desensitizing the dog to that which makes him afraid.

Let's continue with the etiology of fearful aggression. In the case of phobias, such as fear of thunderstorms or trips to the veterinary hospital, the dog may have experienced fearful emotions during the fear-imprinting stage of puppyhood. Phobias are discussed in the next chapter.

Some dogs are fearful of certain types of people (see chapter 2); improper socialization usually plays a part in this scenario. I once had a client, Mrs. Clark, who owned a wire-haired, long-bodied mixed male named Baby Huey. I saw Baby Huey often because he was allergic to almost everything, including one of the medications I used to treat his allergies. When Mrs. Clark remarried, Mr. Jones posed a threat to Baby Huey, who had been raised as an only dog in a single-woman household. Mr. Jones slept next to the now Mrs. Jones, a place formerly reserved for Huey. Mr. Jones was a large man and spoke with a deep voice. Huey lived with mixed emotions: he wanted to stay close to his beloved mistress but wanted to avoid the fearful Mr. Jones.

Desensitizing Huey to men in general and Mr. Jones in particular was one method of dealing with the problem. The goal was to have Baby Huey learn to associate men or Mr. Jones with good events rather than fearful ones. Mrs. Jones would cease all petting and care of Huey, except in the presence of her husband; soon, all petting and care would be performed by Mr. Jones.

Mr. Jones would crouch to Huey's level and speak softly to him while offering a tidbit of a delectable goodie. When Huey finally accepted the goodie, everyone lavished him with praise. If Huey acted aggressively toward Mr. Jones, the man would ignore the dog's misbehavior. When Huey finally accepted his master, he would be introduced to other men at a distance, which would not elicit fear. The

Aggression and Other Misbehavior

distance would be decreased while positive overtures on the dog's part were reinforced and negative ones ignored.

In some cases, temporary treatment with anti-anxiety drugs helps reduce fear-inducing aggression until the patient's behavior is modified.

Territorial Aggression

In territorial aggression, the dog acts with aggression to strangers, either human or animal, while defending his perceived home base. The home base may be the house, yard, car, or other "place." Both sexes are territorial, with males a little more so; neutering has little effect on the behavior. Young adulthood from one to three years seems to be prime time for exhibiting this type of aggressiveness.

A friend who lives in Amarillo recently received severe bites to her legs while jogging by a neighbor's female doberman, who was normally chained. The dog, on most occasions, barked threateningly as my friend ran by on the sidewalk in front of the dog's house, but on the occasion of the bites, the dog broke loose from her chain and attacked. My friend was treated at the emergency room, and the dog was boarded for rabies observation. The dog's owners admitted to my friend that the dog had a history of territorial biting, but, alas, what could they do? They loved the dog.

All owners are liable for the actions of their dogs. It is bad enough that my recently widowed friend, who needs an outdoor outlet, now stays inside her home; even worse is the possibility of the dog's attacking an elderly person or child, who may not have the strength to resist a large dog.

This particular dog should always be attended while outside. A double-fenced yard might add an element of protection. While indoors, the dog should wear a Promise collar with a long lead, so he can be brought under control instantly if a stranger appears at the door. A basket-type muzzle adds additional protection when the dog is taken for walks and trips in the car. If the dog reacts to predatory stimuli, which is covered in the next section, prevention is most important: prevent the dog access to joggers, bicycle riders, and other moving targets.

Behavioral modification starts with obedience training. When strangers appear at the door, the dog is instructed to "stay" in one particular area of the house. Aggressive barking is brought under control with "quiet."

This type of training is termed counterconditioning. The undesirable response (barking and attacking) in response to a stimulus (strangers) is eliminated by training a desirable response (staying and quiet) that is incompatible with the undesirable response (the dog cannot attack or bark at strangers while he is quietly staying on his rug).

Desensitization training involves reinforcing good behavior as strangers approach from a distance. This is the same technique as used to desensitize Baby Huey to men.

Predatory Aggression

Predatory aggression is an extension of the dog's natural ancestral behavior, designed to catch and kill animals for food. Dogs killing chickens, sheep, and cats are exhibiting predatory behavior. The behavior is more likely to occur when dogs associate in packs.

Dinky, a seventeen-year-old dachshund, provides my favorite and least distressing story about a predatory dog. Dinky was smart enough to adopt wealthy owners, and he lives the lifestyle of the rich and famous. Last summer Dinky's mistress was entertaining several of her Dallas friends at the vacation home near Santa Fe. One evening the ladies were eating hors d'oeuvres on the patio, which houses a kiva fireplace and iron kettle for storing wood. Dinky, who has the diminished eyesight and hearing of the elderly, nonetheless detected movement in the kettle. His investigation paid off as he caught a mouse in his teeth, crunched down, and swallowed the critter while the society matrons gasped and screamed.

Mice and other stimuli that trigger predatory aggression have in common certain elements—noise, movement, and running away. Small children, particularly infants, can trigger this predatory instinct in some dogs. The dog's behavioral signs might include agitation, circling, and poking his head in the baby's playpen. Regardless, never leave an infant and dog together unsupervised. Review socialization of dog to baby in chapter 5.

Behavior modification of the predatory dog is difficult because of the rewards to the dog inherent in the chase and/or catch and/or kill. Tiffany, one of my neighbor's dogs, lives with five cats. Tiffany knows and leaves alone her own cats.

Aggression and Other Misbehavior

Francis, Tiffany's caretaker, says, "Tiffany occasionally gets a strange look in her eyes as she buries her nose in the fur on one of our kitties. I say to her, 'Tiffany, stop that right this minute,' and the predatory urge is distracted." Tiffany, however, shows no such restraint when it comes to feral cats who might happen by or to porcupines. Time after time, she has suffered the resulting pain and agony of embedded porcupine quills after chasing one of the dagger-filled critters. Tiffany is now restrained by a chain or lead when outside.

The negative reinforcement of catching a porcupine is quite intense, but it never seems to deter those dogs addicted to the behavior. However, there is a statistical reference in my notes about rabies, citing that more than 90 percent of red foxes (a primary carrier of rabies in Canada) found with porcupine quills are rabid. In other words, only a fox who is brain-damaged would be stupid enough to tangle with a porcupine.

Negative reinforcement and punishment might be methods worth trying with the predatory dog. I've heard of people who tied a dead and rotting chicken around the neck of the chicken-killing dog; probably works as a deterrent because everyone, including the chickens, can smell him a mile away. Another negative reinforcer is the shock collar activated when the dog takes off after the porcupine, cat, or chicken.

Fighting Dogs

Pound per pound, the Chihuahua is the Rocky Balboa of fighting dogs. I've known several of these diminutive dogs who challenged larger dogs and bears (my neighbor, Tiger, for one), and won by chasing away the larger animal. Every once in a while, however, the bigger animal will return the challenge, with disastrous results for the smaller.

My former neighbor in Amarillo owns a small Chihuahua named Sweet Pea who lost a leg to a Great Dane; it was Sweet Pea who made the initial aggressive overtures to the Dane. At a recent rabies drive (not my station, thank God), a poodle challenged a chow, and the attending veterinarian had to cease vaccinating and suture the poodle's wounds.

What makes a four-pounder challenge an opponent twenty-five times or even one hundred times bigger? I think it is one or a number of aggressive personality and/or instinctive traits that kick in before the dog's deductive reasoning power does. If your small dog thinks he's an attack dog, you must take steps to ensure that he is supervised and/or restrained when in a position to challenge a larger adversary.

There are dogs, such as the pit bull, who have been fighting bulls, bears, and other dogs for a couple of centuries. "Pit bull" is a rather generic term; the breeds in the United States associated with dog fighting are the American Staffordshire terrier, the bull terrier, the Staffordshire bull terrier, and the American pit bull terrier.

Commonalities are found in dogs seized by Humane Society officials from humans engaged in the illegal sport of dog fighting. The dogs fought among themselves and had to be separated; they showed evidence of fighting—scars, torn ears, and unhealed wounds about the head, legs, and throat; compared to other dogs, the fighting dogs appeared to react less to pain. They liked to chew and "mouth" food and other objects. They consistently maintained eye contact with people and other animals. They made few threatening gestures such as baring teeth, snarling, or raising hair that other dogs make before attacking. The dogs could seriously injure or kill another dog in minutes; the bite is applied with great force, is difficult to break, and serves to hold and inflict damage (the canine teeth stabilize the hold while the premolars and molars grind into the tissue).

If you adopt a dog with this type of genetic predisposition to fighting, you must take every precaution to ensure that he is socialized to people and other dogs, trained to respond to your commands, and restrained when not under your direct supervision. I'd also recommend carrying maximum homeowner's liability insurance.

Rage Syndrome

Accounts of aggression labeled rage syndrome are appearing in both the veterinary and the lay press. In rage syndrome, the dog attacks without apparent warning; the attacks and resulting injury to humans are severe, and after the attack, the dog acts normal or offers friendly appeasement gestures such as licking the person attacked.

An acquaintance, a middle-aged woman, went with her husband to her daughter's house to care for the dog, a chow, in the daughter's absence. The dog, who knew and had always acted with friendliness to the woman, suddenly attacked her. The woman believes that the

Aggression and Other Misbehavior

dog would have killed her if her husband had not been present to intervene; as it is, the lady is still receiving physical therapy and medical treatment for injuries sustained over a year ago.

Some experts believe that rage syndrome is a form of dominance aggression; that is, inadvertent dominance signals on the part of the owner stimulate the aggressive behavior. Behavioral expert Dr. Ian Dunbar suggests in "Rage Syndrome Reexamined," in the *American Kennel Gazette*, that the bite stimuli comes from what he terms superstitious behavior by the dog. He writes:

> One of my cases involved a dog that attacked its owner when he picked up his car keys. Another dog bit its owner whenever she was about to sneeze. A single chance pairing of the stimulus and the extreme event are all that it takes for some dogs to assume "cause and effect" and to respond dramatically to the stimulus in the future. The car keys and the sneeze were superstitious bite cues for those dogs. Once identified, however, superstitious stimuli are usually easy to desensitize.

In my book about cat behavior, I used the example of a large, despot cat who attacked and dominated a small dog. The cat was brought down a notch in dominance when she was accidentally conked on the head by the owner's walker at the same time that the dog appeared and barked at her. The cat associated the conking on the head with the dog and avoided the dog thereafter.

This had a positive result, in that the cat ceased abusing the small dog. Suppose, however, that a large dog with a genetic tendency toward aggression—say, the chow mentioned above—came to associate his human grandmother with a conking on the head that occurred when the broom accidentally fell out of the closet. The woman appears, and the dog thinks he's going to be conked on the head; he reacts with fearful and/or dominance aggression.

Regardless of the causation, the chow was put to sleep. This is how most such cases are resolved because the very nature of the behavior—rage resulting in severe and multiple bites and mutilation of the victim—makes behavioral modification risky to family members. If, however, you can detect a situational cue that stimulates the dog's aggression, discuss the options of desensitization or other behavioral modification methods with an expert.

Other Aggression

Even though I've divided aggression into different types, there is overlap. I've seen Tiger, for example, display traits of dominance-related aggression, territorial aggression, predatory aggression, possessive aggression, and redirected aggression.

Tiger, as you remember, was raised as an orphan by Nip and Louise, and he despises little people (children were absent during his socialization). One day Nip's ten-year-old granddaughter leaned over to give her grandfather a hug; Tiger, who was sitting in Nip's lap, became agitated and made a swipe at the child with his fangs, missing and slicing open Nip's nose. This scenario includes elements of dominance (the child leaned over, challenging the dominant dog), possessive-protective aggression (Tiger is possessive of Nip as he is of toys and other objects), and redirected aggression (Nip was in the right place at the wrong time).

I might mention that overprotectiveness is more evident in households with numerous family members than in one- or two-person households; aggression in people is more common in families with many members.

Redirected aggressive behavior results in injuries to people breaking up dog fights with their bare hands. A common example of possessive aggression is the pseudopregnant dog protecting her surrogate puppy (covered in chapter 12). Table 10.1 divides aggression into several categories. Let me repeat that rarely is aggressive behavior straightforward or easy to diagnose or to treat. Because of the danger, consult an expert if your dog is overly aggressive.

BITES

Dogs who bite may injure and kill, and aggressive behavior must be taken seriously. It is worthwhile to discuss the statistics, precautions, and treatment concerning dog bites.

Each year in the United States, dog attacks cause between ten and twenty deaths and over half a million injuries severe enough to war-

Table 10.1

Aggression in Dogs

TYPE	DESCRIPTION	SUGGESTIONS
Dominance	Aggressive to family members when competing for coveted resources or when confronted by dominant signals	Castration, drugs, no-free-lunch training, Promise collar and lead, desensitization
Fear-related	Fearful or mixed body language	Anti-anxiety drugs, desensitization, counterconditioning
Territorial	Aggressive to strangers, animals	Supervision, Promise collar, fenced yard, obedience training, desensitization
Predatory	Attacks moving person, animal	Protect target, distraction, negative reinforcement or punishment
Pain-induced	Aggressive when person attempts to touch, medicate, or move injured dog	Get help; don't use bare hands
Redirected	Aggressive when fighting	Don't use bare hands
Play	Aggression directed toward moving extremities of person, play "bows" and gestures	Avoid aggressive play, don't use hands, distract, obedience training, exercise
Interdog	Fighting between dogs	Neutering, muzzles, indoor leads, reinforce dominant dog

rant medical attention or restricted activity. Children, especially those younger than six years old, have the highest incidence of bite wounds. Studies show that in most cases the dog inflicting the injuries is known to the victim. You or your children are more likely to be bitten by your own dog or one belonging to a friend, neighbor, or relative than by a stray.

Most victims are bitten on their arms and hands, although bites from stray dogs are more likely to occur on the legs. Most victims receiving bite wounds to the face are children younger than ten years old.

The profile of the biting dog is as follows: male, intact, trained to be aggressive (guard dog), unrestrained while outdoors, allowed to run in dog packs, and purebred or mixed with a breed known for aggression (pit bulls, chows, Rottweilers, German shepherds).

Many people fail to read correctly the warning inherent in the body language of a biting dog. The clues that a dog will bite include the following: the dog makes eye contact; he bares his teeth and snarls; he stiffens his legs, appearing to walk on the tips of his toes; the hair along his shoulders, rump, and back stands up; the tail is held at an angle above horizontal and begins to move in a rapid transverse flagging motion (he is not wagging his tail). The dog is saying "Back off, buddy!"

"This is my last warning" follows as he prolongs his stare and increases the intensity of barking and/or growling. The dog lowers his body, shows more teeth and flattens his ears against his head, lowering his neck and head to protect his throat and ears in the ensuing attack. By this time, you should be backing away and putting barriers between you and the dog.

Dog bites vary from mere scratches to punctures, lacerations, and crushing injuries. Dogs's jaws can exert a pressure of 200 to 450 pounds per square inch during a bite. The first rule if you are bitten is to prevent further injury. Then immediately flush the wound with soap and water, followed by a quaternary ammonium disinfectant. Call your physician for treatment advice, including the need for antibiotics and tetanus and/or rabies prophylaxis shots.

Report the bite to your animal control officials, who will obtain the biting dog's rabies vaccination history and confine him for rabies observation. If the dog is unknown, describe him to the best of your ability—color, weight, breed, sex, age, identification tags, including rabies (most veterinarians issue rabies tags shaped and color-coded to coincide with year of vaccination).

Be a responsible pet owner and protect your children by teaching them the bite-prevention techniques shown in Table 10.2.

OTHER MISBEHAVIOR

Chewing and Swallowing Nonfood Items

Chewing is part of the puppy's normal exploratory behavior; young dogs learn by chewing what tastes good and what does not and how hard and friable objects are. Chewing also relieves boredom, soothes the gum irritation of teething, and builds strong ligaments and muscles of the jaws and teeth.

The line between normal chewing and destructive chewing is a subjective one. Chewing an old pair of thongs may be okay, but chewing the new Guccis is *verboten*. The problem is that most puppies can't tell the difference. If you don't want the puppy to chew shoes, prevent access to all shoes. If chewing the chair cushion is forbidden, don't offer him a toy made of the same material. Do not play tug-of-war games with the puppy; he's not going to differentiate the frayed rope used in the game from the drapery ties—plus, that type of activity teaches him to use his teeth in an aggressive way.

A puppy is going to chew; therefore, provide the puppy with appropriate items to chew and praise him when he does so. If the puppy shows a preference for a certain type of chew bone or toy, buy him several of that type. If he seems to ignore your offerings, make them more desirable by coating them with peanut butter or bacon grease. You might tuck a small piece of cheese or weeny into the crevice of a hard rubber toy.

Later, you may want to add large bones, such as knuckle and thigh bones, to his supply of appropriate chew items; if the bone is fresh, boil it in water to sterilize and soften. Bones that splinter or small bones should be avoided, as they can cause bowel irritation and constipation.

Teach the puppy to play fetch with some of his toys. If you see him chewing an inappropriate item, you must say "no" while the action is occurring. You might then divert his attention by throwing out a rubber toy for him to fetch.

Older dogs chew, also. There may be a medical reason in a few cases (the dog's teeth or gums are hurting), while in others the chewing behavior occurs in response to anxiety or boredom. Adding stim-

Table 10.2

Bite Prevention Dos and Don'ts

1. Do select a dog with physical and personality traits that fit well within your family.

2. Do socialize your dog to people and other dogs.

3. Do neuter, license, and vaccinate your pet.

4. Do obedience-train your dog.

5. Do provide your dog with exercise and a stimulating environment.

6. Do provide your dog with leash, collar, and ID tags.

7. Don't select a wild animal as a pet.

8. Don't allow your dog to run free or with dog packs.

9. Don't attack-train your dog.

10. Don't bother an animal who is sleeping or eating.

11. Don't approach a mother animal with babies.

12. Don't try to take toys or food from an animal.

13. Don't try to pick up an injured animal. (Call an adult.)

14. Don't attempt to stop a dog or cat fight with your bare hands. (Call an adult.)

15. Don't play roughly with your pet.

16. Don't approach a dog in his own yard or car. (Many dogs are protective of their property.)

Aggression and Other Misbehavior

Table 10.2

Bite Prevention Dos and Don'ts (cont.)

17. Don't attempt to pet or pick up strange animals.

18. Don't try to catch wild animals.

19. Don't stare directly into a strange dog's eyes, lean over, or pet him on the top of the head.

20. Don't run from a dog who chases you. (Stop, face the animal without looking directly into his eyes, talk quietly to him; keep still, especially your hands; back away slowly.)

21. Don't try to outpedal on your bike a dog who chases you. (Stop, get off the bike, placing the bike between you and the dog; back away slowly, keeping the bike between you and the dog.)

22. If you are attacked by a dog or pack of dogs, drop to the ground and curl into a ball; protect your head and throat by tucking your chin and covering your head with arms and hands.

23. Don't scream or squeal. (Call for help in as calm a voice as you can manage.)

---

ulation to the dog's environment, increasing his exercise periods, and spending quality time with your dog does much to alleviate chewing owing to boredom. Treatment of separation anxiety and phobias that can result in displacement chewing is covered in the next chapter.

There are general principles for correcting misbehavior. Remember the story in chapter 9 about the dog who turns over the trash? If the owner punishes too late—after she comes home and finds the dumped trash—the dog fails to make the connection between the misbehavior (turning over the trash) and the punishment; the connection he makes is that the owner is going to act crazy each time she comes home from work. The dog, whose biological clock says it's almost time for the owner to come home, becomes anxious and chews on the dining-room table legs much as you and I would chew our nails. If the owner again uses delayed punishment techniques to correct the problem, she is compounding the dog's anxiety and increasing the likelihood that misbehavior will continue.

Using the training methods cited in chapter 9, you might treat chewing misbehavior with positive reinforcement for chewing appropriate items, while limiting access to and negative reinforcement or remote punishment for chewing the inappropriate ones.

Remote punishment is the setting of loaded mousetraps against the table legs, for example, or squirting the puppy with a water pistol as he places his mouth on a table leg. Aversive conditioning might fall in the remote punishment category.

Aversive conditioning takes advantage of the dog's propensity to smell what he eats. The puppy is forced to smell a foul-tasting substance such as pepper sauce, menthol, or oil of citronella. Then a small amount of the substance is wiped on his gums so he can taste it. It is hoped that the puppy will think "yuck" each time he smells the substance in the future. The aversive substance is then mixed with something like shortening or petroleum jelly and smeared on the objects you want to discourage the puppy from chewing. Grannick's Bitter Apple is a commercial product designed to prevent chewing, available in furniture creams, plant atomizers, sprays, and shampoos at pet stores and veterinary supply businesses.

Most youngsters chew, but they do not swallow the chewed items. There is, however, a group of dogs—canine vacuum cleaners, I call them—that swallow rather than simply chew. I remember one such patient, a young miniature schnauzer named Greta, who ingested everything—an earring, three marbles, and a pair of pantyhose drying in the bathroom. The earring and three marbles (they were swallowed about the same time) showed up nicely in Greta's stomach on radiograph. The facts that Greta was vomiting and the pantyhose were missing served as clues in the second episode. Surgery was successful in ridding Greta of items that were dangerous because of their penetrating or impaction potential. No one knows why Greta swallowed nonfood items; she was well fed and cared for, and received much attention and love. The trick that ultimately works to prevent such behavior is putting everything that might be swallowed

Aggression and Other Misbehavior

out of reach or confining the dog to a crate when you are unable to supervise his activities.

Digging

Dogs dig for numerous reasons: to make a shelter in cold climates and a cool resting place in warm ones; to cache food and retrieve it; to investigate a critter hole; to excavate the garden or flower bed; and, sometimes it seems, to make a new route to China.

A bored dog digs more than one who has a job, so increasing your dog's activity with obedience training, tricks, and exercise are helpful preventives. A consistent and daily routine is more effective than a hit-or-miss approach to training.

Dogs who dig in flower and garden beds are essentially lazy, I think, because it's much easier to dig in loosely turned beds than hard-packed or grass-covered soil. To make the garden or flower bed less attractive, you can booby-trap the area with spraying water or an invisible fence.

My neighbor's adolescent dog, named Bucky, wandered often onto our property and engaged in typical delinquent activity—agitating Bear, chewing my porch rugs, and digging in the wood pile after chipmunks. Much to our delight, Bucky received an Invisible Fence for Christmas. Bucky wears the collar with a small antenna; as Bucky approaches a wire placed around his "yard" and connected to a transmitter, a warning sound is emitted. If Bucky ignores the sound and crosses the wire, he receives a shock. If Bucky's owners were protecting the garden, the wire would go around the outer perimeter of the bed.

Another method of preventing unwanted digging is to give the dog his own sandbox or digging mound. In this case, you use positive reinforcement each time he digs in his area, while using remote punishment or negative reinforcement to discourage digging in your area.

Housesoiling

Keeping the den clean is behavior that is instinctive in most dogs. If, however, the dog is forced to go too long before being let outside, or if he has a physical condition such as diarrhea, making it impossible for him to control the urge to defecate, his natural fastidiousness is overcome by the ease of going in the house.

Understanding and Training Your Dog or Puppy

If there is one place in the house that the dog has established as his indoor toilet, clean the place thoroughly and place the dog's bed, blanket, or food bowl over the spot. When the dog is indoors, confine him by a lead to within a few feet of his bed or to his crate; extend his range as he proves trustworthy.

Take the dog outside and establish a spot that is the approved potty. If he does his business here, praise him. Take the dog outside frequently to his spot; this may necessitate your taking off from work at noon to be sure that he goes outside at least once during the working day. Essentially, you are teaching housetraining all over again.

The same technique is used for dogs who fail to make it through the night without defecating. The dog is confined overnight to his bed. Take him outside at midnight, extending the nightly excursion to his approved potty an hour each night as long as the dog behaves; eventually, you'll get back to your regular waking hour.

I know the above suggestion is easier for me to write about than for you to do. My husband arises at 1 or 2 A.M. to throw another log on the fire; I sleep warm and snug in my bed, but take care of all laundry and cooking. Maybe you can trade with someone in your household to take the dog outside at midnight.

Dogs are creative in finding ways to share our environment; this means that behavior we label as misbehavior will never be the same for each dog. The suggestions for teaching, retraining, and treating must be modified to fit each individual dog and his circumstances.

QUESTION

Dear Dr. Whiteley,

My dog Dozer, a five-year-old Lhasa apso, fell from the porch and suffered a broken front leg about six months ago. The leg healed nicely with a splint, and Dozer's veterinarian has assured us that he is okay. Our baby, however, continues to limp on that leg and cry sometimes, especially at night. Do you think there might still be a problem with the leg?

Concerned in Boise

Dear Concerned,

What does Dozer gain from limping and crying? Do you act concerned, pick him up, or take him into your bed?

Aggression and Other Misbehavior

Dozer learned that injury has its rewards, and decided to continue the sympathy-eliciting behavior after the pain and dysfunction of the limb were gone.

Withdraw all attention from Dozer while he is limping and crying; the action—limping and crying—will extinguish over time if not rewarded. Give attention such as petting only when he is not limping and/or crying.

Good luck!

H. E. W.

11
The Sick, Injured, and Neurotic

GENERAL SIGNS OF ILLNESS

Physical illness is almost always accompanied by behavioral changes. A sick dog or puppy is often depressed or lethargic, with little interest in eating or drinking. His hair coat looks unkempt because grooming behavior decreases in conjunction with a decline in general activity. Yet some animals may go to the other extreme when sick, showing symptoms of excitability and/or excessive grooming behavior.

In dogs experiencing dehydration and anorexia, loss of elasticity of the skin and a sunken appearance of the eyes give clues of illness. The ears and outer extremities may be warm to the touch, giving evidence that the animal has a fever.

The fever response is the body's way of attacking an infection by inhibiting the growth of at least some viruses and bacteria, and by increasing the body's effectiveness in mounting an immunological defense against the infectious agents.

To help maintain the elevated body temperature, a sick dog curls up, reducing body surface and cutting heat loss by convection and radiation. Heat is boosted by shivering and by fluffing the hair, increasing its insulating quality.

When an individual mounts a fever response, there is an increase in the body's metabolic rate of 30 to 50 percent; shivering multiplies the body's need for energy even more. The feverous dog conserves energy by inactivity and by sleeping.

PAIN

Pain has its own behavioral indicators, including moaning, groaning, crying, whimpering, panting, attention directed toward a specific area, limping, licking or biting, decrease in physical activity, and aggression. As noted in chapter 6, individuals and breeds differ in their response to pain; regardless, unrelieved pain is stressful. Animals showing the behavioral signs of pain should be checked by a veterinarian.

The following are signs of pain:

>   Anxious expression, wide-eyed appearance
>   Pain-induced aggression

The Sick, Injured, and Neurotic

- Vocalizations—crying, moaning, whimpering, howling, distinctive bark
- Attention to specific area—licking, chewing, smelling
- Reluctance to bear weight on painful limb
- Reluctance to move or guarding painful part
- Change in breathing pattern—abdominal breathing, panting, heavy or shallow breathing
- Increased heart rate
- Excessive salivation
- Rigidity of muscles
- Head shaking, pawing at eyes or ears
- Restlessness, inability to get comfortable
- Loss of appetite
- Shivering
- Tail between legs
- Unusual posture—head tilt, sitting or standing when exhausted
- Escape activity
- Inactive or overactive

STRESS

Stress increases an individual's susceptibility to physical disease, prolongs healing time from injuries, and predisposes to emotional and mental disease. The body responds to stress by raising blood levels of adrenal hormones, including fight or flight hormones and corticosteroids, and decreases the effectiveness of the body's immune system. By definition, stress is the body's response to a demand. However, clarifying stressors is personal, as one person or one animal's stress is another's stimulating adventure or play activity.

Physical causations of stress include hunting, showing, pregnancy and milk production, trauma, disease, or surgery. Distress may be psychological in origin, and the perception of a situation being stressful is related to an individual's breeding, family background, and early conditioning. A puppy exposed to varied interactions with people, animals, and objects becomes a more resilient adult. Those deprived of adequate socialization will become more susceptible to emotional and physical stress.

Caretakers, too, have a direct influence on how pets perceive and react to their environment. I observe situations in which animals appear to mimic the mental neuroses and physical ailments of their human companions—the hypochondriac with an attention-seeking dog, the nervous owner with an apprehensive dog, the allergic owner with an allergy-suffering dog, for example. When the bond is close, the correspondence between owner and pet is great. Hence, the more stress and tension we perceive and/or experience in our lives, the greater the likelihood that our pets will show the physical and emotional symptoms of that stress.

The physical symptoms of stress occur at the body's weakest link. If the pet is prone to respiratory problems, he may develop allergies or asthma. If he has a weak digestive system, bouts of diarrhea and/or vomiting may follow. The same thing happens mentally. If a dog is shy and submissive, he becomes even more so under stressful conditions. If the dog is overly dependent upon his owner, he may develop the behavioral signs of separation anxiety; if the dog reacts to stress in an active and controlling manner, he is susceptible to obsessive-compulsive disorders.

DISEASES AFFECTING BEHAVIOR

As mentioned, illness and injury are accompanied by general behavioral signs. It is beyond the scope of this book to mention or discuss every known disease syndrome; I include in the following section, however, several physical and emotional conditions that lead to specific behavioral or neurological changes in the affected individual.

Rabies

Few diseases hold the fascination of rabies. The rabies virus, which causes the behavioral and neurological signs of depression, paralysis, and rage, is deadly and infects both people and animals. Fiction writers such as Stephen King have capitalized upon rabies and its fatal time-bomb nature to further their plots, but I find that the most exciting stories about this distressing disease are true.

Consider, for example, the account of Louis Pasteur, a crippled, squeamish, and tender-hearted French chemist, and the mad dog. Pasteur was in his sixties and riding on his successes in the develop-

The Sick, Injured, and Neurotic

ment of anthrax and fowl cholera vaccines when, in 1882, he decided to hunt for the microbe causing rabies, or hydrophobia as it was called in those days.

Paul de Kruif explains, in *Microbe Hunters*, a book I recommend you look for at your local library:

> Pasteur himself said: "I have always been haunted by the cries of those victims of the mad wolf that came down the street of Arbois when I was a little boy...." Pasteur knew the way the yells of a mad dog curdle the blood of everyone. He remembered that less than a hundred years before in France, laws had to be passed against the poisoning, the strangling, the shooting of wretched people whom frightened fellow-townsmen just suspected of having rabies. Doubtless he saw himself the deliverer of men from such crazy fear—such hopeless suffering.

The hunt for the microbe or germ causing a dog to become mad sent Pasteur and his assistants into a crude lab trephining holes into the skulls and brains of chloroformed dogs and other animals and injecting the "guinea pigs" with an emulsion made from the ground brain of a rabid dog. This was terribly dangerous work performed in the days before protective filters and robots.

Pasteur never found the rabies virus, because this was before the electron microscope made viewing such tiny germs possible, but he did find a way of weakening or killing the virus, contained in the dried brain matter of animals dying from rabies, and making a primitive vaccine.

Although Pasteur successfully protected dogs with his rabies vaccine, the protective value in humans was uncertain and unproved. De Kruif notes, "From all over the world came letters, urgent telegrams, from physicians, from poor fathers and mothers who were waiting terror-stricken for their children, mangled by mad dogs, to die—frantic messages poured in on Pasteur, begging him to send them his vaccine...."

Pasteur was uncertain. What if the vaccine failed to protect humans? The scientist intended to inject himself with the saliva from a rabid dog and with his rabies vaccine; he would be the first human testing the cure. But then, De Kruif explains, "This woman came crying into the laboratory, leading her nine-year-old boy,

Joseph, gashed in fourteen places two days before by a mad dog. He was a pitifully whimpering, scared boy—hardly able to walk. 'Save my little boy—Mr. Pasteur,' this woman begged him." Pasteur consulted two physicians who urged him to try his vaccine. "If you do nothing it is almost sure that he will die," they told him.

Fourteen doses of weakened rabies germs were injected into Joseph Meister, while people worldwide anxiously waited for word of the boy's death or healing. It was as if Joseph Meister became a symbol of vulnerable children everywhere. What relief and rejoicing took place when the child healed from his wounds and lived to play ball and go to school. And this is the true story of how we found, as people and animals, salvation from the dreaded mad dog.

Our primary protection from rabies today is a vaccine not that different from Pasteur's. Most people are exposed to rabies by bites or saliva-contaminated scratches inflicted by rabid domestic animals, such as cats, dogs, cows, and horses. These domestic animals are exposed to rabies by bites from wild animals, primarily skunks, bats, foxes, and raccoons. By vaccinating our domestic pets—dogs and cats—we form a barrier between ourselves and rabid wild animals.

I saw recently a TV commentary about a rabies outbreak among coyotes in southern Texas. To prevent a spillover of the disease from coyotes to dogs or cats, health officials were dropping by airplane an oral vaccine contained in bait to vaccinate coyotes and other wild animals.

I could easily devote an entire chapter to rabies, but I'll refrain as I go on to other conditions affecting dogs. Please review the section in chapter 10 about protecting children from animal bites, and observe leash laws and rabies vaccination laws designed to protect us and our canine companions from rabies.

Distemper

Unlike parvovirus, which infected and killed dogs for the first time in the late 1970s and early eighties, the virus causing canine distemper has been around a long time. Distemper infects ferrets, minks, skunks, and raccoons, as well as canids such as dogs, foxes, and wolves. The first vaccine to protect animals against the distemper virus was developed for foxes and minks in the heyday of the fur industry, and was later adapted for use in dogs.

The Sick, Injured, and Neurotic

Distemper, which is mainly transmitted by airborne droplets from infected dogs, is highly contagious, particularly to puppies. Old-dog encephalitis, a neurological disease of aged dogs causing head pressing, pacing, and/or unsteady gait, is associated with the distemper virus.

Signs of distemper in young dogs include fever that comes and goes, depression, a mucopurulent discharge from the nose and eyes, reddening of the white part of the eyes, and diarrhea. Distemper is a nasty disease, and there is no specific cure other than good nursing and drugs to treat the various symptoms.

Nervous-system signs of distemper can occur late in the progression of the disease. These symptoms—twitching of a muscle or group of muscles, paralysis of leg or facial muscles, and/or convulsions known as chewing-gum fits because the dog makes chewing movements with his jaws—occasionally occur in puppies or dogs who show no respiratory and digestive signs or who appear to be recovering from these symptoms.

The lesions that the distemper virus causes in the brain and spinal cord are similar to those caused by the human polio virus. In addition, dogs or puppies drooling during a chewing-gum fit look much like animals suffering from rabies. Differentiation must be made by laboratory tests. After nervous signs develop, three results are possible: death, permanent neurological damage resulting in muscle twitches and/or convulsions, or recovery.

The disease commonly called feline distemper is caused by the feline panleukopenia virus, which is a different virus from the virus causing canine distemper. Recently, however, scientists have cited the canine distemper virus as the cause of an outbreak of a potentially fatal disease in large cats—lions, tigers, and leopards—in the African Serengeti and Tanzania and in zoos here in North America. The symptoms shown by the large cats are the same as those of dogs suffering from canine distemper, and researchers believe that the virus mutated into a form infective to large cats.

In an article in the March 1, 1995, *Journal of the American Veterinary Medical Association*, the fear of domestic cat infection is addressed: "Evidence indicates that domestic cat populations have been exposed to CDV [Canine Distemper Virus]. They have developed antibodies to the virus, but have never gotten sick. According to Dr. Max J. G. Appel, a professor of virology in the

College of Veterinary Medicine at Cornell University, the cat population in the United States has little to fear because no indications exist that they have shown clinical signs of CDV infection, and distemper in U.S. dogs has been under control for the past 30 years."

As a cat lover, I find Dr. Appel's comments reassuring. I'd like to comment, though, about canine distemper being under control. In the nearly thirty years that I've been a veterinarian, I've seen the incidence of distemper cases come and go. I've worked in practices where conscientious clients kept their canines vaccinated and restrained; I saw so few cases of distemper that I began to think that the disease had been eradicated. Then I'd visit another practice, one catering to clients who rarely vaccinated or restrained their pets, only to find that distemper was alive and well in the young dog population.

I use my experience as a warning. The way to control this dreaded canine disease is to vaccinate your dogs, and in the process, you may be protecting Mike the Tiger, mascot of my old L.S.U. alma mater.

Lyme Disease

The first documented human outbreak of Lyme disease in the United States occurred in the 1970s, in Old Lyme, Connecticut. Yet Lyme is not a new disease. *Borrelia burgdorferi*, the bacterium causing the ailment, was found by scientists using DNA fingerprinting techniques in rodents, some collected as far back as 1894, stored in museums such as the Smithsonian in Washington, D.C. According to Rick Weiss of the *Washington Post*, "the finding supports a growing consensus among scientists that many 'new' diseases are simply newly emerging because of environmental changes wrought by people."

The bacterium that causes Lyme illness in both man and dogs is carried by the deer tick. The tick, in turn, bites man or dog, leading to the disease in some individuals. Although the dog can carry infected ticks, he does not directly infect people with Lyme disease. Ticks can become infected by feeding on a dog suffering from Lyme.

The initial symptoms in dogs include fever, loss of appetite, and mild lameness. As the disease progresses, the dog may develop heart and kidney dysfunction and behavioral and neurological signs, including a Bell's palsy-like syndrome and aggression.

Table 11.1

Canine Vaccination Schedule

Disease	Initial Vaccination (Age in Weeks)	First Booster (Weeks Later)	Additional Boosters
Distemper	6–8	3–4	Annually
Hepatitis	6–8	3–4	Annually
Adenovirus	6–8	3–4	Annually
Parainfluenza	6–8	3–4	Annually
Parvovirus	6–8	3–4	Age 4–5 months, Annually
Coronavirus	6–8	3–4	Annually
Leptospirosis	12		Annually
Bordetella	12	2–3	Annually
Lyme disease	12	2–3	Annually
Rabies	12		Annually (Per recommendation; state laws and duration of vaccine may vary)

Avoid tick-infested areas and vaccinate your dog as the recommended methods of preventing this disease. See Table 11.1 for a vaccination schedule.

Thyroid Disease

The thyroid is a small gland located in the neck; in spite of its diminutive size, this gland influences virtually every cell in the body. Because thyroid hormones impact so many types of cells, imbalances of hormone levels produce an array of signs, including weight fluctuations, intolerance to cold, reproductive failure, changes in heart rate, retardation of hair growth, and behavioral abnormalities.

An increase in the level of circulating thyroid hormones is known as hyperthyroidism. This condition, relatively rare in dogs, is often caused by a tumor of the thyroid gland.

Much more common in dogs is hypothyroidism, which causes circulating thyroid hormone levels to be reduced. The primary clinical sign is a reduction of basal metabolic rate, resulting in obesity, lethargy, and exercise intolerance. Classical skin changes associated with hypothyroidism are loss of hair and infection of the skin.

Recent studies show that dogs suffering from aberrant behavior, such as aggression, extreme shyness, or seizures, often show thyroid dysfunction. In one case, a four-year-old Akita, who had been well behaved, suddenly showed aggressive behavior toward the owner. Thyroid tests revealed that the dog had severely reduced levels of thyroid hormones. This corresponds with anecdotal reports of aggression in Akitas associated with hypothyroidism. Treatment, in this case twice daily doses of replacement thyroid hormones, cured the dog of his aggressive behavior.

Hypothyroidism is often seen in older dogs. Bear, now seventeen, has been taking replacement thyroid for over a year. I diagnosed hypothyroidism based on his symptoms of hair loss and skin changes; laboratory tests confirmed my diagnosis. His natural fur coat is now full and protective enough to sustain our mountain winters.

Poisoning

One of the most toxic products to animals and children is ethylene glycol, found in traditional antifreeze. This sweet-tasting substance is lethal in even small amounts: a teaspoonful will kill a five-pound Chihuahua. Common symptoms of antifreeze poisoning include vomiting and diarrhea, depression progressing to seizures, coma, and death. Early diagnosis and treatment are imperative if the poisoned individual is to survive.

Safe Brands Corporation, of Omaha, Nebraska, recently introduced Sierra antifreeze and coolant, a product safe for children and animals. Sierra antifreeze contains propylene glycol in place of the toxic ethylene glycol. Company representatives say that a 50 percent mixture of Sierra and water will protect a car or boat's engine to -26 degrees Fahrenheit. Sierra antifreeze and Flush, a product used to clean a car's system before installing Sierra, are available at large discount stores, pet shops, and auto supply stores. For more information, call Safe Brands at 1-800-432-9306.

Lead toxicity occurs more often in summer and fall because of increased exposure to outdoor sources of lead, which include lead-based paint, solder, putty, hard water from lead pipes, and batteries. Lead is ingested directly or by grooming. Vomiting and diarrhea accompany behavioral changes, which include hysteria, blindness, convulsions, aggression, and head pressing. Diagnosis is confirmed by laboratory tests, and treatment is aimed at preventing further exposure, decreasing absorption from the gastrointestinal tract, and providing supportive care.

Many preparations used to kill rodents contain an anticoagulant, leading to hemorrhage in animals that consume them. Dogs are poisoned by eating the rodent bait or by consuming rodents that have eaten the bait. Signs of poisoning are those associated with blood loss—bleeding from body openings, pallor of mucous membranes, and depression. If bleeding occurs within the brain or spinal cord, nervous system signs and behavioral changes are seen. Treatment for dogs diagnosed with this toxicity is vitamin K administered by injection and/or orally and blood transfusions.

Pesticides containing organophosphates in high doses cause excessive salivation, convulsions, and death in dogs. Organophosphate poisoning occurs most commonly when dogs are dipped or sprayed with products designed for large animals or with products designed for garden or agricultural use.

Illegal drugs, such as cocaine, amphetamines, and marijuana, are occasionally ingested or inhaled by animals, either accidentally or by malicious intent of humans. Cocaine is easily absorbed through all mucous membranes, and dogs suffering from cocaine intoxication are hyperexcitable and hypersensitive to touch or sound. Amphetamine, known as speed or uppers, produces similar signs as cocaine in dogs. Marijuana is often grown as a houseplant or baked into cookies or brownies, which are highly palatable to dogs. Signs of a marijuana high in dogs vary from slight wobbliness and depression to hyperactivity and increased sensitivity to sound.

If you suspect that your dog has been poisoned, contact your pet's veterinarian and the National Animal Poison Control Center (NAPCC), a nonprofit, animal poison center located at the University of Illinois. This center is staffed twenty-four hours a day by veterinary health professionals who are familiar with poisons, symptoms, and treatment of intoxication in small animals.

A charge for NAPCC services is made on your VISA, MasterCard, or American Express card at the rate of $20 for the first five minutes and $2.95 each additional minute if you call the 900 number and $30 a case if you call the 800 number. If the product suspected of causing poisoning is covered by a sponsoring company, the call is free. Telephone numbers for NAPCC are 1-900-680-0000 or 1-800-548-2423.

Seizures and Epilepsy

An animal undergoing a seizure or convulsion loses control of his muscles and limbs; may salivate, defecate, and urinate; and may show behavioral changes. Personality alterations such as aggression, jaw snapping, flank sucking, persistent licking of the anus, and staring behavior may be due to seizure activity in the brain.

It is the brain where the abnormality causing the seizure originates. Yet the causes of brain dysfunction can be as varied as brain tumor, stroke, trauma, poisons, liver and kidney damage, hypoglycemia (low blood sugar), congenital disease such as hydrocephalus (water on the brain), drugs and inflammatory diseases including those caused by viruses (canine distemper, for example), bacteria (bacterial meningitis and Lyme), rickettsial organisms (those causing tick fever in dogs or Rocky Mountain spotted fever, as it's known in man), or parasites (roundworm larva). When all of the above have been eliminated as the source of the seizure behavior, epilepsy is the probable diagnosis. Epilepsy is a chronic disease, for which there is no specific cure, and is often inherited.

Treatment of seizure disorders is aimed at controlling convulsions with medication and at eliminating underlying causes of the convulsive behavior. If a brain tumor is diagnosed, surgery or chemotherapy may be options. If liver, kidney, or thyroid disease is present, treatment to restore organ function is instituted. Removal of toxic substances, such as organophosphates or lead, causing the convulsions is the first step in treatment of these poisons.

Bosley is a two-year-old Lhasa apso who has experienced seizures for six months. His first seizure occurred during a boisterous greeting with family members who had been away on an overnight trip; successive seizures occurred approximately every two weeks thereafter, until anticonvulsant therapy alleviated the symptoms. Bosley was diagnosed as an epileptic after physical examination and laboratory tests failed to reveal a specific cause of seizure behavior. Breakthrough seizures occur occasionally when Bosley becomes agitated or excited, and his family has learned to maintain a calm environment for everyone's peace of mind.

The following central nervous system abnormalities cause behavioral changes in dogs:

> Brain tumors
> Epilepsy
> Encephalitis (canine distemper, rabies)
> Liver disease
> Drugs (marijuana, tranquilizers, anticonvulsants)
> Brain trauma
> Hydrocephalus
> Oxygen deprivation (respiratory and cardiac disease)
> Poisoning (lead, antifreeze, organophosphates, chlorinated hydrocarbons)
> Inherited disorders (lysosomal enzyme deficiency)
> Intracranial meningitis

Dancing Doberman Disease

A neuromuscular disorder in doberman pinschers produces symptoms that mimic dancing in affected dogs. The muscles of the hind limbs are affected, causing the animal to alternately flex and extend the legs, hence the dancing movement. Over a period of time, the muscles weaken and the dog prefers to sit. The disease is chronic and progressive, but most dogs remain functional pets. There is no treatment.

EMOTIONAL DISORDERS CAUSING BEHAVIORAL CHANGES

Obsessive-Compulsive Disorders

Obsessive-compulsive disorder (OCD) is a popular diagnosis in the human health field, affecting up to 3.3 percent of the U.S. population. Someone who washes his hands over and over throughout the day suffers from this disorder; a dog who licks his paws over and over exhibits the same syndrome. Patients with OCD are character-

Table 11.2

Signs Associated with Obsessive-Compulsive Disorder

Type	Signs
Grooming	Self-licking, air licking, chewing hair, flank sucking, lick granuloma
Eating, drinking	Ingestion of shiny objects, rocks, dirt, excessive drooling
Movement	Pacing, head shaking, running fence, freezing, tail chasing, floor digging, prey searching with nose to ground
Vocalization	Barking at food, aggressive growling associated with tail or foot biting
Hallucinatory	Staring into space, fly-biting, jaw snapping, imaginary prey chasing
Neurotic	On-off aggression directed toward people, vicious biting of feet or tail

ized by repetitive, ritualistic behaviors in excess of those required for normal functioning and by the interference of normal daily functioning during their performance. Table 11.2 shows the types and signs of obsessive-compulsive disorder.

I believe that both people and animals desire a safe and predictable environment. The lack of predictability and control can be extremely stressful to some individuals. When the person or animal becomes highly aroused because of stress-inducing factors, and cannot control or avoid the source of the stress, the resulting behavior can develop a repetitive rhythm, designed to soothe and take one's mind off the problem. Later, this behavior is indulged in during any period of high arousal. But as a coping method, compulsive behavior fails: research shows that obsessive-compulsive actions do not change the body's physiological reactions to stress.

The Sick, Injured, and Neurotic

Some of the personality changes associated with atypical seizures—such as jaw snapping, flank sucking, persistent licking, and staring—mimic those of OCD. If the animal showing these signs fails to respond to anticonvulsant drugs, indications are strong that a diagnosis of OCD is correct, and that the origin of the behavior is psychological rather than physical.

I find it interesting that certain breeds are prone to specific obsessive behaviors. Dobermans tend to suck their flanks; jaw snapping or fly biting occurs in Cavalier King Charles spaniels and dobermans; tail chasing is common in spaniels and bull terriers.

Smokey, my huge malamute neighbor, suffers from lick granuloma. Acral lick dermatitis or lick granulomas are seen most frequently in large, active breeds; Smokey is a typical representative. To develop a lick granuloma, the dog continuously licks, bites, and scratches at one or more areas on front or rear legs until those areas are raised, reddened, denuded of hair, and perhaps oozing.

Inciting factors for the dog to self-mutilate include boredom, loneliness, confinement, and in some cases local irritation of the skin owing to injury or parasites. Smokey again fits this profile, as he stays confined to a small area with a ten-foot chain. Unfortunately, most dogs continue to lick compulsively after their environment has been enriched, exercise programs instituted, and skin irritation treated, leading veterinary clinicians to include this condition in the OCD category.

For years, we veterinarians treated lick granulomas by wrapping the wound, treating the itching with corticosteroids, muzzling the dog, and other various remedies that worked in a few cases but failed in most. Then Judith L. Rapoport, a physician, wrote a book on OCD titled *The Boy Who Couldn't Stop Washing*. Readers with dogs who couldn't stop washing, or licking in this case, noticed a connection between the symptoms of people with OCDs and their dogs, and contacted Rapoport for her suggestions. *Scientific American* reported in 1992:

> Rapoport prescribed clomipramine, one of the three known antiobsessional drugs, and the dog stopped licking. To prove that clomipramine had worked purely against the compulsion, without any coincident antidepressant effect, Rapoport recruited 42 dogs with acral lick [referred by their veterinar-

ians] and put them on either antiobsessional drugs or conventional antidepressants. The antiobsessinal worked; the antidepressants did not.

Antiobsessional drugs like clomipramine act by preventing nerve cells from reabsorbing serotonin, a neurotransmitter in the brain. I wish I could say OCDs, including lick granulomas, are cured forever by clomipramine therapy, but it's not that simple. People, as well as dogs, with OCD often relapse when the drug is decreased in dosage or treatment stopped.

These drugs are also expensive, and labeled for human, rather than animal, use. When your veterinarian prescribes antiobsessional drugs like clomipramine or antidepressants such as Prozac, he will ask you to sign a release form, acknowledging consent to the use of experimental drugs.

Other factors impact the expression of OCD in dogs. If you bestow attention upon your dog when he is chasing his tail or chewing his leg, for example, you are reinforcing the OC behavior. Better to ignore the dog when he is whirling after his tail or gnawing his leg, and pay attention when he is leaving his extremities alone.

Identifying and removing the stress triggering the OCD is the first goal of treatment. If the stressor cannot be removed, behavior modification that helps train the dog to cope with stressful situations is an alternative. Distracting the dog or training him to perform an incompatible behavior diverts his attention away from the obsessive-compulsive behavior. For example, teach him to lie still on his favorite blanket in response to a command such as "Rover, blanket down." Removing sources of stress and enriching the dog's life with appropriate toys, exercise, and obedience training are recommended.

Drugs such as clomipramine serve to alleviate the symptoms of OCD patients until behavior modification and training an incompatible behavior have time to be effective deterrents to OCD. In some cases, the dog must remain on drug therapy for the rest of his life.

Panic Attacks

Panic attacks occur when acute anxiety (out-of-proportion to the situation) causes stimulation of the autonomic nervous system, triggering bodily responses such as trembling, rapid heart beat, sweating

The Sick, Injured, and Neurotic

or panting, shortness of breath, choking spells, and fear of isolation or crowds.

An acquaintance of mine experienced panic attacks that commenced shortly after her daughter revealed she had been sexually abused, and they occurred most often in places where my friend felt trapped or cornered, such as the shopping mall. Thankfully, my friend overcame her panic as she and her daughter began that long road toward emotional healing.

A similar syndrome occurs in animals experiencing separation anxiety and the terror induced by phobias.

separation anxiety

In separation anxiety, the panic attack occurs when the dog is separated from his owner to whom he has become overly attached. Although most separation anxieties are triggered by the owner's leaving the premises, some animals become overly anxious when merely separated by a fence or closed door.

The panic induced by the separation stimulates the physiological responses cited above: trembling, panting, drooling, defecation, urination and in some cases, vomiting. These responses occur soon after the beloved person leaves—within fifteen to thirty minutes. Destruction of exit sites, vocalization (howling and barking), and aggression are other symptoms of the dog's extreme agitation. In some cases, the dog self-mutilates or engages in other obsessive-compulsive behavior.

Dr. Victoria Voith, formerly of the Animal Behavior Clinic of the Veterinary Hospital of the University of Pennsylvania, found the following: "Dogs with clinical separation anxiety were significantly more likely to greet their owners in the following ways: bark at the owner, jump on the owner, and run around a lot." Not only do dogs with separation anxiety greet their owners with exuberance, but they can't stand to be alone in the house; they follow their owners from room to room, often pestering them for attention.

How does the dog become overly dependent? He was perhaps sheltered from separation as a puppy, suffered a traumatic separation experience during the fear-imprinting stage, failed to adjust to the absence of an owner who went back to work after an extended period at home, or experienced a stressful event such as a move to a new home.

Treatment aimed at specific symptoms of separation anxiety, such as housesoiling or destruction, rarely cures the inciting anxiety and can worsen the signs. Therapy is aimed at desensitizing and counterconditioning the animal to accept your absence and departure. In many cases, drugs—tranquilizers and antidepressants—serve to reduce anxiety levels until retraining has effectively changed behavior.

If the dog has a room or crate in which he feels secure and safe, send the dog to this area prior to departure. Leave him with soft music and a long-lasting chew bone.

Unfortunately, most dogs with separation anxiety feel anxious in the cage or in any room of the house. Retraining for them involves gradual exposure to departure cues, such as putting on one's coat, picking up a briefcase, and turning out lights, without triggering the dog's anxiety. While the dog is calm, the owner departs for a very short period—five minutes, for example. During the training period you may have to take the dog with you or hire a dog sitter until the dog has been completely desensitized to your departure and absence. An anxiety-provoking experience will serve as a severe setback to retraining.

As training progresses, periods of absence should become increasingly longer in duration. Avoid activities that will stimulate the dog prior to your departure; do not respond to his demands for attention during this time; vary your departure routines and length of time you are absent. Reward appropriate behavior.

Owners of dogs subject to separation anxiety are encouraged to distance themselves in general from their pet—refusing pet access to the bedroom at night and no-free-lunch training (giving attention and petting in exchange for performance).

phobias

A phobia is an irrational fear; I mentioned dogs who were fearful of certain people in chapter 2. More common are dogs who develop a phobia to loud noise, thunderstorms, lightning, gunshots, or fireworks. Desensitizing to noise involves exposing the dog to short periods of low-volume noise and rewarding the dog for nonfearful behavior.

Bear is afraid of rain, thunder, and lightning. When we lived in Amarillo, he tried his best to escape by climbing over, through, or

The Sick, Injured, and Neurotic

under the fence or gate. Of course, dogs who use escape tactics to run away from thunderstorms rarely succeed, for the storm seems to follow them. Here, Bear paces the porch or crawls onto the wood pile from where he can peer into the house, displaying all his symptoms of fright—whining, panting, trembling. If I walk outside and attempt to calm Bear during a storm, he reacts even worse during the next storm; I have positively reinforced his fearful behavior.

I decided during our last rainstorm to test the desensitization practice. First, let me digress and tell the story of the gourmet dog food. I received a coupon in the mail for a case of small cans of premium dog food. Bear, like most vet's pets, was used to eating whatever was left over at the clinic or whatever I received free as samples. Those freebies had never before been gourmet food designed for little dogs like Tiger; Tiger, not realizing he's a dog, however, eats people food. The first time I offered Bear one of the little cans of food, he was beside himself with excitement. I fought to keep him from consuming the can, and yes, I felt a little guilty about our feeding practices.

Here's where the dog food ties in to desensitization. I picked a rainstorm that had barely begun, if that's the correct description. The rain smell was in the air, and a few drops were falling. I showed Bear the can, and rather than his fearful expression, he plastered an "Oh boy, it must be Christmas" look on his face. Bear's usual fearful behavior never materialized; I lucked out in that the storm never fully materialized, either.

It is very difficult to pick storms that will work just right for retraining the phobia-suffering dog. For that reason, most experts recommend playing tapes of thunderstorms while positively reinforcing calm behavior on the part of the dog. Once the dog shows fear, you've gone too far in the training session.

Tranquilizers and antidepressants are useful to calm the fear response while retraining is in progress.

Hyperactivity

Hyperactivity, known also as hyperkinesis, is rare in dogs. Most dogs who misbehave in an overactive manner are indulging in puppy behaviors, receive too little stimulation and exercise, or elicit attention by their hyperactive behavior. These animals respond to exercise and training, which rewards calm behavior.

Dogs who are hyperactive are unable to slow down. They move to the point of collapse and exhaustion, and show the bodily signs of dilated pupils, increased heart and respiratory rates, and reddening of vessels of the eyes. Response to stimulants can differentiate between dogs who are truly hyperactive and those who are misbehaving. Dogs who are physiologically normal are stimulated by drugs such as Ritalin and the amphetamines; hyperactive dogs are calmed by the same drugs.

Different types of conditions can cause behavioral changes, and physical and emotional problems often lead to the same behavior. Dogs suffering from rabies, thyroid dysfunction, and separation anxiety might all show aggressive symptoms. A destructive dog may be misbehaving or suffering a panic attack.

It takes an expert to make an accurate diagnosis and to design a program of treatment appropriate for an individual patient.

QUESTION

Dear Dr. Whiteley,

I believe that my fox terrier, B.J., is allergic to his food. He chews, licks, and scratches at his feet until they are red and raw; plus, he has started biting my wife when she attempts to discipline him. Our veterinarian thinks B.J. is allergic to grass, but he bites and scratches during the winter when our grass is dead. Is B.J. a bad or a sick dog?

Frustrated in Lincoln

Dear Frustrated,

Regardless of the motivation behind B.J.'s behavior, I would not call him bad. He may be physically or emotionally sick, however. One of the most common indicators of an allergic condition is biting and licking of the feet; allergy testing and other dermatological and laboratory tests are indicated. Because food has been implicated as a causation in allergies and in certain types of aggressive behavior, I suggest that you ask your veterinarian about changing his food to a hypoallergenic and low-protein diet.

Withdraw all attention from your dog when he self-mutilates his paws or when he acts with aggression toward family members. Make sure that he receives plenty of play and exercise time and that he is taught basic obedience commands.

Good Luck!

H. E. W.

12
Sex, Pregnancy, and Parenthood

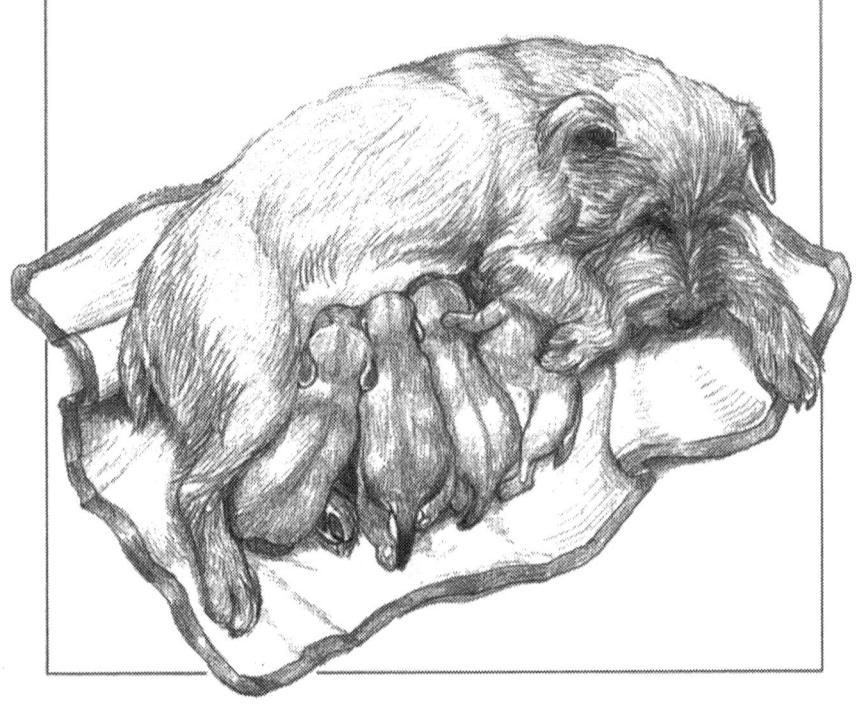

The Female

The female genitalia include two ovaries, each connected to a uterine horn by oviducts or Fallopian tubes. Uterine horns converge at a single small uterine body closed by the muscular cervix. The cervix, which dilates during labor, joins the vagina, which becomes the vulva, the external genital visible to the eye.

At puberty ovaries become active and secrete estrogen, the hormone eliciting signs of heat in the bitch, and produce ova or eggs, which are shed during ovulation. After ovulation, or release of eggs during heat, ovaries secrete the hormone progesterone in both the pregnant and nonpregnant bitch.

It is in each of the uterine horns that puppies develop in the pregnant female; after fertilization and before implantation of embryos into the uterine wall, the eggs space themselves evenly in each horn regardless of which ovary produced the most eggs.

Small breeds reach puberty as early as five months of age while larger breeds take longer—as long as eighteen months in some cases. The average age of puberty is six to nine months for small dogs and nine to twelve months in large breeds.

Although older dogs do not generally experience menopause as women do, they may go longer between heat cycles and produce smaller litters when bred. The number of ova or eggs that can be shed from the ovaries is estimated to decline from 250,000 at puberty to approximately 500 by age ten.

Female dogs commonly have two heat cycles per year; as mentioned earlier, wolves and basenjis have only one heat per year, which is timed so that young are born in the late spring, when prey is abundant and the weather is mild.

The initial heat of maturing puppies may be normal or may manifest as a split-heat cycle, in which a short interval of proestrus appears and subsides. Within a few weeks, the pup again shows signs of proestrus that progresses to full heat or estrus. Mating should be delayed until the second complete heat cycle, occurring in most dogs six months later.

Proestrus is that part of the dog's cycle characterized by swelling of the vulva and dripping of blood. Males are attracted to the female at this time, but she refuses intercourse. Play behavior is often part of the courtship exhibited by the female in proestrus. She will run

Sex, Pregnancy, and Parenthood

around and bow to the male and may lick his body and genitals. If he attempts to mount, however, she will turn before he can mount and perhaps rebuff him with a growl. This period lasts approximately seven to fourteen days, with nine days being the average duration of proestrus.

As her hormones bring her into true heat, the female accepts and may even court the male, and ovulation occurs. The vulva is at peak swelling, but secretions have changed from bloody in appearance to straw or clear colored. This period of receptivity is termed estrus, and persists for six to seven days.

The surge of estrogen that brings the bitch into heat triggers her to be more active and nervous, especially in the presence of male dogs. She increasingly indulges in urine marking and may even cock her leg to do so; both urine and secretions from the vulva contain pheromones that attract males. A particularly amorous female may mount males or other females.

Females are choosy, accepting some males as mates and rejecting others. This rejection ranges from avoidance to actively chasing and biting him. In a few cases, the dominant female refuses to allow a male to stand over or to approach her from behind. Dominance on the part of mothers may serve to inhibit mother-son matings and to prevent close inbreeding. The submissive behavior of a timid female—lying down and rolling onto her back—in deference to a dominant male can also interfere with breeding.

When I married George and blended families, I obtained Snowball, an older female German shepherd, as well as Bear. Bear, then seven, was the younger of the two dogs; he had spent his life since adoption at six weeks under the dominance of Snowball. Neither dog was neutered, and as far as I know, Bear never attempted to mate with Snowball. The trouble with obtaining a vet for a stepowner is that I immediately spayed Snowball, castrated Bear, and proceeded with all kinds of fun procedures like heartworm checks, vaccinations, and dewormings.

When the female chooses a mate, she does not necessarily pick the macho biggest and dominant male; she often prefers one who is familiar or who appeals to her for some other reason that she alone seems to know. An occasional female imitates her wolf ancestors by maintaining a monogamous relationship with one male. According to one report, the female is less receptive in general and less rejecting of nonpreferred males when there are lots of males gathered together waiting for her attentions.

If the female makes her choice and the male does not follow through by mounting, she will turn so that her hindquarters are directly in front of his nose and even back into him with her tail elevated. It doesn't take a behavioral expert to determine that she is saying with her body language "yes" and "get on with it."

When her answer is no, a strong and persistent male can pursue her to the point of exhaustion, grasp her along the back with his teeth, and force himself on her. Rape is, however, a rare occurrence in the animal population.

THE MALE

The male genital system consists of the penis, urethra, prepuce, two testicles, scrotum, epididymides, spermatic cords, deferent ducts, and prostate gland. The prepuce is a protective sheath of skin covering and protecting the penis, the external copulative organ of the male. In some species, including the dog, raccoon, mink, and beaver, a bone called the os penis adds support to the penis.

Two testicles are located within the scrotum; these sex organs produce sperm and the male hormone testosterone. An epididymis located on each testicle stores sperm prior to ejaculation and is continued in the spermatic cord as the ductus deferens, a pathway for sperm to the prostate gland and then the urethra.

As the only accessory sex gland in the dog, the prostate secretes a fluid that increases the volume of semen and influences the motility of sperm in the female reproductive tract after mating.

Male pups reach sexual maturity between six and twelve months of age. The ability to mate and produce puppies can continue in some males until death takes away that sexual longing. Although neutering will render a dog incapable of producing sperm and testosterone (circulating testosterone is gone within six hours of removing the testicles), it does not necessarily take away the incentive or ability to mate. Learning and memory play a part here, and the more experienced the male, the longer sexual behaviors persist after castration.

Sex, Pregnancy, and Parenthood

Parts of the male puppy's brain become masculinized by male sex hormones prior to birth; the female brain is feminized by the lack of male hormones. The male simulates the postures needed for copulation when he starts mounting and clasping his littermates at around five weeks of age. Puppies raised without peer-group modeling are often unable to function sexually. They seem not to know what is expected or how to do it.

A timid male rebuffed by a more aggressive female may become impotent, as he associates fear with the sexual act. The same thing can happen if he is frightened by something in the environment during sex. This is a similar situation to the dog exhibiting what appears to be unprovoked aggression in response to superstitious bite cues (see chapter 10).

The presence of a dominant male may inhibit a submissive male from even attempting to mount a female in heat; and like the female, certain males have their own preferences for mates, refusing some individuals and accepting others.

Dominance in males is associated with increased levels of the male hormone testosterone. Studies in humans show that losing a competition can cause a temporary drop in circulating testosterone levels in men. I wonder—does the sexist phrase "having balls" actually have a scientific basis?

Dominance and lust do have a price. In a study linking dominance rank and copulatory behavior in male reindeer, Japanese scientists found that top-ranking males monopolized access to females in heat. As the mating season of reindeer is restricted to a few weeks, courting and copulating with as many females as possible is an intense activity in terms of energy expenditure and reduced food intake. The high-ranking males soon became exhausted, allowing the lower ranking males access to females during the latter part of the breeding season.

Using the male propensity for lust, scientists have found a way to eliminate the peach borer, an insect that destroys fruit trees. The insects try to mate daily for about two weeks, the lifespan of adult borers. The problem for the borers is that they are mating with a dispenser containing a strong artificial sex scent and not with their natural mates; the female insects remain barren, producing no offspring to bore into peach trees.

Masturbation

The action of mounting people and objects is an extension of puppy-play sexual behavior, and the puppy will often grow out of these behaviors. In a few cases, however, sexual imprinting occurs (remember the dog with a sexual attraction to the vacuum cleaner bag?) toward objects or people.

Because the action is more likely to occur in dogs overly attached to their owners, treatment is aimed at encouraging owners to distance themselves from the dog—removing the dog from the bedroom, giving positive reinforcement to appropriate behavior, and isolating the dog or puppy who masturbates on people or objects.

Objectionable mounting and masturbation are more likely to occur in males, but occasionally a female will indulge in this behavior. Neutering resolves the problem in approximately 60 percent of cases. Those dogs who masturbate after spaying or castration are treated with behavioral modification and hormonal therapy.

THE MATING ACT

During estrus, the bitch will stand and flex her body toward him as the male attempts to mount. The male grasps the female's body just anterior to the pelvis and begins thrusting with his penis. She will deviate her tail and move her rear from side to side, assisting him with intromission.

Once intromission has been accomplished, the male pulls his front legs backward, deflects his tail downward and initiates a stepping activity with the rear legs while the penis is undergoing intense oscillations. At the time of ejaculation of sperm, the bulb of the male penis engorges inside the female's vagina, and the two are locked together in what is commonly called a "tie."

During the first part of the ejaculatory reaction, the female stands rigid, but then starts twisting and turning, occasionally throwing the male off balance. Within a few minutes of ejaculation, the male dismounts, swings one hind leg over the bitch's back, and turns around so that the pair are facing opposite directions. The male must be quite a contortionist to perform this feat of mating, for the axis of the dog's penis is bent through an arc of nearly 180 degrees; yet if the

Sex, Pregnancy, and Parenthood

dog experiences distress, he is quite good at hiding it. Theories about why dogs adopt the tail-to-tail position range from helping ejaculation to the idea that this position leaves the pair less vulnerable to attack.

The average tie lasts from ten to thirty minutes, and during this time, prostatic fluid continues to be ejaculated. When the swelling of the male penis subsides, the tie is broken and the two can separate. It is generally thought that a tie is necessary to impregnate the bitch; however, sperm deposited at the vulva may successfully travel though the female reproductive tract to impregnate the ovulating female.

I have heard stories about people throwing water on and beating with sticks the canine lovers locked together. The tie is a physiological phenomena and not under conscious control by the dog, so tactics such as these are cruel. If the dogs have difficulty separating, gently and quietly place the male back on top of the female and press him toward her. This will sometimes work to release the tie.

The male and female recover quickly after copulation, and both can continue to mate with each other or with other partners. As the example of the amorous reindeer proves, overindulgence will tend to tire the pair.

The female who mates with several different males may deliver puppies who are half-siblings. If the female has mated with more than one male, the paternity question can be resolved only through DNA testing.

One benefit of the O. J. Simpson trial is that now everyone in America is familiar with DNA fingerprinting. However, DNA technology offers us more than forensic information. DNA fingerprinting is helpful in determining bone marrow matches for both humans and animals needing transplants, and could prove a means of detecting difficult-to-find viruses.

In this chapter, however, the emphasis is on DNA fingerprinting to determine the sire of litters with questionable mating history. International Canine Genetics (ICG) is a company that offers DNA testing, as well as ovulation timing and pregnancy tests and sperm banks. If you have a question about any of these services, ask your veterinarian or call ICG at 1-800-248-8099.

I recall the furor caused in the country community where I grew up when Mr. Rison's prize blue tick hound's first litter of puppies showed a remarkable resemblance to old Shep, the mongrel from next door. What bothered Mr. Rison most was his belief that Betsy was ruined for life, that she could now never have a litter of purebred blue tick puppies. This, of course, is just an old husband's tale, although I've heard dog owners express the same concern today. Shep may very well have been the begetter of Betsy's first litter, but he could not "taint" successive pregnancies unless he mated with her each time.

Breeding Management

The only legitimate reason in my book for mating two dogs is the desire to improve the breed. Care should be taken that animals with congenital and inherited defects are not mated. Beware of genetic disorders prevalent in breeds that have been highly inbred; genetic counseling by your veterinarian is advised.

Research into canine genetic disorders has come a long way, and tests are now available to detect certain disorders. For example, early radiographic screening with a new technique can detect hip dysplasia in pups as young as four months of age, allowing breeders to eliminate young dogs with poor hips from their breeding program.

Before mating, both partners should be examined by a veterinarian for general condition and health of the reproductive tract. Vaccinations and deworming are administered before breeding, and both male and female should be tested for brucellosis, a disease which can cause fetal death and reproductive problems.

As mentioned, the virgin female should not be mated before her second complete heat cycle; if that cycle is missed, breeding before she reaches her third birthday is recommended. The female's readiness for breeding is determined by physical signs—swelling of and discharge from the vulva—and by laboratory tests to reveal time of ovulation.

Laboratory tests, performed by your veterinarian, include blood tests for determining progesterone and luteinizing hormone concentrations (two days before the time of ovulation, these hormones increase in the blood) and microscopic examination of cells lining the vulva. These cells change in accordance with the stage of the heat cycle, allowing the veterinarian to determine if the female is entering, in, or past estrus.

Sex, Pregnancy, and Parenthood

After a female ovulates, eggs are expelled into the oviducts, where they require another forty-eight hours to mature into fertilizable ova. If not fertilized, these mature eggs begin to disintegrate within seventy-two hours. Canine sperm lives in the female tract after natural mating for two to seven days. There is a relatively narrow window of time—three to four days—when the sperm and ova can meet to produce puppy embryos. According to some experts, incorrect timing of breeding accounts for 60 percent of infertile matings.

After determining that the female is receptive and ovulation imminent, the lovers are introduced. The female is generally brought to the male, who performs better in quiet and familiar surroundings. Matings are usually scheduled for every other day during the estrus period.

Assistance is sometimes needed when breeding inexperienced dogs to prevent one partner from injuring the other. A few dogs do not tolerate an audience and breed only when granted privacy.

Artificial Insemination

Artificial insemination (AI) is a consideration when natural mating is impractical owing to physical or behavioral problems of the partners or when prospective mates live great distances apart. Using AI cuts shipping costs, eliminates stress to shipped dogs, and overcomes the long quarantine periods for dogs entering some countries.

The AI procedure involves collecting semen from the male by ejaculation into an artificial vagina. The semen is then injected via a syringe and pipette directly through the vagina and cervix into the uterus of a bitch in heat (determined by physical signs and laboratory tests). If the collected semen is not to be used immediately for a mating, it can be frozen. Sperm banks, operated by private or public institutions like veterinary schools, serve to collect, freeze, and ship canine semen.

A new technology involving cell separation may allow breeders in the future to select sperm that will allow sex selection of offspring. Remember the discussion in chapter 3 about the chromosomes that determine sex? An XX configuration becomes a female and an XY becomes a male. The mother always contributes an X, but the male can contribute an X or Y chromosome, thereby determining the sex of each puppy. Using the same technique that researchers use to separate cells in bone marrow for cancer therapy, veterinary scientists hope to separate sperm cells into the two types (X or Y) for artificial insemination.

Pregnancy Determination

In the old days, we veterinarians relied solely upon our powers of palpation to determine pregnancy. At approximately three weeks after conception, fetuses can be felt between the fingers when palpating the abdomen of the pregnant bitch. Palpation is a subjective art, and we were sometimes wrong.

I remember one veterinarian who believed he could tell the number of puppies a bitch was carrying just by looking and feeling. He determined that Sally, a large doberman pregnant with her first litter, was going to deliver at least eight puppies. I was on call when the dog's owner notified me that Sally was in labor and having trouble. I finally delivered by cesarean section one gigantic puppy, named Cheever by Sally's owner, for Dr. Cheever who missed the litter size by seven.

A blood test for pregnancy and ultrasound testing are helpful for evaluating pregnancy. Samples for blood tests are taken between days 28 and 37 after mating, while ultrasound is performed twenty-three to twenty-five days after the last breeding date. Radiographs can determine the number of puppies after day 38 of gestation (pregnancy length in dogs averages sixty-three days); earlier exposure of fetuses to X-rays may be damaging to developing puppies.

PREGNANCY AND LACTATION

As mentioned earlier, the average duration of pregnancy is nine weeks or sixty-three days. Generally, there is no appreciable change in body shape or weight of the pregnant bitch the first thirty days. During the second month, however, she gains weight and exhibits the enlarged abdomen of pregnancy. About the fifth week after conception, the mammary glands begin enlarging, accompanied by a reddening of the unpigmented skin around the nipples. Milk may appear shortly before term.

Sex, Pregnancy, and Parenthood

Nutrition is one of the important considerations in caring for the pregnant and lactating bitch. Overfeeding during early pregnancy may lead to obesity, which can predispose to whelping problems. Most of the weight of developing fetuses is gained during the last half of gestation; that is the time to increase the bitch's food.

Veronique Legrand-Defretin, a canine nutritionist, recommends that the bitch's food be increased by fifteen percent each week from the fifth week of gestation, so that by the time of whelping, she will be eating 60 percent more than when mated. Feeding several small meals over the course of the day is recommended over one large meal.

In terms of energy requirements, lactation or giving milk enacts the heaviest toll on the mother. The quantity of extra calories needed is dependent on the normal energy intake of the mother and the size and age of the puppies she is feeding. Generally, the mother must eat from two to four times her normal maintenance requirement to satisfy her own nutritional needs and that of her litter. This is best fulfilled by feeding her a growth-lactation diet, which is palatable and nutrient dense. Again, small meals evenly spaced throughout the day are preferable to once-a-day feeding. This same diet can be moistened for puppies as they reach weaning age.

Whelping

The act of giving birth is termed whelping, and can be divided into three distinct stages. Stage one heralds the coming birth and lasts from a few hours to one day prior to the onset of obvious contractions. This stage is indicated by restlessness, increased licking of the abdomen and genital area, and nest-making activity. Nest-making ability varies greatly from dog to dog. Some ignore the impending birth and your efforts to provide a nice box lined with fleecy diapers, and opt to give birth amidst the dust under the bed, while still others make an elaborate nest or den.

Barbara Woodhouse addresses the subject of nest building in *No Bad Dogs:*

> I clearly remember my Alsatian, Argus, choosing a wife and going off with her to our orchard and digging a fifteen-foot underground passage and bedroom at the end for her to have her litter in.... We allowed her to have her nine pup-

pies down there, and seeing Argus standing erect on top of the entrance the day the mother whelped was a thrilling sight, for we felt the true nature of the dogs had been allowed to develop by choosing their own home and bringing up the babies in a homely atmosphere.

Although male involvement in building nests and caring for pups is a natural phenomenon in wolf families and a rare dog like Argus, most canine fathers invest only their sperm and genetic material in the family, leaving the bitch as a single mother. If she's going to have help building nests and delivering puppies, you, the human caretaker, are going to have to provide it.

Uterine contractions, which mark the onset of labor or stage two, are accompanied by straining; the soon-to-be mother will lie down but may get up to shift positions, and appears unable to get comfortable. Prolonged labor with contractions signals a problem. After hard contractions begin, the first puppy should arrive within a few minutes to, at the most, a couple of hours. The same goes for successive puppies.

Uterine and abdominal contractions become more intense as the first fetus is passed through the birth canal. The bitch breaks the water bag as the head or buttocks of a puppy is presented at the vulva. After the puppy is born, the mother consumes the fetal membranes, bites the umbilical cord, and licks the puppy to stimulate breathing. Some mothers, however, stop the process of taking care of the infant to clean themselves and eat the placenta. If the bitch abandons the puppy before the sac has been removed, cord severed, or breathing stimulated, you must step in to assist the newborn.

Wash your hands before handling the infant. Remove the sac from around the puppy, exposing first his nose to the air. The cord can be tied with string approximately one inch from the pup's body and severed below the knot. Rub the puppy with a clean diaper or towel. If the infant is not breathing, remove fluid from his nose and mouth with a bulb syringe. Continue rubbing to stimulate breathing.

The third stage of labor is delivery of placentas. This brownish tissue is expelled with each puppy, or shortly thereafter. It is not necessary that the bitch eat this tissue, and if placentas can be removed without disturbing the new mother, the diarrhea that often accompanies eating of the placentas may be prevented. In the wild, eating the placentas serves a worthwhile function: it provides nutrients, allowing the mother to spend more time with the young than if she had to hunt for food immediately, and also serves to keep the nest clean. In the midst of birth, it is difficult, if not impossible, to keep up with the placentas. However, an accounting of each placenta is helpful for the veterinarian who is trying to diagnose postdelivery problems. A placenta remaining in the uterus predisposes the bitch to infection.

Whelping occurs frequently at night or on the weekend, making the decision to consult your pet's veterinarian a judgment call. Of course, the best time for the first consultation is before breeding and potential problems crop up, as discussed in the section on breeding management (see page 218). Bitches with the potential for problems should be seen before the onset of labor. For females without prior problems, the veterinarian should be consulted as soon as serious problems are detected (see Table 12.1). For bitches with a normal delivery, the mother and puppies should be checked the next day, or on Monday if whelping occurs during the weekend.

Pseudopregnancy

Pseudopregnancy is a condition in which the nonpregnant female shows the behavioral signs and some of the physiological signs, such as milk production, of pregnancy and motherhood. In wolf families, only the dominant pair mates. However, wolf aunts who produce milk and exhibit mothering traits are able to contribute to the survival of the offspring by acting as nursemaids. Female dogs often retain this ability, which serves no useful purpose in dog families.

The syndrome in dogs usually starts prior to the date of whelping if the dog had been bred. The affected female shows the enlarged abdomen and mammary development associated with pregnancy. The symptoms either begin to subside near the whelping date or the bitch adopts toys and other objects for mothering. Pseudopregnancy has a hormonal causation, and spaying is curative.

Parenthood

As mentioned several times, parenting in wolves is a family affair with all relatives—mother, father, aunts, and uncles—involved in

Table 12.1

When to Consult the Veterinarian

1. Dogs having a history of pelvic fractures, gross obesity, chronic illnesses, or previous cesarean sections. Consult before onset of labor or, better yet, before breeding.

2. Passage of bright red or greenish discharge from vulva without onset of labor.

3. Prolonged gestation (over sixty-eight days).

4. Prolonged contractions without producing a puppy (over ninety minutes).

5. Puppy stuck in birth canal.

6. Weak, diminished contractions without producing puppy.

7. Mother or puppies depressed, cold, with pale mucous membranes (can be determined by examining the color of gums, tongue, membranes surrounding eyes) during or after birth.

8. Uterine prolapse following birth: presence of one or two turgid tubular structures extending from the vulva.

9. Mother not eating twenty-four hours following whelping; mother with body temperature over 103 degrees Fahrenheit; mother showing malodorous discharge from the vulva.

10. Mother having no milk or refusing to let puppies nurse following birth. Puppies too weak to nurse.

raising the young. Except in rare instances, parenting in dogs is in actuality mothering. The father invests his genetic material during mating, and that is his sole contribution to the family. The mother is the primary parent ensuring the survival of the species.

Eytan Avital and Eva Jablonka, writing in the journal *Animal Behavior*, note:

> According to the conventional view, the female invests more in the offspring but transmits the same amount of hereditary information as the male; females compensate for their proportionally greater investment by being very choosy, and selecting the genetically superior males as fathers of their offspring. According to our view, the female does indeed invest more, but she also transmits more; she transmits behavioral phenotypes in addition to her DNA contribution. The female thus contributes more to the next generation than the male.

Are good mothers born with that ability or can mothering be learned? It is both, I think. In one experiment using rats, microscopic changes were found in the brains of maternally behaving rats that are different from those of nonpregnant or nonlactating rats. These tiny brain differences occur in conjunction with the hormones of pregnancy, and with the sensory stimulation induced by the presence of rat babies. The changes are reversible, and after weaning are no longer detectable.

Diane Ackerman, author of *A Natural History of Love*, says in a *Parade* magazine article:

> Oxytocin, a hormone that encourages labor and the contractions during childbirth, seems to play an important role in love, especially in mother love. The sound of a crying baby makes its mother's body secrete more oxytocin, which in turn erects her nipples and helps the milk to flow. As the baby nurses, even more oxytocin is released, making the mother want to nuzzle and hug the baby. It has been called the "cuddle chemical" by zoologists, who have artificially raised the oxytocin level in animals and produced similar behavior.

Other hormones aid in making mothers attentive to their young. In humans, preliminary studies indicate that during the first three days following the birth of their infant, new mothers show an increase in the hormones associated with mothering (estrogen, prolactin, pregnancy steroids) and an increased ability to detect the infant-related odors, sounds, and feel of their own young.

There is a hormonal component to respond maternally to one's young, but there is a learned component, too. Rhesus monkey mothers who were themselves deprived of maternal stimulation during their early developmental years often failed to care for their young at the end of their first pregnancy. However, these same mothers overcame their earlier deprivation and displayed relatively normal maternal behavior toward their young after the second and third pregnancies.

In the wild, good mothers pass their genetic material to future generations, because the offspring of superior mothers survive and the young of those with inferior mothering ability do not. Because of our intervention, bitches today may lack both the innate and learned components of mothering behavior.

Cannibalism

Cannibalism is the eating of offspring by the mother. In the wild, cannibalism eliminates sick or malformed puppies, increasing the likelihood that healthy pups will survive. Occasionally a domestic dog will take care of a malformed pup in the same way. The behavior becomes abnormal, however, when the mother systematically eliminates the entire litter.

This behavior may be due to nervousness, anxiety, and possibly hormonal abnormalities. A decrease in progesterone—the pregnancy hormone—after delivery triggers depression in some individuals; others may suffer a lack or imbalance of the mothering hormones. Although we can do little to alter hormonal imbalances in dogs at this time, we can take steps to ensure that the canine mother is exposed to as little environmental and mental stress as possible.

BIRTH CONTROL

Compared to humans, dogs and cats reach sexual maturity quickly and produce young quickly. Between 2,500 and 3,000 dogs and cats are born every hour in this country, according to an estimate by the Humane Society of the United States. Unfortunately, that's more animal babies than we can take care of and train as pets. The answer to this problem is birth control.

Neutering

Spaying (ovariohysterectomy surgery) not only prevents pregnancy but also significantly decreases the incidence of canine breast cancer and eliminates the possibility of uterine disease in later life. Castration (removal of testicles) eliminates tumors of the testicles and significantly decreases behavioral problems such as intermale aggression, urine marking, roaming, and masturbation.

Traditionally, veterinarians recommend spaying the female when she reaches physical maturity and before the first heat, usually at six months of age, and neutering the male at physical maturity between six and nine months of age. Recently, however, the practice of pediatric neutering of both sexes at seven to twelve weeks of age is increasing in popularity. The advantages of early neutering include reduction of unwanted pregnancies and improved adoption chances for pet-quality puppies. The disadvantages are increased incidence of urinary incontinence and small external genitalia of females and possibly growth and weight deficiencies in both sexes.

Scientific studies to determine the long-term results of pediatric neutering on both physical health and behavior are being conducted now. While we are waiting for results, I suggest that you adhere to the advice of your veterinarian.

For the surgical procedures of castration and spaying, general anesthesia is required. It is best that your pet be in good health and have received protective vaccinations prior to scheduling surgery. Surgery itself is a stress, both physically and mentally; vaccinations and other medical procedures add to that stress when combined with surgery.

In the female, the abdomen is opened, and both the uterus (uterine horns and body) and the ovaries are removed. Your pet cannot get pregnant, nor will she come back in heat following surgery. Several stitches will be required to close the abdominal incision.

It is best to schedule ovariohysterectomy surgery at a time when the dog is not in heat or pregnant, although it is better to spay in heat or within the first three weeks of pregnancy than risk an unwanted litter. After four to five weeks of pregnancy, the surgery poses an increased risk to the mother because of engorgement of blood vessels and loss of fluid during surgery.

In males, a small incision is made anterior to the scrotum and both testicles are removed; a few sutures close the incision.

Pets recovering from surgery should be given as much love and attention as possible. Dogs with stitches should be confined and closely monitored until the sutures are removed or dissolve, depending on the type used, usually in ten to fourteen days.

Morning-After Shot

An unplanned pregnancy can be prevented with a morning-after, or mismate, shot. An injection of the female hormone estrogen within forty hours of mating will usually terminate the pregnancy. The hormone prevents the implantation of fertilized eggs in the uterine horns. Because of the potential for harmful side effects from the drug, such as increased risk of uterine infections, most veterinarians are reluctant to recommend this means of terminating pregnancy, especially on a routine basis. Another side effect of estrogen therapy is that it prolongs the behavioral signs of heat.

Abortion

Drugs in the prostaglandin category cause abortions in the dog and other domestic animals. The drugs must be given after day 30 of pregnancy in dogs; they work by causing a cessation of progesterone (the pregnancy hormone) production by the ovaries. Because these drugs have not been approved for clinical use in dogs, most veterinarians are reluctant to use or recommend them for canine abortions.

Birth Control Pills

There are two birth control "pills" for preventing estrus or heat in the bitch. Cheque Drops is actually a liquid that is administered orally starting one month prior to the anticipated onset of proestrus. This drug can be given for as long as twenty-four consecutive months; while it is given, the female will not come into heat. The bitch returns to normal heat cycles within seven to two hundred days after the drug is withdrawn.

Ovaban is a progesterone-related drug in pill form that is started at least one week prior to the expected onset of proestrus. This medication is given for a month and prevents ovulation and signs of estrus for that particular heat cycle. The drug is contraindicated in dogs with a history of uterine and mammary gland disease or diabetes mellitus.

Although there are a lot of exciting birth control methods, such as intrauterine devices and sterilizing vaccines, on the horizon, the only sure way to date of preventing pregnancy in dogs and cats is neutering.

Methods that don't work—disposable diapers that prevent spotting but not copulation, fences that are climbed or copulated through, dogs who perform hanky panky despite four-foot and hundred-pound size differences and others—prove the old adage "Where there's a will, there's a way."

QUESTION

Dear Dr. Whiteley,

My dog Muffin has been miserable ever since she came into heat at age five months. She continually drips blood from her vulva and stays swollen down there; she licks constantly and can't seem to get comfortable. Don't tell me to spay Muffin because I want her to have one litter of puppies. I am waiting until I retire next year and have more time to devote to Muffin and the little ones. What can I do in the meantime?

Distressed in Hot Springs

Dear Distressed,

Why do you want Muffin to have puppies? Motherhood is not a requirement for a fulfilling life for dogs or for women. If you want another dog, adopt one from a reputable breeder.

My advice is to get Muffin spayed. She is displaying all the symptoms of continual heat, called nymphomania. The causation of nymphomania is a hormonal imbalance, which is cured by spaying. Veterinarians who specialize in reproduction are called theriogeniologists; you might consult a reproductive specialist for a second opinion.

Best Wishes!

H. E. W.

13
Aging

I've noticed that most articles about the aging of Americans focus on the graying of the baby boomers, those of us born between 1946 and 1964. Let's face it, I missed the boat again by being born in 1945. That makes me older than the boomers; I fit as an expert about aging.

Dogs in this country are graying, too. Statistics gathered in 1991 by the American Veterinary Medical Association revealed that of the 52.5 million pet dogs in this country, 13.9 percent were eleven years of age or older. An eleven-year-old dog is about the same age as a sixty-year-old person (see Table 13.1).

Bear, at seventeen, should be older than me, but, dang, if we don't have about the same amount of gray hair, mine on my head and his on his muzzle. Hair color is produced in both people and dogs by cells called melanocytes, which produce pigment called melanin. In an article in the *Boston Globe*, Dr. Robert Stern, a dermatologist at Beth Israel Hospital in Boston and professor at Harvard Medical School, explains graying: "As the years march on, the melanocytes that provide hair color 'sort of run out of gas.' And as melanin production slows, hair turns gray; when it stops completely, the result is white hair."

Okay, I am stretching the analogy; dogs and people have different types of hair, and ours grows continuously while dog hair grows in cycles. Guess that's the reason graying is not as definitive a sign of aging in dogs as in people.

Life Expectancy

The life expectancy of both humans and dogs is increasing, yet there is a limit. "While an individual's chance of living longer has grown, thanks mostly to curing childhood diseases, our species has not increased its life span for the past 100,000 years, says [Leonard] Hayflick [a gerontologist]. Then, as now, the most a human can live is about 115 years. Few of us become centenarians, however, because something in our aging cells makes us more vulnerable to disease." So it was reported in the March 1995 issue of the American Association of Retired Persons *Bulletin*.

The article gave one theory about why cells age and eventually die. The end region of each chromosome within a cell has a telomere,

Table 13.1

Canine-Human Physiological Age Comparison

CANINE	HUMAN	CANINE	HUMAN
6 months	12 years	11 years	60 years
1 year	15 years	12 years	64 years
2 years	24 years	13 years	68 years
3 years	28 years	14 years	72 years
4 years	32 years	15 years	76 years
5 years	36 years	16 years	80 years
6 years	40 years	17 years	84 years
7 years	44 years	18 years	88 years
8 years	48 years	19 years	92 years
9 years	52 years	20 years	96 years
10 years	56 years	21 years	100 years

which consists of repeating subunits of DNA, "like a pattern of colored beads on a string." Each time a cell divides, it loses one or more of those beads comprising the telomere. When there are no more beads, the cell will cease dividing and eventually die. Dr. Hayflick noted the increased vulnerability of aged cells and aged individuals to disease. This occurs because of decreased immunological responses, longer exposure to toxins and carcinogens, and decreased ability of cells to repair their own DNA, the genetic material regulating cell function.

This might explain why none of us is going to live to be 175 years old, like Abraham of the Old Testament (they must have counted birthdays differently in those days). But why is a person old at eighty, a dog at seventeen, and a peach borer at two weeks? One theory states that a biological clock controls the aging process, and that this clock, genetic in origin, does so by influencing the body's hormonal systems. I'm still not sure why dogs have a shorter life span than people, but I have found some general principles that govern longevity.

Animals who produce only one or a few offspring per pregnancy generally live longer than species that produce multiple offspring. The average lifespan for a species tends to increase with the size of the species. For example, elephants—the oldest of which is seventy-nine years old—live longer than dogs, who live longer than peach borers. The exception seems to be man, who is smaller than—but lives longer than—the elephant. For example, maximum life spans of the following are:

>Man, 115 years
>Elephant, 79 years
>Horse, 50 years
>Cat, 36 years
>Dog, 32 years
>Mouse, 4 years

Within a species, the smaller sex tends to live longer than the larger sex. In humans, women outlive men; in hamsters, the female is the larger gender and the male is longer lived.

In dogs, small and medium breeds live longer than giant breeds. For example, miniature poodles are not considered old before eleven years, and border collies before ten years, but a six-year-old Saint Bernard is elderly. In one study, the average life span of Saint Bernards was 6.5 years (6.2 for males and 6.8 for females).

Experiments with mice given growth hormone show that increased body size results in a shorter life span and greater incidence of degenerative and proliferative diseases. Drs. Barbara Deeb and Norman Wolf of the University of Washington, analyzing the ages at death of six giant breeds and seven small breeds of dogs, found that giant dog breeds have a significantly greater risk of developing cancer and diseases affecting the heart, skin, muscles, and bones. The risk of musculoskeletal diseases in giant dog breeds increases significantly with age.

Extremely small dogs have an increased risk of early death. Drs. Deeb and Wolf write:

> When percentages of deaths in various age groups are compared, giant-breed dogs died significantly earlier than small-breed dogs did. When the percentage of dogs dying before seven years of age was correlated with adult shoulder height, we found that mortality rose with increased height in giant breeds and with decreased height in small breeds. However,

the correlation between earlier deaths and increased height in giant breeds was stronger than the correlation between earlier death and decreased height in small breeds.

(See also the discussion about size and health in chapter 3.)

Chilla, a cross between a Labrador and a cattle dog, died recently at age 32 in Sydney, Australia. Thirty-two must be close to a record in dog longevity. According to one report, the average life span of dogs is twelve years.

The longevity of individuals within a species is genetically determined. Long-living parents tend to produce offspring that live to a ripe old age. Hybrid vigor is also a factor. Genetic diversity of offspring produced by mating two different but pure lines (breeds or varieties) increases strength and resistance to disease in the resulting organism, and it doesn't matter if the organism is a radish or a dog. Breeding of closely related individuals tends to produce shorter-lived offspring.

Other Factors

Preventive medicine—dental care, parasite control, vaccinations against infectious diseases—and neutering contribute to lengthening our dogs' life span.

Nutrition also plays an important part in health and longevity. Extremely malnourished animals suffer slower wound healing, impaired disease resistance, increased susceptibility to cancer and, thus, early death. But overfeeding to the point of obesity also has a damaging effect on health and longevity. Most damage is due to a reduction of cellular immunity, organ dysfunction, and increased susceptibility to autoimmune diseases.

Moderate caloric restriction, however, has a positive effect upon extending life and retarding disease development. Dr. Roderick Bronson, a scientist at the U.S. Department of Agriculture Human Research Center on Aging, found that laboratory rodents fed 40 percent fewer calories than normal-fed controls lived 29 percent longer and suffered less from cancer and other diseases. This correlates with reports that the longest-lived humans reside in mountainous regions where diets are low in calories and life is hard and strenuous. People in these remote regions are also free from crowding, reducing their exposure to disease-causing viruses.

An active lifestyle and exercise tend to increase an individual's life span. Adequate physical activity is important to maintain muscle tone and lean body mass, to enhance circulation, and to improve waste elimination.

My friend, veterinarian Terry Adkins, tells of old Oscar, his favorite lead dog for the 1,049-mile Iditarod Sled Dog Race. "I've seen Oscar pull eleven dogs to their feet when he, himself, was personally very tired and going only on my command. I've been behind him when he has pulled eleven dogs, a heavy sled and myself over the last ridge in Nome [Alaska]." Old Oscar no longer pulls Terry's sled in the Iditarod. After his retirement, Oscar spent his last days racing over Terry's Montana big sky country home. He died accidentally at age fifteen, when he fell into the water tank and drowned.

Oscar acted young until his death, and his active life as a sled dog may have contributed to his health and longevity. Researchers found that rats receiving ten minutes of exercise each day on a motorized exercise wheel lived 32 percent longer than nonexercised controls. Exercised rats were calmer and more exploratory than those who did not exercise.

A stimulated rat is apparently a happy and smart one, for rodents given a stimulating environment show an actual increase in the size of the brain's cerebral cortex. This correlates with my observations of Bear, who seems to have "come alive" when we moved to the mountains. Perhaps Chilla, the long-lived Australian dog, lasted as long as he did because he had the important job of caretaking sheep. An interest in life does wonders for the psychological health of all of us, human and animal, and it is my belief that state of mind controls much of what is thought of as state of body.

OLD DOGS AND NEW TRICKS

K. Warner Schaie, director of the Gerontology Center at Pennsylvania State University, suggests in a *Reader's Digest* article that the factors most associated with strong mental function in older humans include an above-average level of education, a complex and stimulating lifestyle, and being married to a smart person. Benjamin Franklin said, "There are three faithful friends—an old wife, an old dog, and ready money." It seems to me that if you are fortunate enough to be married to a wise older spouse and own an elderly dog with his own trust fund, you are doubly blessed.

Dr. Schaie mentioned that stimulating lifestyles tend to improve mental ability in the elderly. This applies also to animals. When old rats were put into cages with new toys, their brain cells responded to the new stimuli by sprouting fresh connections. When the novelty wore off, the rats became bored and the effect was diminished. Other experiments showed that "watching" doesn't count—rats who passively observed other rats playing didn't improve their mental ability. Makes me think that watching TV isn't making me or my house rats any smarter.

The longer an animal lives, the more meaningful the learning process is. A dog who learns tricks or obedience commands is going to benefit from that learning more than a shorter-lived but well-trained hamster. And that learning contributes to the dog's living longer under the survival of the fittest principle.

The wise old woman or man is not a myth; neither is the wise old dog. If learning continues throughout life, and I believe it does, an older individual accumulates a wealth of knowledge that could be passed on to younger generations.

Research on elk behavior showed that groups of elk containing old animals survive better during periods of severe weather conditions than herds without older animals. The scientists proposed two explanations for the phenomenon: older animals survive only in well-fed herds, thus these herds are in the best condition; and older females remember the procedures followed during the previous drought or storm, thus enabling the rest of the herd to follow their direction in finding shelter and food.

Elizabeth Marshall Thomas, who observed the behavior of her own dogs as research for her book, *The Hidden Life of Dogs*, talks about older dogs teaching the younger ones: "I made no effort to train them, even for housebreaking or coming when called. I didn't need to. The young dogs copied the old dogs, which in their case resulted in perfect housebreaking, and all the dogs naturally came when called most of the time. . . ."

Wisdom, defined as good judgment based on knowledge, is accumulated over a lifetime of learning. It is not the same thing as mental acuity. An older dog is going to learn new tricks slower and forget details more readily than a younger one. His reflexes and his sense of spatial relationships wane, making it harder for him to maneuver obstacle courses or to find his way in unfamiliar surroundings. But this very learning of new tricks, visiting unfamiliar surroundings and maneuvering obstacle courses, is going to keep his brain agile, just as exercise keeps his body limber. The key is to make the new learning and environment stimulating and fun rather than stressful and anxiety provoking.

The Aging Body

Our physical shell—the body—changes with age. We look and move differently at seventy than we do at twenty; it is easy to distinguish an eight-month-old puppy from an eight-year-old dog.

In humans and dogs there is a progressive waning of the senses, slowing of movement, shortening of stride, and decrease in muscle tone (the sagging syndrome). When Bear and I go for a walk, he may accidentally scare up a rabbit, or once a porcupine, but he either fails to see the critter until it's gone or is too slow to catch it (even the slow-moving porcupine got away).

The percent of body weight represented by fat increases while metabolic rate decreases with age. Cholesterol levels tend to increase while sexual and thyroid hormones tend to decrease. The ability to withstand stress and immunological competence decreases, making the aged individual more susceptible to disease. See Table 13.2 for the dog's body changes associated with aging.

Geriatric Care

Feeding

Healthy older dogs should be fed diets based on their individual needs, which are related to body weight, condition, and physical activity.

Owing to changes in metabolic rate and reduced activity, many older animals become obese; these dogs should be fed less or fed diets containing fewer calories. Other individuals who suffer reduced appetite or intake should be fed highly digestible diets in amounts that will allow them to maintain optimum weight. Feed the reluctant eater several small meals; if decreased saliva production causes the

Table 13.2

Body Changes in Dogs Associated with Aging

Body	Change
Senses	Hearing—earwax production decreased; eardrum becomes hardened and less elastic; loss of hearing in higher frequencies occurs. Sight—tear production decreases; the lens thickens and becomes cloudy; visual acuity decreases; cataracts and glaucoma more common. Taste—taste buds are lost and taste sensitivity decreases; takes more food to satisfy because taste perception is diminished; saliva production declines, producing dry mouth. Smell—diminished.
Skin and hair	Loss of elasticity of skin; skin becomes thickened; hair becomes thin and brittle; sebaceous glands located around face, flank, and tail decrease production of waxy secretions, leading to dryness of hair coat; nails become more brittle and footpads become thicker.
Bones, joints and muscles	Bones become thinner and brittle, increasing susceptibility to fractures; cartilage hardens, elasticity decreases, and joint stiffness increases; loss of muscle mass and tone; arthritis increasingly common; muscle tremors in some individuals.
Blood	Bone marrow, which produces components of blood, does not respond to the stress of blood loss or infection as rapidly as in young dogs.

(cont.)

Table 13.2

Body Changes in Dogs Associated with Aging (cont.)

BODY	CHANGE
Immunity	Immunity decreases, leading to increased susceptibility to disease and cancer.
Respiration	Vital lung capacity and efficiency decreases; the ability to clear mucus declines; susceptibility to respiratory diseases increases.
Heart	Decreased cardiac output and thickening of heart valves may lead to congestive heart failure.
Urination	Ability of kidneys to filter decreases, leading to increased drinking and urination and possible incontinence; chemicals such as drugs may not be excreted effectively; reduced dosage of certain medication is indicated.
Reproduction	Irregular heat cycles, decreased conception rates and increased fetal mortality; increased incidence of tumors of reproductive tract in both males and females.
Digestion	Decreased liver function, intestinal absorption, and colon motility; increase in constipation and gas.
Oral cavity	Inflammation and infection of gums and teeth, leading to bad breath and loss of teeth; increased incidence of oral ulcers.
Other	Decreased sensitivity to thirst may lead to dehydration; cold and/or heat intolerance; decrease in amount or depth of sleep increases restlessness and irritability; decrease in activity and metabolism, leading to reduction in caloric needs and obesity.

dog to suffer from dry mouth, add water to a dry food or feed a canned diet. Soft food is also indicated for the dog with missing or diseased teeth.

Aging of internal organs accompanies aging in general, and some older dogs suffer from kidney, liver, and heart insufficiency. By middle age—seven years for most dogs—routine (every six months) laboratory tests and physical examinations are indicated to monitor organ function. Organ insufficiency detected early can be treated with medication and prescription diets.

Dr. Veronique Legrand-Defretin, in "Feeding Dogs for Life," *Waltham Focus*, says "protein requirements in elderly dogs can be considered from two aspects. On one hand, older dogs may have a higher protein requirement than younger adult dogs, whereas on the other, high levels of protein increase stress on renal function." The debate about protein levels in geriatric diets has been going on for a long time; your pet's veterinarian, who is familiar with his individual history and organ function (particularly kidney function), is best qualified to make recommendations.

Supplementation of the older dog's diet with vitamins, minerals, or fatty acids is not recommended unless prescribed by your pet's veterinarian.

Exercise

I've mentioned that exercise benefits both longevity and mental alertness. The idea bears repeating in regard to caring for the aged pet. Dr. Jacob E. Mosier, professor emeritus at Kansas State University, stresses the bodily benefits of exercise for the aging dog: "Exercise acts to appease the appetite, increase muscle tone, improve circulation and glucose tolerance, decrease retention of dietary fat and enhance elimination."

Grooming

Grooming, including hair, teeth, and nail care, is especially important for the older dog. The aged dog should be brushed often—daily in the case of long-haired dogs. If fecal matter soils hair around the tail, trim the hair with scissors and wash the area gently with soap and water. Hair obliterating the external ear canal can be gently pulled or cut, while hair under the eyes soiled with ocular secretions should be trimmed and washed. Commercial preparations to remove staining under the eyes in light-colored dogs is available at pet stores and veterinary clinics. The nails should be cut every couple of weeks to prevent splitting and breaking. Dry and hard footpads can be massaged with cocoa butter.

Teeth care includes regular checkups and cleaning by your pet's veterinarian and brushing at home. In addition to improving the dog's quality of life, proper dental care can extend an animal's life span up to 20 percent, according to some experts.

The experts didn't know Bingo. A less than handsome terrier with scanty hair, skinny legs, and terrible breath, Bingo was twenty-one and a regular boarder at the veterinary hospital where I worked two days a week.

Bingo's owners usually spent a half-hour telling him goodbye, while instructing me about Bingo's habits, food, and medication. I knew all of those things after the first trip, but stood by for each admonishment, loaded with Bingo's favorite blanket, chew bone (Bingo had only six teeth), prescription diet, and heart pills.

One day I decided to clean Bingo's teeth; he had seven at that time and breath so bad everyone at the hospital avoided him. With an assistant holding his upper jaw, I inserted the dental scraper against a premolar to chip off the tartar. To my horror, the loose, decayed tooth fell out. I cleaned the remaining six teeth, and felt very pleased, because I had removed a constant source of infection from Bingo's mouth.

Bingo's owners were, however, irate that I had relieved him of one of his chewing appendages. From that day hence, I avoided any unsolicited maintenance on Bingo, and lived in fear that Bingo would die while I was attending doctor at the veterinary hospital. When I left that hospital to start my own practice, Bingo was still going strong at the ripe old age of twenty-three.

Hormones and Steroids

Hormones are not an elixir of youth for any of us, but may be indicated for certain older individuals. Spayed females suffering from bladder incontinence are often helped by the administration of estrogen. Overly lethargic dogs may be stimulated to activity with testosterone-estrogen combination therapy. Older dogs suffering from hypothyroidism are aided by thyroid hormone replacement.

Aging

Anabolic steroids are a class of drugs receiving bad press because of their abuse by young athletes. These drugs can rejuvenate some older dogs by increasing general metabolic activity, appetite, and feelings of well-being.

Accommodating the Older Dog

When we moved to the mountains, Bear abandoned his familiar doghouse, complete with heating lamp and blankets, for the wood pile. I think he likes the container of stacked wood because it is elevated, and he can see into the house and over the porch rail to survey his territory.

One day Bear peered into the kitchen window and barked. "What's he trying to tell us?" I asked George.

"Oh, he wants us to come out and lift him off the wood pile," my husband replied.

Bear was having an increasingly difficult time jumping up on and down from the woodpile, and he tried to train us to lift him on or off. Neither my husband nor I want to be at the beck and call of our dog, so we didn't rush out and lift him down from the wood pile. After all, his doghouse is available two feet away.

What we did was make a rather crude ramp to the top of the wood pile, and we bought Bear a dog basket with a fluffy pad, which we placed next to the wood pile. He now spends his loafing and sleeping time divided between the bed and the roost on top of the wood. I suppose that as he gets older, he'll favor the bed, but I've given up on the doghouse.

Sometimes, the little things make life easier—things such as ramps, runners on the stairs or furniture shifts to make navigation easier for the arthritic patient; carts for those with rear-limb paralysis; more trips outside for the elderly dog; the bed in a more accessible (for him) place; a cold-air humidifier for house dogs who sleep under a drying furnace and a heated blanket; a hot water bottle or knit sweater for dogs sensitive to cold. Suggestions for blind and deaf dogs are addressed in chapter 6.

Aged animals are especially affected by the physical and mental ravages of stress. Providing a refuge for the dog disturbed by noise and visits from the grandkids, or having a trusted friend or dog sitter care for your old dog in his own environment while you are on vacation, may be helpful.

Behavioral Problems Associated with Aging

Older dogs experience the same behavioral problems as do younger ones. A behavior such as excessive barking or aggressiveness may become worse as the pet ages. Also, the physical stresses associated with aging—arthritis, for example—exacerbate an existing behavioral problem. When I don't feel well, I am more aggressive and cranky with family members. It's the same with dogs.

As the senses of sight and hearing diminish, the dog's ability to assess his environment decreases. The cliché "let sleeping dogs lie" comes from the fact that dogs startled when resting often react with sudden aggressiveness. It is easier to startle an older animal while he is sleeping or eating if his senses fail to alert him that you are approaching.

Behavioral problems also sometimes appear for the first time after the pet is old. Dr. Wayne Hunthausen, a small animal behavioral specialist, reports that he sees in his practice a higher number of panic-induced behaviors—thunderstorm phobias and separation anxiety—in older dogs than in younger ones.

At the University of Pennsylvania's Animal Behavior Clinic, the five most frequent complaints about geriatric dogs are as follows: destruction (38 percent), housesoiling (38 percent), excessive vocalization (27 percent), fear of noises (8 percent), and aggression toward people (8 percent). As discussed in chapter 11, separation anxiety might manifest as one or more of the above behavioral symptoms.

The treatment of behavioral cases in old dogs is the same as for younger ones, and includes methods discussed in chapter 10: behavior modification, drugs, neutering, environmental changes, and obedience training. Diagnosis and treatment of underlying physical problems causing or contributing to misbehavior are especially important in the geriatric patient, because elderly patients are more likely to have one or more physical ailments.

Neurological Conditions in Aged Dogs

Senile Dementia

The clinical signs of senile dementia include failure to recognize familiar places or people, confusion, excessive barking or howling, abnormal wake-sleep cycles, obsessive-compulsive behaviors such as pacing or circling, and apathy. The symptoms are very similar to people with Alzheimer's disease.

Although the direct cause of mental deterioration in these patients may be unknown, physical conditions such as hypothyroidism, chronic epilepsy, encephalitis, and tumors may mimic or aggravate the symptoms.

Several drugs that help alleviate signs of senile dementia are under study. Present recommendations, however, include those covered earlier in this chapter: providing mental and physical stimulation, exercise, health and nursing care, and geriatric accommodations.

Tremor

A tremor is a regular, rhythmic, oscillating movement, usually evidenced by alternating contraction and relaxation of certain muscle groups. A tremor syndrome of the hind legs that may progress to the front legs is found in certain geriatric terrier breeds. The tremors become worse during stressful or panic-inducing situations. Treatment is aimed at reducing stress; anticonvulsant drugs are helpful in some cases.

Old-Dog Degenerative Myelopathy

Animals with this disease show a slowly progressing weakness and unsteadiness of the hind limbs. The condition is seen primarily in large breeds of dogs who are middle-aged or older. The clinical signs result from a degeneration of the spinal-cord white matter, but the cause of the spinal-cord deterioration is unknown. Although physical therapy and exercise are helpful early in the disease, dogs with progressive symptoms usually become totally incapacitated.

Brain and Spinal Cancer

Cancer is primarily a disease of older dogs. Over a lifetime, inflammatory events cause increased cell division and mutation. Tumors occur when the body fails to mount an immunological response sufficient to eliminate mutated cancer cells. Because the immune response to these cancer cells peaks at puberty and gradually decreases with age, most tumors occur in geriatric patients.

The incidence of various cancers varies with breed, leading one to surmise that there is also a genetic predisposition to certain types of cancer. For instance, the Boston terrier is cited as a breed with a high incidence of brain tumors.

The clinical signs associated with brain tumors depend upon the location and cancer type. For example, tumors affecting the cerebral hemispheres typically cause behavioral or personality changes and seizures. Brain-stem tumors cause altered states of consciousness, such as depression and coma, while tumors affecting the cerebellum cause head tilts, circling, and tremors. Muscle weakness progressing to paralysis is a sign association with cancers affecting the spinal cord.

These tumors are difficult both to diagnose and to treat. Veterinarians use the same diagnostic tools as physicians: analysis of cerebrospinal fluid, EEG, CAT scans, and MRI. Few private practitioners offer CAT scans or MRI, as the cost of this equipment is astronomical. For this reason, patients suspected of suffering from brain or spinal tumors are often referred to specialists.

Veterinary oncologists (cancer doctors) are becoming more common, and treatment is aimed at prolonging the quality of life for canine cancer patients. Therapy is the same as for people—surgery, radiation, and/or chemotherapy.

QUESTION

Dear Dr. Whiteley,

My two dogs, Lavern and Shirley, have always been great buddies, but recently Lavern, who is four years younger and ten pounds lighter than Shirley, has been picking fights with and refusing to let her older sister eat. Both dogs are spayed dachshunds.

I feel sorry for poor Shirley, who is now twelve and can hardly get around because of several episodes of back trouble. What can I do to prevent Lavern from picking on her?

Fair-minded in Jones County

Aging

Dear Fair-minded,

I am guessing that until recently Shirley was top dog owing to being larger and older. Now, however, she is old, overweight, and partially crippled. Lavern is making her bid to become the dominant dog.

Aggressive behavior on the part of Lavern most probably occurs during competitive and social encounters—soliciting petting from family members, and guarding territory, food, and possessions. If the threat of injury is great, you must protect Shirley by separating the dogs when you are not available to supervise or by muzzling or using a Promise collar on Lavern.

I encourage you to acknowledge Lavern's status as top dog by petting and feeding her first, for example. The alternative is to reaffirm the family's dominant role over both dogs.

Obedience commands are taught to or reinforced for Lavern and Shirley. Next, you institute the "no free lunch" rule for both dogs. This means that the dogs must respond to your commands before eating, sleeping, playing, or receiving attention. They are never allowed to jump up on or hover over you or other family members who are now the "top dogs" in the family. When either dog approaches family members, a guest, a doorway, or the food bowls, she should be commanded to "stay" until you release her. Vary the order in which each dog is spoken to and released from commands.

Good luck on ruling your house as top dog.

H. E. W.

14
Preparing for the Inevitable

Death is inevitable for all of us; however, because the life span of dogs is much shorter than ours, most of us will outlive our canine companions.

GRIEF

Many years ago Mrs. Griffith, a frail middle-aged woman, brought a young squirrel monkey named Toby to the veterinary hospital for me to examine and treat. Toby had a nonresponsive respiratory infection, and despite all of my efforts and medicine, his condition deteriorated with each passing day and week.

Toby was cold, limp, and barely breathing and Mrs. Griffith was hysterical when they entered the hospital for what would be their last visit. I placed the small monkey in an incubator and watched hopelessly while he closed his thin eyelids and took his last shallow breath.

Mrs. Griffith expressed more grief—crying, screaming, and pulling her hair—over Toby's death than I had ever encountered at the time, and would have collapsed had I not been there to lend physical support. I remember how helpless I felt, and how relieved I was when Mrs. Griffith was finally able to go home. Later, I learned about the void that the small monkey had filled in Mrs. Griffith's life of loss and loneliness. Maybe now, brought to my knees at times by my own losses and sorrows, I could offer her an understanding word or touch.

Coping with Loss

Of fifty-four telephone calls to the pet-loss support hot line at the University of California at Davis in 1987, severe grief was most often associated with the loss of a dog or cat, and occasionally other animals such as horses, birds, and rodents. Of the callers, 22 percent were in such despair and depression as to allude to feelings of hopelessness and to suicidal thoughts.

The degree of bonding between us and our dog is the primary factor in how we view and experience the loss or death of a canine companion. If you view your dog as a child or as the remaining tie to a beloved human, the bond is strong and the loss great. Toby was Mrs.

Griffith's surrogate offspring. In my book about cat behavior is the story of a man who had bonded with his son's cat after the young man's death in Vietnam. When the cat died, the father experienced the worst grief of his life, for he grieved not only for the cat but also for the last living tie to his son. It was a final letting go.

As a testament to the bond between people and their pets, Hallmark Cards recently test-marketed a line of cards called Pet Love Greetings. Sentiments expressed by the 200-card line include happy pet birthdays, "sorry you got fixed" cards, and sympathy cards for friends who have lost a pet.

Other factors impacting our ability to cope with the loss of a pet include our view of death and life after death for ourselves and animals, our relationships with other pets and people, and the degree of stress that we are experiencing now or in the recent past.

view of death

The study of life after death is fascinating to me. In the article "Do Animals Survive Death?" by Scott Smith that appeared in *Veterinary Forum*, near-death experiences (NDEs) are discussed:

> Betty Preston slipped into a coma for several days after heart surgery at a Seattle hospital. She related that "suddenly I was floating through a tunnel with other people and animals. I knew that we were all dying."
>
> A young boy with little understanding of what it all meant, claimed that when he left his body during an NDE he was met by his deceased pets.

How we view death is crucial to letting go of the deceased. If death is the end of all existence, dying brings with it a finality that is hard to bear. If we believe those who report NDEs, we are comforted by the thought that we will be reunited with our loved ones, including pets.

relationships with others

A study of bereavement counseling for grieving pet owners at the University of Pennsylvania shows that clients who have the most difficulty recovering after the loss of a pet are those who have lost an only pet with which they have spent over seven years and those who live alone or with a spouse only. People who have multiple pets or live with an extended or nuclear family including children seem to bounce back sooner after the death of a pet. Thus, significant others serve as an in-house support group, and carrying on for the sake of remaining pets and/or children may help direct our focus away from the loss.

life stress

The ability to cope with the death of a pet is related to last-straw syndrome. If past losses such as the death of a loved one, loss of a job, or children leaving home have not been resolved, the fresh loss is like pouring alcohol into an open sore.

Any loss from the smallest, such as the loss of an article of clothing, to the largest, such as those here, must be grieved. Losses accumulate, and if not processed and accepted, lead to depression.

Acknowledging impending loss is often as painful as processing the loss itself. Many people with aging or terminally ill pets start the grieving process prior to death.

Stages of Grief

Dr. Elisabeth Kübler-Ross was the first physician to study the dying process and to develop a guideline for the stages that people go through in coming to terms with death, the ultimate loss. Kübler-Ross coined the stages of grief: denial, anger, bargaining, depression, and acceptance.

Although the stages are set down in a stepwise fashion, one's grief is personal and individual in nature. The grieving process may last only minutes for small losses or forever for life-shattering ones. You may think you have finished the whole process with the sentiment, "Thank God, I managed to get through that," only to find the old grief surfacing again and again until it is truly over and completed. You may bypass a stage and return to it later, or may vacillate between various stages.

Denying, feeling angry, blaming, regretting, bargaining, feeling guilty, being depressed, and accepting are all part of the grieving process. When we feel these emotions, we are not the only ones who

Preparing for the Inevitable

have ever felt this way after a loss, and it may be helpful to accept ourselves and our common human reactions. Grieving is a normal part of living, and physical or mental illness may be the penalty for unresolved grief.

For example, denied anger will express itself in other ways, such as yelling at family members or coworkers, or as bodily ailments—headaches, digestive tract upset, and high blood pressure. Sleeping and eating problems and an inability to concentrate are physical symptoms associated with the depressive stage of grief.

During my divorce, which was a major loss, I stopped eating and sleeping. My attention span dropped to practically zero; I would be talking with someone and forget completely what we were discussing. It took a couple of years, but as soon as I resolved my grief and came to terms with the loss of my first marriage, I started eating and sleeping again. Alas, the only time I have been thin was when I was grieving.

Support

People are finally becoming sensitive to the feelings of those who have lost a beloved pet. Rarely today does someone carelessly say, "Oh, you'll get over it. After all, it was only a dog." Who among us has not suffered the intense pain of losing a cherished animal companion?

When my sister-in-law lost Abby, a schnauzer who suffered a fatal respiratory disease, she took the day off from work to grieve. Her coworkers and friends sent flowers and cards.

If you are in the unfortunate position of living with others who refuse to acknowledge or who ridicule your feelings of grief, you must be kind, gentle, and understanding with yourself. Seek out those friends who will allow you to vent your true feelings, without judging. It may be worthwhile to talk with someone from a pet-loss hot line, support group, or individual counselor. See Table 14.1 for pet-loss resources.

EUTHANASIA

Selecting euthanasia is, in my way of thinking, one of the kindest decisions a pet caretaker can make if his pet is experiencing minimal

Table 14.1

Pet-Loss Resources

1. Pet Grief Support Service Hot Line of Phoenix, Arizona: 24-hour hot line staffed by trained volunteers and weekly support group for bereaved pet owners; 602-995-5885.

2. Grief counseling by University of California at Davis: Staffed weekdays by veterinary student volunteers from 6:30 to 9:30 P.M. PST (you must call in; volunteers cannot return long-distance calls); 916-752-4200.

3. The Animal Medical Center of New York: On-staff social workers for counseling 11 A.M. to 7 P.M. EST Tuesday through Saturday, and a pet-loss support group meeting every other Saturday; 212-838-8100.

4. The Delta Society: This organization devoted to studying the human-animal bond offers resource material and a listing by state of organizations and individuals offering pet-loss hot lines, support groups, and counseling dealing with pet loss; 206-226-7357.

5. Most colleges of veterinary medicine provide grief counseling for owners of ill and dying pets.

---

quality of life, requires extensive life support that the owner cannot offer, or is a danger to others. The option of euthanasia can be abused, of course, but I have found that owners often wait too long rather than act too quickly to elect euthanasia.

Deciding the "if and when" is a personal decision. Ellen Goodman, columnist for the *Washington Post*, had many questions concerning making a decision about terminating the life of her dog, Sam. In the end, however, Goodman's dog spared her from making the euthanasia decision by beginning the dying process at home. One day she fell down and couldn't get up, and the choice was clear.

Preparing for the Inevitable

Euthanasia should be a choice made jointly by all members of the dog caretaking group. Your veterinarian may be able to guide you by offering a prognosis (a prediction of the future course of illness or behavioral problem). All options should be considered. Guilt about a euthanasia decision—for or against—serves no useful purpose, and talking the decision over with personal and professional support groups helps us let go of guilt.

Once the decision for euthanasia is made, the time and place can be selected, the grieving process begun, and plans for burial, cremation, or other means of honoring the pet put into action. The veterinarian will ask you to sign a form that gives legal permission for him or her to perform euthanasia. It states that the animal has not bitten anyone within the last fourteen days (otherwise, he should be quarantined for rabies before euthanasia).

The current method used by veterinarians is an injection into the pet's vein of a concentrated drug used for anesthesia. The animal literally goes from sleep to death. I like to administer a tranquilizer before the IV to relieve any anxiety that may be associated with the injection itself. Occasionally, a dying animal will gasp, vocalize, eliminate, or twitch. This is the body's natural response; it does not mean that the animal is experiencing pain.

Most veterinarians will permit you to be present at the time of euthanasia. This, again, is an individual choice for both you and the veterinarian. An alternative might be spending a few private minutes with your pet prior to and/or after the procedure to say goodbye. The latter may be the best choice for children, who might misunderstand or be upset by the procedure. Explaining that the veterinarian is helping Rover to die is more accurate and less confusing than "putting to sleep," which might be associated with actual sleep or anesthesia.

If your veterinarian offers home service, euthanasia can be performed in the dog's home environment. If this option is elected, make sure that other pets are not in the immediate area; animals are sensitive to the intense feelings and to the dying act.

Your veterinarian can take care of the dog's body, or you may make your own arrangements. This should be decided before making the appointment. It may be a good idea to ask a friend to be with you to drive you home or offer other support. And yes, it is okay to cry.

Making Arrangements

People from many cultures have derived comfort from the burial or cremation ceremony. The oldest remains of domestic dogs are from burial sites, one of the most ancient being the 12,000-year-old human owner and puppy found in Israel.

Mummification is an ancient rite that is reemerging today (see the following section on mummification), whereas freeze-drying is a relatively new procedure for preserving bodies. More people use taxidermy to prove that they caught "the big one" than to preserve Rover, but this too is an option for those who like to have their deceased pet nearby.

Burial or Cremation

The animal control facility in Amarillo, Texas (my former home), offers private cremations at what I consider a modest fee. By informing clients who faced the loss of a pet about this service and, on occasion, providing further assistance by making the appointment with animal control, suggesting a proper receptacle for the ashes, and delivering the body to and from animal control, I may have extended my job as a house call veterinarian to that of funeral director. These services were, however, worthwhile and highly appreciated by most bereaved pet owners.

Other clients, however, preferred for me to take care of the body. I paid a fee, which I passed on to the client to have the remains cremated in mass with other bodies at the same animal control facility. I add this detail so that you will know that you have the right to ask your veterinarian about his specific policy concerning the deceased pet's body. If those plans are unacceptable, you can make your own.

If you opt to bury your dog in his own yard, you might want to check local laws governing this practice. In general, seal the body in an airtight container, such as a heavy plastic bag or animal casket. Bury the remains at a depth of at least three feet. Make sure that the burial site is located distant to water sources, such as streams or water pipelines. Caskets can be hand made or bought from several sources. Ask your veterinarian, pet store owner, or animal control staff for sources of burial containers.

Preparing for the Inevitable

According to the International Association of Pet Cemeteries (IAPC), a not-for-profit organization devoted to the advancement and ethical operation of pet cemeteries, approximately 600 pet cemeteries are located across the United States. The oldest operating pet cemetery is the Hartsdale Pet Cemetery in New York, established in 1896. New York is, by the way, one of a handful of states with laws regulating pet cemeteries and crematories. To locate pet cemeteries, ask your veterinarian, consult your yellow pages, or write IAPC at 13 Cemetery Lane, Ellenburg Depot, New York 12935 or call at 518-594-3000 for a list of guidelines and location of member cemeteries.

Pet cemeteries perform the duties of both a funeral home and a cemetery. You can pick a variety of caskets, vaults, plots, urns, and markers. Services include private and communal burial or cremations; the body may or may not be embalmed.

With a private burial, the pet is separately prepared and buried in a lot with an individual marker. With mausoleum burial, the casketed body is placed in a crypt. Cremated remains, called cremains, can be interred in a recessed compartment called a niche, or can be stored in an urn at home or scattered in a place favored by the pet. A columbarium is an arrangement of niches for storing cremains.

Not all pet cemeteries offer every amenity nor are all pet cemeteries created equal. I encourage you to thoroughly check each facility you are considering. A pet cemetery should be deeded so that pet owners will know that their pets' remains will not be disturbed by land development or the cemetery closing. The cemetery should maintain a care fund like human cemeteries to ensure that funds are available for continuing maintenance of the ground and roads. The land on which the cemetery is located should be owned by the proprietors rather than be rented or leased property.

Costs for burial or cremation services vary from a couple hundred dollars to several thousand dollars for elaborate trappings, such as marble engraved stone and a mahogany casket.

Freeze-Drying, Mummification, and Taxidermy

In my files are articles featuring companies offering freeze-drying for pets; when I called, however, the businesses had ceased operating. Freeze-drying services do exist; it may take some detective work on your part to find one.

This is how it works: You must wrap the pet's body in plastic, and keep it frozen after death; after receiving the body, the freeze-drying company will defrost, clean, and position the body (sitting, lying, or standing); the body is then refrozen and placed in a vacuum chamber where the temperature reaches minus 4 degrees centigrade (this process gradually removes moisture).

The freeze-drying procedure takes around six months, and the pet is preserved in a lifelike condition. Some people display their pet in his favorite resting spot; others store the body so that it can be buried with them when they die. Costs range from $500 for a small dog to around $2,000 for a giant breed.

Mummification is a different process. The remains are wrapped in plastic and stored in a cooler with ice packs (do not freeze, as this will damage cells) until shipped to the company; the remains will then be embalmed, soaked in a secret solution for one to two months, wrapped in linens and bathed with herbs, oils, and resins to make the skin supple, and then encased in a mummiform. The mummiform comes in a standard bronze variety or can be custom-made in gold and embedded with diamonds or whatever else you might want. The mummification process takes at least two months.

Photographs of mummified pets prepared by Summum, the only company of which I am aware that offers this service, show an animal who looks like a statue or sculpture. The difference is, of course, that the pet is inside; radiographs show the bones intact and in correct position; fur and skin are supposedly soft and supple ("pristine" is how a company representative described the body). By the way, the first mummy produced by Summum was the founder's doberman, Butch.

Summum is a nonprofit organization offering mummification of both animals and people. Because mummification is a religious rite, preparing the body (in this case, human) may be a tax-deductible item. I doubt, however, that you will be able to convince the IRS that Rover is a practicing member of a religion that encourages mummification.

For animal mummification, Summum prefers to work through veterinarians to ensure that the animal was treated humanely prior to death and that the body is optimally prepared for shipment. Because dogs vary in size, the metal encasing must be custom-made by an artist. The cost begins at $14,000. For more information, contact Summum at 707 Genesee Avenue, Salt Lake City, Utah 84104; telephone 801-355-0137.

Taxidermy differs from mummification and freeze-drying in that only the shell of the animal is preserved. The skin is tanned and formed around a mannequin; the eyes are glass. Taxidermy requires at least six months, and costs vary with the size of the animal and the business performing the service.

I spoke with one taxidermist who said that he refused to work with pets. In his experience, pet owners in the throes of grief over an animal's death are anxious to preserve that animal; however, after the six- to eight-month period that the taxidermy process requires, many have changed their minds.

Funeral Services

Funeral services are for the survivors. It is a gathering to honor a long-lost buddy, which allows those honoring a chance to remember, to express their gratitude, and to celebrate the life of the deceased.

Sinbad, a mongrel who served on the Coast Guard cutter *Campbell* during World War II, was honored at the site of his grave in Barnegat Light, New Jersey, in 1986. Sinbad was a favorite because he was a dog with whom the sailors identified—he was a common dog who worked hard protecting the country from German U-boats and played hard with his comrades during shore leave.

A news article about the event described the moment:

> Sailors from almost a dozen states gathered around their comrade's seaside grave to honor him with taps and a headstone, placed atop the Coast Guard's "most famous dog" 38 years after his death.
>
> A nine-man color guard stood with flags dipped as a rifle squad sounded a salute while King Reynolds, a *Campbell* veteran from Tallahassee, Fla., raised the flag over Sinbad's grave.
>
> As taps filled the sea air, the men of the *Campbell* bowed their heads and cried.

The article explained that Sinbad had been smuggled aboard the *Campbell* and then adopted by the entire crew. "Sinbad made Chief Dog, the highest rank the animal could attain in the Coast Guard, and the crew partied till dawn. But a few drunken binges had him busted back to Dog First-Class."

Sinbad served aboard the *Campbell* from 1937 until he was retired in 1948 to a Coast Guard station along the New Jersey shore, where he died at age fifteen.

Funeral services can be elaborate, like the one for Sinbad, or simple, like one in which a picture or photograph of the pet is affixed to the grave site and a poem and/or prayer read at the interment.

Memorials

Memorials are another way of honoring and sharing. Some people write poems, stories, or books about beloved dogs. Others volunteer at a humane shelter or pet-visitation program for schools or nursing homes; they fund a scholarship or wing of a veterinary hospital; they donate to favorite animal-related charities; or they plant a tree in memory of a beloved pet.

At least one newspaper—*The West Chester County Daily Local News* of West Chester, Pennsylvania—publishes a pet obituary column, called "Pause to Remember." A pet memorial, sponsored by the Massillon Public Library of Massillon, Ohio, encourages owners to place a book matched in subject matter and type of pet in the library in memory of deceased pets. A donation of $25 allows the library to purchase the book and affix a bookplate denoting the owner's name and the pet's name inside the front cover.

SURVIVING PETS

Animal Grief

In 1858, a Skye terrier named Greyfriars Bobby joined his master's funeral procession and then remained at his grave site in Greyfriars churchyard in Edinburgh until his own death, fourteen years later. By one account, Bobby died lying stretched across his owner's grave; the grave was then opened and Bobby interred alongside his beloved human.

Preparing for the Inevitable

Does a dog grieve when a human member of his family dies or is hospitalized for a lengthy period? What does he feel when a canine sibling of fifteen years goes away to the veterinary hospital and never returns? Although it is hard to assign the emotional stages of grief—denial, anger, bargaining, depression, acceptance—to dogs, they do miss and long for the return of a familiar and loved human or animal companion.

What can you do to help a dog say goodbye? Do as much as you can to eliminate other stress from his life. Accumulated stress acts on dogs just as it does on people: it makes each event more stressful. This is not the time to bring a new puppy into the household, board the dog in strange surroundings, change his food, or leave him at the vet's for teeth cleaning.

If possible, spend time talking to and reassuring the dog. In some cases, providing familiar objects with the deceased's smell or playing ball with the dog just as his missing family member did is helpful. Provide a safe, quiet environment away from the friends and relatives who always gather at this time; offer nutritious food and plenty of fresh water. If a friend who is familiar to the dog asks to help, let him oversee the care of the dog during this stressful time for all household members.

Wills and Codicils

The primary reason to include disposition of pets in your will is to ensure that your wishes are carried out in the event of death or incapacitation. Spelling out your desires for surviving pets helps prevent legal disputes and family squabbles. Because laws vary from state to state, the decision to include pets in wills and codicils should be discussed with a knowledgeable attorney.

Generally, the law considers pets the same as property, like the family car or the living room sofa. But unlike the sofa, the dog can't wait until the will is located, read, and probated before receiving custodial care. A codicil is useful for speeding up the process.

A codicil (sometimes called a letter of instruction) to a will is an amendment; it is used for minor changes or items that are updated frequently. In the case of pets, an update is needed each time an animal is added or lost, or every time the designated guardian is changed. The codicil should inform the executor of the estate of the name, address, and telephone number of the guardian or guardians, plus names, descriptions, and identification (tatoos, microchips) of the pets involved.

Specific details about the care and disposition of pets, such as the name of the veterinarian, location of records (medical, vaccination and registration), how and when to consider finding good homes, or reasons to consider euthanasia can be added here.

Codicils must be witnessed by two or more people and a copy attached to each copy of the will. The codicil should also refer to the date of the current will ("codicil to my will of June 1, 1995," for example).

In some cases the wording should include compensation to be legally binding. It might read: "I bequeath my dog, Bear, to my daughter Sissy Bartlett, for the sum of one dollar. Sissy Bartlett will act as guardian for my dog and will provide for his care as follows. . . ." A copy of the codicil should be left with the person designated as the pet's guardian, so that the guardian can legally provide care as soon as needed.

It is better to err on the side of too many people knowing your intentions for pets than too few; copies of the codicil might be left with neighbors, friends, relatives, and veterinarian so that they will know your wishes in case of sudden death or illness. Animal control and humane society workers tell horror stories about animals being sent to shelters by unknowing or ruthless friends and relatives of deceased or hospitalized pet owners.

In one case, an elderly woman set aside $10,000 for the care of her two dogs. The owner's will designated that if the dogs predeceased her, the money would go to her brother. Before the woman's death, and while she lay critically ill in the hospital, the brother had the two dogs euthanized at the local veterinary hospital. If a codicil with the guardian's name, address, and telephone number—in this case, a humane society offering surviving pet care—had been in the possession of friends and neighbors, this travesty of the pet lover's wishes might have been averted.

Emergency decals for home and cars, and wallet cards that list pets and emergency telephone numbers of temporary or permanent guardians, are recommended. If a surviving-pet program has been designated the guardian, the program will usually supply decals with pertinent information and will pick up pets, meet airplanes, and the like.

Preparing for the Inevitable

Financial arrangements for the care of pets are specified in the will. Monetary provisions for surviving pets vary, depending upon the nature of the owner's estate; a trust fund and a life insurance policy designated for the care of surviving pets are two common methods. Fewer legal hassles emerge if the trust or insurance is bequeathed to a human guardian, rather than to the animals themselves; pets are property and cannot inherit directly. It can be spelled out in the will, however, that the money is for the maintenance of pets; if the guardian fails to provide for pets as stipulated, the executor of the estate can withdraw funds. Money may also be paid directly to each provider, such as veterinarian, groomer, or pet store, by the executor.

One of my favorite patients when I practiced in New Orleans was a five-pound Pomeranian named Pom Pom. Pom's caretaker, a Mr. Smith, stayed at a trailer park located near the clinic where I worked when traveling through town in a small RV about every six weeks.

The clinic visits were routine—bathing and grooming by my assistant, Richard, or vaccinations or dewormings performed by me. One night Mr. Smith called me to meet him at the hospital; Pom had been attacked in the trailer park by a couple of German shepherds. The little dog was in critical shape—his abdomen had been lacerated and intestines were peeking out. After emergency surgery and intensive care, Pom hovered for several days in a twilight zone between life and death.

Mr. Smith called Pom's attorneys in New York so that I might speak with them about the dog's condition. I discovered that Mr. Smith was Pom's guardian rather than owner, and that Pom's expenses and extensive care had to be cleared through the attorneys acting as executors of a trust left for the little dog's care. After a long recovery period, Pom and Mr. Smith left in their RV for other adventures traveling around the southern United States.

The bond between Mr. Smith and Pom was a close and loving one. Although I know none of the details, I like to think that Pom's original owner was a true matchmaker, enriching the life of both man and dog in ways that money helped but could not completely buy.

Matching guardians and pets, and selecting an amount to leave in trust, should be done carefully and with professional advice. An elderly mother living in a small apartment might be a poor choice for guardian of a two-year-old Rottweiler belonging to a twenty-five-year-old son. A surviving pet program located within the state might be just the answer to the question of "Who will care for Rover when I'm gone?"

One thousand dollars seems a tidy sum to many of us, but is rarely enough to provide for the lifetime financial support of several young pets unless they are all white mice. Yet leaving millions and a mansion with a swimming pool to three aging poodles might be excessive. The Association of the Bar of the City of New York offers excellent advice in a pamphlet titled "Providing for Your Pets in the Event of Your Death or Hospitalization." They suggest:

> The owner should leave only a reasonable amount of money for the care of any pet. A large sum of money may prompt relatives to challenge the Will and the court may invalidate the bequest for pet care. The attorney may want to include an "in terrorem" clause in the pet's owner's Will to reduce the challenge to the Will. This clause provides that if a person unsuccessfully challenges a provision in the Will, he or she cannot then receive property under *any* provision of the Will.

Surviving-Pet Programs

Programs or agencies providing care for pets belonging to owners who can no longer care for them offer a wide array of services, arrangements, and accommodations. Shelters that advertise no-kill policies may be overcrowded and understaffed for obvious reasons, whereas others may offer the finest of everything.

A surviving-pet program may accommodate only one species, such as those catering to cats, ferrets, rabbits, and horses, or may attempt to care for every living creature needing care. An organization may offer several different programs.

The Associated Humane Societies of New Jersey provide three options that might be considered surviving-pet programs: Limited Guarantee Adoption Program is a boarding situation—for a set rate per day, the dog or cat is ensured residence as long as there is need or until he is adopted; Lifetime Boarding Program allows the animal to live at the Animal Haven Farm located near Forked River for the rest of his life or until adoption, requiring a one-time donation paid in advance; and the Foster Pet Program allows the animal to live out his life at the Animal Haven Farm, requiring monthly payment with the first year paid in advance.

Preparing for the Inevitable

Programs that offer lifetime care for pets are nonprofit, yet most require yearly donations averaging $1,000 for a cat and $2,200 for a dog. The Pet Life Care Program located at Texas A & M requires a one-time $25,000 bequest for each pet. If you are interested in such a program, please visit and evaluate the services for yourself. Then the specific arrangements can be made legally binding in a will.

Table 14.2 lists surviving-pet programs but is not comprehensive and is subject to change as policies change. Ask humane society and veterinary staff about programs in your area.

QUESTION

Dear Dr. Whiteley,

My old shepherd, Whitney, is in his final weeks or months. Due to hip dysplasia, he is unable to pull himself to his feet any longer, and the veterinarian says that his liver and kidneys are going, too. I am opposed to putting an animal to sleep, and want Whitney to live out his natural life.

I am hoping to find a home hospice for animals in my area, but I can't locate one. If I had help once or twice a day moving Whitney and administering medication such as fluids, life would be easier for both of us.

Do you know of a hospice-type service for animals in my area?

Hopeful in Memphis

Dear Hopeful,

The idea of a hospice for animals is a good one—it is less stressful in many cases for the pet with a terminal disease to be cared for in his home. Although I am not aware of a formal hospice program for animals, I suggest that you contact several veterinarians offering house-call or home services about your idea. A veterinary technician working under the direct supervision of an attending veterinarian might be just the medical helper you are seeking.

I, too, am hopeful that your last days with Whitney will be treasured time.

Good luck!

H. E. W.

Table 14.2

Surviving Pet Programs

Animal Haven Farm
1 Humane Way
P.O. Box 43
Forked River, New Jersey 08731

Assisi Animal Foundation
P.O. Box 143
Crystal Lake, Illinois 60014

Bosler Humane Society
P.O. Box 520
Barre, Massachusetts 01005

Helen Woodward Animal Center
6461 El Apajo
P.O. Box 64
Rancho Sante Fe, California 92067

Kent Animal Shelter
River Road
Calverton, New York 11933

Last Post
Belden Street
Route 126
Falls Village, Connecticut 06031
203-824-0831

Living Free Animal Sanctuary
P.O. Box 5
Mountain Center, California 92361

North Shore Animal League
750 Port Washington Boulevard
Port Washington, New York 11050

Pets Alive
Middletown, New York 10940
914-386-9738

Pet Life Care Program
% Dr. E. W. Ellett, Director
P.O. Drawer AQ
College Station, Texas 77840
409-845-2351

Pet Pride
P.O. Box 1055
Pacific Palisades, California 90272

Pet Rescue
151 N. Bloomingdale Road
Bloomingdale, Illinois 60108

Sido Program
San Francisco SPCA
2500 16th Street
San Francisco, California 94103

Index

Abortion, 228
Ackerman, Diane, 82, 92, 128, 225
Aesthetics, 100–102
Afghan, 40, 42, 50
African basenji, 6, 69
Aggression, 169–178, 179
Aging. *See* Elderly dog(s)
Air, 128
Allergies, 28, 30, 208–209
Altitude, 128
Ambidextrousness, 119–120
American Kennel Club, 156
American Veterinary Medical Association, 5, 18
Anal sac, 113–114
Ancestral type, 32–33
Anderson, Robert K., 117
Anorexia, 136–138
Antifreeze, 198–199
Antiobsessional drugs, 203–204
Anubis (Egyptian god), 8
Appel, Max J. G., 195–196
Arctic dogs, 141
Art, 101
Artificial insemination, 219–220
Automobiles, 143–144
Avital, Eytan, 225

Baer, Ted, 160
Balance, 86
Barking, 120–124, 165
Barometeric pressure, 128
Barry, Dave, 160
Basset hound, 115, 116

Beaver, Bonnie, 78, 110, 154–155, 171
Beck, Alan, 140
Begging, 139–140
Behavior problems, 168–187
  aggression, 169–178, 179
  aging and, 244
  disease and, 192–201
  emotional disorders, 201–209
  modification of, 170, 173, 174
Binocular vision, 87
Birth control, 226–229
Biting, 115, 178, 180–181, 182–183
Blindness, 88–90
Bloodhound, 42, 82, 92
Body changes, 238, 239–240
Body language, 114–120
Body rhythms, 98–100
Boyd, L. M., 60
Brainstem auditory evoked response, 85
Breed(ing), 6–7, 37, 39, 40, 41, 42–43, 59, 89, 121, 218–219
Bronson, Roderick, 235
Brown, Donna, 7, 14
Budiansky, Stephen, 4
Bullmastiff, 43
Burial, 256–257
Busch, Heather, 101
Butcher, Susan, 121

Cancer, 36, 245–246
Canidae family, 2
Cannibalism, 226

267

Caras, Roger, 93
Castration, 141, 170, 227
Catahoula hog dog, 10–11
Cat(s), 7, 52, 68, 101, 130, 143, 196
Cherry eye, 88
Chewing items, 181, 183–185
Chihuahua, 7, 33, 34, 35, 175
Circannual rhythms, 98
Classical conditioning, 151–152
Clomipramine, 203–204
Cocaine, 199
Cocker spaniel, 43, 169
Codicils, 261–264
Cold weather, 130
Collar, 117–118, 123, 155, 160–161, 173
Collie, 40, 42
Commands, 160–162, 163–164
Communication, 109–125
Companion dogs, 6
Coppinger, Raymond, 120
Coprophagia, 138–139
Coyotes, 120, 194
Crate training, 159
Cremation, 256–257
Crotch sniffing, 113

Dachshund, 43
Dancing doberman disease, 201
Deafness, 84–86
Death of dog, 250–260
  arrangements for, 256–260
  coping with, 250–252
  pet-loss resources, 254
  support for, 253
Death of owner, 260–266
Deeb, Barbara, 234
Degenerative myelopathy, 245
De Kruif, Paul, 193
Dens, 140–141
Dental care, 133–134, 242
Diets, 133, 136
Digging, 185

Disease(s)
  affecting behavior, 192–201
  inherited, 38, 40, 89
  See also specific diseases
Distemper, 194–196
Diversity, 6–7
DNA, 217, 225, 233
Dobermans, 138, 201, 203
Domestication, 2–4
Dominance, 114–120, 169–171, 215
Dorsal tail gland, 114
Drewnowski, Adam, 95
Druyan, Ann, 108–109
Dunbar, Ian, 177

Eating
  of dogs by humans, 11–12
  of grass, 138
Economics, 12–13, 49
Edwards, Edwin, 11
Elderly dog(s), 232–247
Elk, 237
Emotional disorders, 201–209
Energy requirements, 132, 221
English bulldog, 36
English springer spaniel, 169
Epilepsy, 200–201
Escaping, 142
Estrogen, 213, 228
Estrus, 213, 216
Euthanasia, 253–255
Exercise, 135, 162, 236, 241
Expense. *See* Economics
Extinction, 150
Eyes. *See* Vision

Facial expressions, 114–120
Falling, 142–143
Fear, 13–14, 76–77, 171–173
Feces, 111–112, 138–139
Feeding, 131–134
  diets, 133, 136
  food selection, 129–131

nutritional needs, 131–134
of older dogs, 238, 241
problems, 134–140
Feinstein, Mark, 120
Female dog(s), 212–214
Fighting dogs, 175–176
Fleas, 97
Flexor dominance, 67
Foster, Ruth E., 117
Fox, Michael W., 67, 101
Fox terrier, 6, 42, 51
Freeze-drying, 257–258
Fremont, John C., 12
Frustration, 168
Funeral services, 259–260

Gender
dog's, 58–59
human, 20–21
Genetics, 37–39
Genital sniffing, 113
George, Jean Craighead, 110
Geriatric care, 238–243
German shepherd, 35–36, 40, 162
German shorthaired pointer, 42
Glands, 114, 135, 197–198
Goodman, Ellen, 254
Graves, 8
Great Dane, 20, 42
Greyhound, 6
Grief
animal, 260–261
human, 250–253
Grinning, 110
Grooming, 241–242

Habituation learning, 150
Hall, Rich, 139
Hart, Benjamin and Lynette, 69, 116
Hayflick, Leonard, 232–233
Health insurance, 26–27
Health maintenance organizations, 27

Hearing, 82–86
Heat (female), 212–213
Heat (temperature), 97
Herding dogs, 6, 9
Herriot, James, 22
High-rise syndrome, 142–143
Hip dysplasia, 35
Hogs, 10–11
Homing sense, 100
Hormones, 242
Hounds, 82, 83, 115, 116
Houpt, Katherine, 95, 130–131, 136
Housesoiling, 185–186
Housetraining, 157–159
Howling, 121
Human-animal bond, 18–22
Humidity, 128
Hunthausen, Wayne, 244
Hunting dogs, 6, 9
Hyperactivity, 207–208
Hyperkinesis, 207–208
Hyperthyroidism, 198

Illness, 190
Imprinting, 76–77, 151
Inherited disease, 38, 40, 89
Insight learning, 151
Intelligence, 106–109
Invisible Fence, 142, 185
Irish setter, 42

Jablonka, Eva, 225
Junkyard dog, 32–33

Katcher, Aaron, 18
Kennel-dog syndrome, 141
Kilcommons, Brian, 159
Kübler-Ross, Elisabeth, 252

Labor, 222
Labrador retriever, 7, 41, 42, 49, 133, 162
Lactation, 220–221

269

Large dogs, 35–36, 37
Lassie, 58–59, 154
Latent learning, 150–151
Lead, 160–161
Learning, 148–151
Left-pawedness, 119–120
Legrand-Defretin, Veronique, 221, 241
Lemonick, Michael D., 39
Lemon laws, 57
Lhasa apso, 40, 200
Life expectancy, 232–236
Life stress, 252
Lifestyle, 236
Livestock, 150
London, Jack, 7
Lorenz, Konrad, 39
Love, 13–14
Lust, 215
Luttgen, Patricia, 84–85
Lyme disease, 196–197

McManus, Patrick, 157
Male dog(s), 214–216
Marijuana, 199
Mastiff, 6
Masturbation, 216
Mating, 212, 216–218
Memorials, 260
Miller, Dare, 83
Miller, Ron, 59
Misbehavior. *See* Behavior problems
Morning-after shot, 228
Morphogenetic resonance, 106
Mosier, Jacob E., 241
Mummification, 256, 258

Naming, 156–157
Narcolepsy, 99
National Animal Poison Control Center, 199–200
Near-death experience, 251

Negative reinforcement, 154–155, 175
Neurological conditions, 244–246
Neutering, 58, 141, 227–228
Newfoundland, 42
Nutrition, 131–134, 221, 235

Obedience training, 160–162
Obesity, 134–136
Observational learning, 149
Obsessive-compulsive disorder, 201–204
Ocular disease, 89
Ovaban, 229
Overfeeding, 131–132
Ovulation, 213
Ownership
  alternatives to, 50–51
  expenses of, 49–50
  pet matching for, 48, 61
  and role of dog, 48–49
Oxytocin, 225

Pain, 96–97, 190–191
Panic attacks, 204–207
Parenthood, 223, 225–226
Pariah dogs, 32–33
Pasteur, Louis, 13, 192–194
Patterson, Donald, 39
Pavlov's dogs, 151
Paws, 119–120
Pekingese, 6, 43
Percy, Carol, 132
Perianal glands, 114
Personality, 39–45, 59–60
Pesticides, 199
Pet clubs, 26
Phobias, 19–20, 77, 206–207
Pit bull, 44, 176
Placenta, 222–223
Pliny, 8, 13
Poisoning, 198–200
Police dogs, 9

Pomeranian, 34, 112
Poodle, 43, 83
Porter, Jessica, 5
Positive reinforcement, 152–154
Potty area, 158
Predatory aggression, 174–175
Pregnancy, 220–221
Prescription diets, 133, 136
Preventive medicine, 235
Problem solving, 107–108
Proestrus, 212
Progesterone, 229
Promise collar, 117–118, 123, 155, 173
Prostaglandin, 228
Prozac, 170
Pryor, Karen, 152, 153
Pseudopregnancy, 223
Puberty, 212
Punishment, 122, 155–156, 175
Puppies
 development of, 64–77
 imprinting in, 76–77
 as infants, 67–68
 learning by, 148–149
 orphans, 69–72
 recommendations for, 77–80
 socialization of, 72–75, 168

Rabies, 13, 24–26, 180, 192–194
Racial attitudes, 21–22
Racing dogs, 9
Rage syndrome, 176–178
Rapid-eye-movement sleep, 99
Rapoport, Judith L., 203
Rat poison, 199
Receptors, 97
Redirected aggression, 178
Reinforcement, 152–154, 154–155, 175
Reisner, Ilana, 171
Religion, 8–12
Rented premises, 53
Rewards, 152–153

Right-pawedness, 119–120
Riser, Wayne H., 35
Roaming, 141–142
Roommates, 51–53
Rotweiler, 50
Roy, Aaron, 75

Sagan, Carl, 2, 108–109
Saint Bernard, 7, 36, 43, 234
Saluki, 6
Samoyed, 141
Savant, Marilyn Vos, 90
Scent, 93–94, 111–114
Schaie, K. Warner, 236–237
Scott, J. P., 73, 120
Scrotum, 214
Seizures, 200–201
Selection of dog, 53–55, 58
Selling of dogs, 11
Senile dementia, 244–245
Senses, 82–103
 See also specific senses
Separation anxiety, 205–206
Service dogs, 9
Shar-pei, 36
Shelter, 140–145
Short dogs, 36–37
Siberian husky, 43
Silver, Burton, 101
Sled dogs, 129, 133
Sleep, 99–100
Small dogs, 33–35
Smell, 90–94
 See also Scent
Smiling, 110
Smith, Scott, 251
Sniffing, 113
Snorting, 144–145
Socialization, 72–75, 168
Sources of dogs, 55–57
Spaniels, 83, 169, 203
Spaying, 227
Specieism, 101
Staring, 110

Steger, Will, 133
Stern, Robert, 232
Steroids, 243
Stress, 191–192, 252
Submission, 114–120
Sucking, excessive, 138
Surviving pets, 260–266
Swallowing items, 181, 183–185
Swimming, 162–163

Tartar Check biscuit, 133
Taste, 94–95
Taxidermy, 259
Teaching, 148–165
Teeth. *See* Dental care
Territorial aggression, 173–174
Territory, 140–141
Testicles, 214
Testosterone, 214, 215
Thomas, Elizabeth Marshall, 107, 140, 237
Thunderstorm phobias, 77
Thyroid disease, 135, 197–198
Time expense, 49–50
Touch, 95–97
Tracking, 92–93
Training, 152–165
Travel accommodations, 143
Tremor, 245
Trial and error, 149–150
Tricks, 163–164

Urination, 111–113, 118–119
Uterine contractions, 222

Vaccination schedule, 197
Veterinarian(s), 22–24, 27, 28, 29, 133, 224, 255
Vision, 86–90
Vocalization, 120–125
Voith, Victoria, 205

Watchdog, 120–121
Water, 129
Waterman, Charlie, 107
Watson, Lyall, 106
Weight control, 137
    See also Diets; Obesity
Weiss, Rick, 196
Whelping, 221–223
Whining, 124
Whiskers, 96
Wild dogs, 4–5, 68, 120, 130
Wills, 261–264
Wisdom, 237
Wolf, Norman, 234
Wolf-girl, 75–76
Wolves, 4–5, 34, 68, 114–115, 120, 140
Women, 133
Woodhouse, Barbara, 221
Working dogs, 7–8, 9, 13
Wright, John C., 69–70

Yorkshire terrier, 51

www.ingramcontent.com/pod-product-compliance
Lightning Source LLC
Chambersburg PA
CBHW030136170426

43199CB00008B/86